Company Rescue

Company Rescue

How to manage a company turnaround

O. P. KHARBANDA
and
E. A. STALLWORTHY

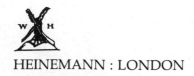

HEINEMANN : LONDON

William Heinemann Ltd
10 Upper Grosvenor Street, London W1X 9PA

LONDON   MELBOURNE   JOHANNESBURG   AUCKLAND

First published 1987

British Library Cataloguing in Publication Data
Stallworthy, E.A.
   Company rescue: how to manage a company turnaround.
   1. Industrial management
   I. Kharbanda, O.P.
   658.4   HD31
ISBN 0 434 91855 5

Photoset by Deltatype, Ellesmere Port
Printed in Great Britain by
Redwood Burn Ltd, Trowbridge, Wiltshire

Contents

Preface

Corporate failure, though it often appears to be sudden, seldom occurs without prior warning. Of course, the warning signals are often ignored – as is often the case with our own health. We have demonstrated in our earlier book, *Corporate Failure: Prediction, Panacea and Prevention*, that it is possible to predict corporate failure. We then went on to demonstrate that the ability to predict should be used to find a suitable remedy or, better still, the company management, headed up by the chief executive, should go on to 'do something about it'. That is, review their management approach, reappraise their corporate strategy and proceed to take such action as will avert failure and disaster.

Regrettably, decisive action is rarely taken when a company is at risk, for such action would be tantamount to an admission by management that its previous approach had failed. Many companies are so concerned about the health of their executives that they insist upon and pay for an annual medical check-up, yet they fail to check up on the 'health' of their own company. The reason for the medical check-up is to discover latent problems and hopefully thereby to prevent them. The same approach should be adopted in relation to companies. The techniques are there to be used: early warning signals can be developed in time for decisive action to be effective, but more often than not management fails to act until it is too late. Of course, the annual report to the board and to the shareholders is supposed to serve this purpose, but it rarely does so, since such reports often hide more than they show.

We believe that while the best teacher of all is our own experience it is far better, quicker and cheaper to learn from the experience of others. We have therefore included in this book a wide range of illustrative case studies. By analysing the way in which impending disaster was handled and averted, we can learn and devise our own road to recovery, should we be in a similar position. In our earlier book on this subject the theme was, in effect, failure, but now we want to look at a number of success stories and learn how the rescue and revival of ailing companies was achieved.

The rescue and revival of failing companies is an exciting subject. The term now often used in this context is 'company turnaround', so challenging a job that some managers seem to thrive upon it. Such managers, or 'company doctors' as they are now being called, were a rare breed a few years ago, but their number seems to be growing to meet the growing need. More and more companies, large as well as small, seem to be at risk these days all over the world. Seeing how others have dealt with such situations can help us to deal with a similar situation on our own doorstep. Of course, as noted earlier, prevention is always better than cure, so we also highlight those aspects of management that should ensure that our company never gets into such a disastrous situation in the first place.

The 'doctor' or 'turnaround manager' who seeks to accomplish a turnaround is putting both his reputation and his career at risk if the turnaround is not successful, since it will be seen as a personal failure. To effect a turnaround one has to be tough, ruthless: take hard, unpleasant decisions and implement them. The company 'doctor' has to have a free hand if he is to be effective, and acts very much alone. So, when assessing turnaround case studies, we also have to assess this *man*. We shall assess not only the problem and its resolution, but the qualities and the attributes of the *man* who achieved that result.

There is no way in which we can write down a set of rules in this context. Each company is unique, just as each human is unique and has his own personal 'body chemistry'. The turnaround strategy has therefore to be specifically developed for each individual case. The 'doctor' has to make his diagnosis and then write his 'prescription'. Fortunately, there are many turnarounds worldwide that have been well documented, so that we have a wide range of data and a most valuable body of knowledge upon which we can draw and from which we can learn. We have chosen selectively, taking case histories that are representative of the various strategies that can be employed, highlighting the lessons that are there to be learnt. In the first part of our book we set the scene, as it were, by defining the role of management. Parts Two to Four present the case histories themselves. Then, in Part Five, we go on to draw conclusions, setting out broad guidelines for success.

We believe that this is the first comprehensive approach to this particular subject, our case histories coming from all over the world and covering a very wide spectrum of industries. Returning to our analogy between the company and the human body, we might well call this present book a sort of *materia medica* on the subject. We have paid very special attention to the indexes and cross-referencing, seeking to make them as comprehensive as possible. This, together with the extensive references given at the end of each chapter, should help our reader find what is most relevant to his own situation with ease.

Our case studies highlight the style and approach of the 'doctor' who brings the company back to health. Just as the *'materia medica'* is a starting point, so we believe that this book can be a suitable starting point for those likely to get involved with a company in trouble. We are sure that real learning comes, above all, from 'doing' and the newcomer has to learn by a process of trial and error, the errors becoming less and less frequent as experience grows. Once again, we can draw an appropriate analogy with the doctor of medicine. He too has to spend many years learning 'on the job', so that when he starts his practice, and stands on his own, he has behind him a wealth of experience and wisdom – both his own and that of others that can guide his judgment. Just as there is no universal remedy for sickness in the human body, each case being unique, so it is with the corporate body. Just as some societies have particular diseases that run rampant among them, so it is with companies. Countries differ and the nature and cause of the 'sickness' can be very different from one country to another.

It is asserted throughout that management, in particular the chief executive, is primarily responsible for the health of its company. Good management should ensure that the road to failure is never followed, but we all make mistakes. Then others, particularly if they are on the outside looking in, can often see where we are going wrong before we see it ourselves. It is here that the company auditor and the bank manager have an effective role to play, if only they will. They should be watchdogs, keeping their eyes and ears open. There is some movement in this direction of which we have taken due note and we believe that such officers can do far more to protect the public interest, the interests of their customers and their shareholders, than they often do.

Summing up, our extensive presentation of case histories and the lessons that they bring is an attempt to learn from the experiences of others. But if we are to do this successfully we *must* listen. It is most difficult to get people to listen, let alone learn. It is our sincere hope that this book will help in this direction.

O. P. Kharbanda, Bombay
E. A. Stallworthy, Coventry

Acknowledgements

The reader will notice that we have put a list of references at the end of each chapter. While they are there, in part, to allow those who are interested to research further into any particular aspect of this subject should they wish to do so, they are so numerous that we realize that they will never be scrutinized in detail. Why then are they there? Well, not only do we wish to acknowledge our debt to the many who have written on the various subjects we touch upon in the course of our work, but we believe that a simple perusal of the references can be in itself an education. They bring, we feel, a 'flavour' to the subject. The titles of the articles, papers and books to which we refer are sometimes quite arresting and thus give quite an insight into the attitudes of those involved. So please do not 'jump' the references when you get to the end of a chapter. Give them a glance – it's well worth it!

Librarians are among our best friends, particularly those looking after the libraries of the American Library, the British Council, the Industrial Credit and Investment Corporation of India, the Indian Institute of Technology, the Tata Energy Research Institute and the University of Bombay, all in Bombay, together with the librarians at the British Institute of Management, the Institute of Bankers, the London Business Library and the Science Reference Library, all in London, and last, but not least, the New York Public Library, the Fairleigh Dickinson University Library at Rutherford, New Jersey, and the Library of Congress at Washington, in the United States. Our grateful thanks go to them and their staff for their labour of love in tracking down the material we were seeking.

Lastly, and as always, our special thanks to our families for their patience, understanding and loving support while this book was being written.

Part One

The role of management

1 The profile of failure

When we start to consider company rescue, we have to discuss the management of companies who have reached a state of crisis in their affairs: companies that will become insolvent unless steps are taken to effect a turnaround in their financial performance. The term 'turnaround' has now become popular usage in this context. A turnaround becomes necessary when it looks as though the company will fail in the near future unless corrective action, usually of a drastic nature, is taken. There are some writers who see a turnaround situation as a situation where there is a cash crisis.[1] This places certain restrictions on their assessment of the situation. For instance, a study in the US made by Bibeault showed that a quarter of US companies quoted on the Stock Exchange needed turnaround during a ten-year period. But that was according to his definition of a turnaround: a somewhat limited definition in our view. Slatter, who combines practical experience with an academic approach, in that he was once managing director of a subsidiary of a UK public company, but became director at the London Business School, in his appraisal of the subject, takes a broader view and includes those companies who, while they do not have a cash crisis, nevertheless are displaying symptoms of potential failure.[2]

One in five companies at risk

Slatter undertook a study of publicly quoted companies in the UK over a fifteen-year period, defining a turnaround situation as one where the 'real' profit of a company before tax, measured at constant prices and so eliminating the influence of inflation, declined for three or more successive years. Then a successful turnaround was said to have been accomplished once a company, after such a period of profit decline, had increased its profit in four of the six following years. Notice that such an assessment requires that the company has to be in business for some ten years before it can even be considered. However, the study showed that some 20 per cent of the companies assessed in this way were in need of a turnaround. Of the companies in need of a turnaround, some 25 per cent were turned around successfully, as indicated in Table 1. We introduce you to the subject of company turnarounds in this particular way in order to give you some idea as to the magnitude of the problem. It seems that any one time, whether we look at the US or the UK, something like one in five of the companies in business are in danger of becoming insolvent, going into receivership or going bankrupt. We are very sure that this situation is not peculiar to these two countries: the statistics tell us that a similar situation prevails worldwide. This then is a very real and a very substantial problem.

Table 1   *What is the chance of successful recovery? This table indicates that roughly one company in four under threat manages to make a successful turnaround*

Number of years of declining earnings	Firms requiring turnaround	Firms successfully turned around	Success rate (%)
3	335	81	24
4	84	23	27
5	13	2	15
6	5	1	20
Totals	437	107	24

Source: S. Slatter, *Corporate Recovery*, Penguin, 1984, p. 19.

The assessment that one in five companies are always at risk seems to be quite realistic. Performance Analysis Services Ltd once estimated that among the 850 largest UK manufacturing companies, once again 20 per cent, or one in five, were running the risk of insolvency at any one time. Their assessment of potential failure was made using their own proprietary predictive technique, referred to as the PAS score, a sort of company 'health' chart.[3] It is claimed that by using PAS a credit manager can 'monitor his credit risk exposure, focus attention on the high risk debtors and highlight opportunities to promote products and services to the healthiest companies'. Notice the objective in view. It is not a diagnostic tool designed to help 'sick' companies by identifying their sickness and point the road to recovery. Not at all. It is designed to assist companies avoid dealing with sick companies and work only with the healthy ones. The suggestion is *not* made that companies should use the technique in order to see whether they themselves were sick and in need of treatment. This omission we find quite remarkable and we shall return to it later. However, for the moment the point we wish to make is that there are many many companies continually at risk worldwide. Slatter speaks of 'healthy' companies, but he doesn't seem to speak of 'sick' companies, although that term seems very appropriate for those companies – and there are so many of them, it seems – who are at risk. They need treatment.

Enter the doctor

This discussion of companies and their problems in symptomatic terms, as if a company were a person, seems to be very widespread, so much so that the term 'company doctor' is applied to the person primarily instrumental in achieving a turnaround: bringing that company back to health. Headlines in the technical press and management journals worldwide often use the phrase. Even what we might call the popular press seems to do the same without fear of misunderstanding, since the *International Herald Tribune* captioned an article on Sir John Cuckney: 'For "company doctors" rescue cases are routine'. Another title is even more 'medical' in its terminology. The journal *International Management* headed an article on a Japanese exponent of the art of 'turnaround', one Umeo Oyama, with the words: 'This corporate doctor with homespun remedies is no quack'. It is obviously possible for there to be some confusion of ideas, for many companies, especially those running factories, employ a medical practitioner (doctor) to take care of the health of their workforce, and he or she would then be referred to, quite properly, as the company doctor. But this is no medical tome, even although our theme is to be 'company doctors'. For us the company doctor is the person, most often the chief executive, who brings health back to, or rejuvenates, a sick company, accomplishing a turnaround. Such individuals are also referred to as 'turnaround managers' or 'rejuvenators' because, it seems, there are some who, in effect, make a profession of it, moving from company to company, just as a doctor goes from patient to patient. Sir John Cuckney, Umeo Oyama and others like them fall into this category and their 'cures' are most instructive, as we shall see. They are a relatively new phenomenon in the business world, but their numbers are growing fast to meet an urgent need. There is no formal training for this particular managerial skill, only a few short-term seminars, including one that we have introduced.

The medical analogy we keep on using is popular, we believe, because it is appropriate. It simplifies discussion and the analogy assists in an understanding as to what is happening. Indeed we may venture to draw a fairly complete parallel between a company and the life of any one of us as follows:

The person	*The company*
Conception	Concept
Pre-natal care	Feasibility report
Birth	Company start-up
Healthy person	Profitable company
Patient	Company with a problem
Sickness	A problem, usually financial
Doctor (GP)	Management consultant
Specialist	Consultants technical and financial
Hospital	Bank or other financial institution
Intensive care	Turnaround techniques
Cured	Turnaround
Death	Financial collapse
Undertaker	Receiver

As with the person, so with the company. While there is usually ample warning of trouble (sickness) the warning signals are ignored. Indeed, at times they are even hidden. The management just does not want to know, much less let others know. Companies are usually very concerned about the health of their employees, often insisting that their executives have a regular annual medical check-up, for which the company is prepared to pay. Yet management is totally oblivious when it comes to its own check-up! As we said earlier, while there are techniques available which would assist in such a 'check-up', they are not used by management for this purpose. Either they are completely ignorant of their benefits or over-confident: perhaps both in many instances. It is only those who have to come into contact with the patient who use them. To press the analogy a little further, we can liken the 'financial difficulty' that a company gets into to an infectious disease, which no one else, naturally enough, wants to catch. So they take preventive measures. They take a look at the company – assess its credit rating – and if its rating is poor they keep away.

Just ten years ago most specialists would have ridiculed the suggestion that the mind can influence the body, but today this concept is being taken very seriously indeed by the medical profession. It would appear that a company also has a 'mind', so it is possible for us to continue the medical analogy even further. Indeed, we have seen 'sick' companies referred to as

neurotic   psychotic   sociopathic

The analogy is thus being taken to the extreme.[4]

None are immune

We have all been young once. Perhaps some, even many of our readers still regard themselves as 'young'. The point we wish to make is that when we are young death always seems remote, although of course accidents do happen. Yet death is inescapable, unavoidable. Death is the inevitable consequence of life, and this is just as true of companies as it is of people, although the lifespan can vary considerably. Infant mortality has its parallel in the companies that never really get going, even though they may sometimes survive for a few years. But 'growing up' doesn't bring complete immunity from sickness or accident, although one may be much less vulnerable than when one was a child, and the same holds true with companies. However large they become, they call still collapse and 'die'. This fact was driven home to the financial world in the early 1970s by the failure of such giants as Penn Central and Rolls Royce. These dramatic failures came as a complete surprise to the business world at the time: no one ever imagined it to be possible. Examining the statistics, it was indeed true that prior to 1970 companies with assets greater than US$25 million hardly ever failed, but since then some forty industrial companies with assets greater than US$125 million have collapsed.[5] Why this is so no one really seems to know, but the warning is there. No company or group of companies, however large, is safe. Later, we shall be taking a look at the experience of General Motors, one of the largest, if not *the* largest

company in the world. Yet General Motors tripped up, hurt itself
and needed a 'doctor'. General Motors did not present itself to the
world as an ailing company: using the financial criteria for assessing
a company in need of a turnaround the company did not qualify.
True, there was a collapse in profits, but that was sudden: it was not
a case of profits declining over a period of years. But all this tells us
that there are more symptoms to be assessed than financial ones.
The financial symptoms may be very apparent, when they are there,
but once again the human analogy can make the point for us. The
very purpose of an annual medical check-up is to forestall trouble.
One feels quite fit, yet one goes to the doctor, just to make sure that
there is not some hidden danger, which he will discover by a detailed
examination. It is the same with companies. By the time the sickness
is manifest in the company accounts, it may already be too late to do
anything about it. Certainly the measures that will have to be taken
to accomplish a turnaround are going to be much more drastic than
they would have had to be were the problem diagnosed earlier.

Now we are in the area of 'preventive medicine'. There is the
well-known saying that 'prevention is better than cure' – and it is
true. If only companies would take a careful look at themselves – or
get someone else to do so – at regular intervals, rather than allow the
hidden 'cancer', if we may call it that, to grow in secret until its
presence can no longer be ignored – but then it is all too often far too
late. We are going to look in detail at the way in which the 'doctor'
heals the patient. Sometimes radical surgery is called for, a most
unpleasant experience for all involved, so preventive measures are
also of great interest. However, we have assessed them elsewhere[6]
and since we are very sure, such is human nature, such the
reluctance to admit that things can go wrong, that there will still be
one in five, perhaps even one in four companies throughout the
world in decline and in need of treatment, more and more 'doctors'
are going to be needed. So it must be helpful to look at the way the
doctor goes about his job. A study of what happens – what *has* to
happen if the patient is to recover, may well be a sort of 'shock
treatment' in itself. A company turnaround can be a most distressing
thing for those who have to experience it. It can affect not only those
most immediately concerned, the employees and those trading with
the company, but also industry in general and even the overall well-
being of the country or countries where the company operates.
Thousands can be thrown out of work and whole communities can
die. But for the 'doctor', the banks, the shareholders and those

employees who remain it is most satisfying to see a company brought back to normal 'health'. In the long run, of course, the community as a whole will also be better off.

Making a diagnosis

It is most difficult to assess the reasons for the decline and failure of companies, because we lack diagnostic tools. The only consistent statistics we have are those relating to bankruptcy. These are available from a variety of agencies and are prepared for a great many countries, but of course many companies who get into trouble never go bankrupt. The smaller ones, in particular, just cease to exist. So while the bankruptcy statistics tell us that bankruptcies are on the increase worldwide, they cannot be an absolute measure of the problem. The reason for this steady growth is not at all clear. It has nothing directly to do with the depression, since the recent improvement in the economy in certain countries seems to have had no impact on the growth in the number of bankruptcies. A more likely cause, we believe, although probably not the only cause, is the sharp increase that has occurred over the past few years in the number of companies being set up, largely due to the rapid expansion in electronics and other computer-related activities. A proportion of new companies will always fail, so the more new companies there are that appear on the scene, the more failures there are going to be at some later stage.

Altman has established that nearly half of all company failures occur within the first two years of operation.[7] We have plotted his data in Figure 1. This being so, an upsurge in company formation will be followed, over the next two to three years, by an upsurge in company failures. Once those early years are past, the climate of failure is different according to the country. If we now look at the average age at failure of companies in a number of very different countries, remembering that failure equals bankruptcy, that being the only statistic we have, we have the following picture:[5]

	UK	USA	Israel	Japan
Average age at failure *(years):*	5–7	5–7	9–13	31
Failure rate (per year, as %):	1–2	0.5–0.7	0.2–0.7	0.5

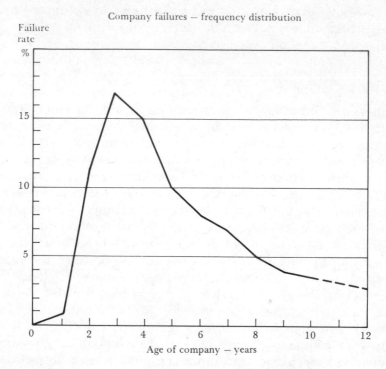

Figure 1   *The frequency of company failures. This graph demonstrates that most failures occur in the early years of a company's life. (Derived from data presented by Altman, see Reference 6.)*

While the above pattern is very interesting, it does not tell us very much. Tamari, who made the study, thinks that the pattern of financial failure is independent of the social, political and cultural factors prevailing in the four very different economies he surveyed. He then goes on to suggest that the theories and the techniques established in relation to the US economy, where a great deal of research has been done, would be equally applicable in these other economies, but we cannot agree. To take but one example, the abnormally long life of companies in Japan is explained by the specific financial structure existing there, a structure which we discuss in some detail in Chapter 14. As you will see then, the banks in Japan play a very protective role there and bankruptcy is very much the 'court of last resort'.

Now that we have introduced the word 'failure' let us make the point that failure is nothing to be ashamed of. It is something that can come to the best of us. Unfortunately most of us are so obsessed with success that failure is something one does not talk about. But its study can be an education. Even more is this true of a study of recovery from imminent failure, which is our purpose in this book. You cannot have success without failure. Why is that? Because in order to be successful you have to make decisions, and some of those decisions are liable to be wrong. Those who are outstanding in terms of decision-making still make mistakes, but the best of them have the courage to admit to their mistakes and the resolve to do something about it. It usually takes courage because it almost always involves a change of course and a public confession. It was General Johnson, the founder of the world-famous company *Johnson and Johnson*, who is quoted as saying: 'If I wasn't making mistakes, I wasn't making decisions'.[8] Successful business executives have to choose between alternatives and can sometimes make a decision that leads to failure – or could lead to failure if not reversed. But one should learn from failure: that is the theme of our latest book on the subject.[9]

Where the trouble starts

We are always very good at finding excuses when things go wrong and the common tendency is to blame anyone else rather than ourselves. This human weakness is as manifest in company management as it is anywhere else, since what else is a board of directors but a group of human beings, with both the vices and the virtues that all human beings have. Man is behind and is the cause of all the troubles that come upon us, once we exclude the impact of natural disasters such as earthquakes and floods – though even their effect can be mitigated to a great extent by proper management.

So when a company is in trouble, it is man that is the cause – and in this case the man in charge of the company. It is our thesis that company failure comes from bad management, *not* from external causes and we believe that the case studies to which we shall come in due course demonstrate this very clearly. The fact that external conditions, such as competition, business depression, excessive taxation and the like are blamed is no evidence. They would say that, wouldn't they! Who is going to blame himself when he can find someone or something else to blame. The truth of this dictum is demonstrated by the fact that there *are* 'company doctors' who manage a turnaround. What does the 'doctor' do? He examines the patient, makes a diagnosis and writes out his prescription. He looks at the *patient* because it is the patient that needs treatment and that treatment can cure. Yes, it is certainly true, to revert to the human analogy, that much sickness and disease is due to the conditions in which people live, but they themselves can stay well if they take the appropriate steps. It is just the same in a declining industry, to take but one example in the commercial field. While some companies suffer and others go under, there are yet others who manage to prosper in the same industry, since their management knew how to handle the situation with which they were faced and resolved the problem. So we cannot blame the declining market. We must blame the management of those companies that cannot cope with the changing situation. Management is what matters. So let us now go on to see what management can do about it. We think that deserves a chapter all to itself, so important do we feel it to be.

References

1 Bibeault, D., *Corporate Turnaround*, McGraw–Hill, 1981.
2 Slatter, S., *Corporate Recovery*, Penguin Books, 1984.
3 *The PAS Microcomputer System. A Confidential Customer Information System*, Performance Analysis Services Ltd.
4 Frost, T. R., 'The sick organization', *Personnel*, no. 62, May 1985, p. 40 and June 1985, p. 44.
5 Tamari, M., *Some International Comparison of Industrial Financing*, Technicopy, 1977.
6 Kharbanda, O. P. and Stallworthy E. A., *Corporate Failure: Prediction, Panacea and Prevention*, McGraw-Hill, 1985.
7 Altman, E. I., *Corporate Financial Distress: A Complete Guide to Predicting, Avoiding and Dealing with Bankruptcy*, Wiley, 1983.
8 Peters, T. J. and Waterman R. H., *In Search of Excellence: Lessons from America's Best-Run Companies*, Harper & Row, 1982.
9 Kharbanda, O. P. and Stallworthy E. A., *Management Disasters*, Gower, 1986.

2 Management can prevent failure

Business failure is not something that comes to companies as 'one of those things'. While the statistics lead us to believe that it is widespread that does not mean that it is in any way inevitable under certain circumstances. Having said in the heading to this chapter that management *can* prevent failure, we are prepared to go one step further and both assert and demonstrate that *good* management *can* and *will* prevent failure. Instead of the word 'good', we could use the word 'sound', or 'effective', but that statement opens up a question: what is good, sound, effective management? When we come to our case studies, and see the 'company doctors' at work, we shall of course be looking at examples of 'effective management' but it will be a rather specific management style, referred to in financial circles as 'turnaround management', or sometimes 'crisis management'. But of course, a company should never get into a situation where its directors have to cope with a crisis and the company is in need of a turnaround. It is all very well for us to write about corporate failure, or for Slatter to write about corporate recovery, or for Kibel to tell us how to turn around a financially troubled company,[1,2,3] but such situations should not arise. The company doctors, who turn around troubled companies, are obviously very good managers indeed and by looking at the way they approach and handle a crisis situation we are going to learn a great deal about effective management techniques, but if there had been effective management in the first place, some of those 'techniques' would not have been necessary. That, perhaps, is the first point that we should make. Prevention is always better than cure. If you prevent trouble (preventive 'medicine') then a 'cure' is not necessary!

Management style

We have already said and demonstrated that the comparison made between a company and the human being is very apt: perhaps more so than you may realize. A company is a living and dynamic entity. Each company is different, just as no two people are ever the same, and each company has a life of its own. Each company, therefore, has its own management style, often referred to in the literature as the 'company culture'.[4] In an unusual and interesting article Uttal points out that all companies with a record of outstanding financial performance have very powerful corporate cultures.[5] The definition of 'culture' in this context, as it relates to those who work in the company, from chief executive all the way down to the post boy (not forgetting that some chief executives started off as post boys) is:

A system of shared values, and
A system of shared beliefs.

The company values tell everyone, from the chief executive downwards, what is important to the company, while the company beliefs tell them all how things work in the company. With a successful multinational or conglomerate this culture should and will be seen operating throughout all the companies in the group, whatever the country. In fact an important but not too easily readable book on this subject stresses the point that the main characteristics of the most efficient companies are the same, irrespective of country. To quote:[6]

> Despite their differences, well-run factories around the world share many similarities. . . .A well-run German factory is more like a well-run Japanese factory than German society is like Japanese society. And well-run American factories have important similarities to both.

The authors' advice in relation to establishment of well-run factories is that there is no 'quick fix'. What is required is that one does 'the basic things a little better, every day, over a long period of time. It's that simple – and that difficult'.

The company culture, it appears, is very powerful. A system of shared values and beliefs ensures that there are behavioural norms in relation to company administration and control that prevail throughout the organization. That then becomes 'the way we do things round here'. When we seek to learn about company culture we have to look closely at the way specific companies operate, and it will be the successful companies that have a successful culture. What are the outstanding features in the management style of very successful companies? Well, with IBM it seems to be customer service, while everyone that visits a Toyota office or factory tells us of the 'company song' that the workers sing every morning. Hewlett Packard, on the other hand, looks for long-term growth and seeks to make every employee an entrepreneur. They are all very different, but then we ought to have expected that: people are all very different!

Company culture – a set of beliefs

It seems that the company culture is, in effect, a set of 'beliefs' and it is these beliefs that establish values. Some companies go so far as to publish their beliefs not only to all their employees, but also to such of the public as are prepared to listen. Donaldson and Lorsch, to whose work we shall refer more than once, carried out a very detailed examination of twelve successful, mature companies in an endeavour to learn what are the factors within companies that bring success. The companies they chose were all very different from one another, but of course they found many common characteristics. The companies selected all promised to allow complete access to their papers and people against the promise of complete confidentiality and the sample was small enough to allow an intensive investigation to be carried out, yet large enough to establish what were common factors. There were, it seems, company beliefs and objectives that they all shared. It was hardly surprising, perhaps, that one belief they all shared was that making a profit is a *must!*[7]

As we have said, some companies publish their 'beliefs', and we are told that one brochure set out the basic concepts in their culture as follows:

1   Do a good job, make a genuine technical contribution, not just 'me too' products.
2   Keep [the company] on a 'pay-as-you-go' basis; grow through our own resources.
3   Make [the company] a stimulating, fun and secure place to work.
4   Don't be a hire/fire company.
5   Make a profit to benefit the shareholders.

he best companies have the best culture

We ourselves came across and read with interest a booklet published by Standard Telephones and Cables (STC), available to all its employees, called *The Best Company Book*. STC is an old, mature company. It celebrated its centenary in 1983, but in the early 1970s it was in need of a turnaround, and got it. The 'doctor' then was Sir Kenneth Corfield, who took over as chairman and chief executive and transformed the company's managerial approach. The booklet encapsulates the approach he instituted and developed in co-operation with his staff, and four main priorities are indentified:

1   Be efficient and profitable, giving good service to customers.
2   Do business straightly and honestly.
3   Treat all employees with respect and help them develop and contribute fully.
4   Have an open and participative style of management.

The foreword, written by Sir Kenneth Corfield, includes the following statement:

> It is almost nine years since we set ourselves the aim of being the Best Company in the United Kingdom. It is for others to judge the extent to which we have succeeded or failed. What is certain, however, is that the Best Company Book is a constant challenge to us to live up to our ideals.
>
> (November 1983 edition)

One wonders why its target was limited to the UK: why not strive to be the best company in the whole world. But the important point for us is that the company – that is, all its employees – *had* a goal and an objective, or objectives. It knew where it wanted to go and that is a tremendous help in getting there, for if it did not know where it is going how can it ever get there?

Obviously space does not permit us to quote from the booklet at any length, but it opens with a chapter headed 'Overall objectives'. This talks of 'profit' as an objective, enabling the company to meet its responsibilities towards its shareholders, employees, customers and suppliers, and indeed to the community as a whole. So once again we see profit set up as a desirable objective, and this time seen not only as something that the shareholders deserve, but as something that benefits everybody. Profit is not only desirable but essential for the 'health' of a company. Without it, the company will inevitably cease to exist. This is a subject we have dealt with earlier, this present work being but the obvious sequel.[1]

Innovation is another basic objective. Ideas for new and improved products, new applicatfiions of technology and improvements in manufacturing skills and efficiency are to be encouraged. This goes hand in hand with a recognition that full consideration must be given to both problems and opportunities before entering new fields, while accepting that properly quantified risks must some-times be taken. Don't forget, as we enunciate these management principles, that they are being put before *every* employee. We already have two concepts in common with that earlier list and have seen that making a profit is indeed a continuing and abiding theme, but we must not give too much attention to any one particular culture. As we have said, each culture will be different and what we have to discover, that we may learn, are the common factors that *all* companies should have incorporated in their culture. To revert to the human analogy once again, we know we are all different the one from the other, yet we have quite a number of things in common.

Man is the crux

The company name IBM is synonymous with computers and the company has a long and successful history. A history of the origins and growth of this company, known worldwide, makes fascinating reading.[8] IBM came into existence back in 1924 as the successor to CTR (Computer-Tabulator-Recording) but the man who gave the company its 'culture' was a certain Thomas Watson. His basic philosophy, which seems to have been preserved as part of that company's culture right down to the present day, was expressed by him thus:

> A company is known by the *men* it keeps. We have different ideas, and different work, but when you come right down to it there is just one thing we have to deal with throughout the whole organizatïon – that is the MAN.

This was said all of seventy years ago and today we have to allow that generic term 'man' to include 'woman', but it remains true and we shall revert to the importance of the individual a little later. But what was Thomas Watson's view of the organization. That is equally interesting and his words must carry weight, seeing the successful course taken by the company he influenced so much. He is reported as saying:

> Consider any great organization [this was said before IBM became great] – one that has lasted over the years, and I think you will find that it owed its resiliency not to its form of organization or administrative skills, but to the power of what we call beliefs and the appeal these beliefs have to provide.
>
> This, then, is my thesis: I firmly believe that any organization, in order to survive and achieve success, must have a sound set of beliefs upon which it premises all its policies and actions. Next, I believe that the most important single factor in the corporate success is faithful adherence to these beliefs. *And finally, I believe that if an organization is to meet the challenges of a changing world, it must be prepared to change everything about itself except those beliefs as it moves through corporate life.* In other words, the basic philosophy, spirit and drive of the organization have far mor to do with its relative achievements than do technological or economic resources, organizational structure, innovation and timing. All these things weigh heavily in success, but they are, I think, transcended by how strongly the people in the organization believe in its basic precepts and how faithfully they carry them out.

We agree with his philosophy, except in relation to the portions we have set in *italics*. We agree that a company's beliefs, or culture, are all-important, but we cannot agree that they should be kept inviolate, once established. We feel that while the culture should be very stable, yet it must change to deal with a changing economic reality. There are those who maintain that once established, a company culture *cannot* be changed. The director of management development at Hewlett-Packard, a company noted for its excellent record and said to have a strong company culture which is at the heart of its success, has been quoted as saying: 'I don't think John Young (*president*) could fundamentally change our values if he wanted to'.[5] Perhaps not: company culture must be strong and all-pervading if it is to be effective. But while it may not be subject to fundamental change, it must surely be open to such changes as may be required by events.

The lowest common denominator

What should all companies have in common, in terms of their culture? Well, let's start by asking ourselves where that culture comes from in the first place. It seems that with most successful companies the company culture can be traced back to the founder of the company, or some top manager who both lived and preached the concepts he set in motion. Constantly hammered home as the 'way to do it', his ideas become the company culture, kept alive by those who follow after. The culture comes from within and not from without. It cannot be imposed, as it were, upon a company. This is one reason, we believe, why the company doctor can never operate effectively outside the company, just by giving advice. He has to join the company, become its chief executive, to achieve his results. He has to both assimilate and then most probably modify the company culture.

Once again, it seems, we learn our lessons best by looking at failure. Seeking an answer to the question 'why do companies fail?'. Two management experts, Ross and Kami conclude that it is bad management that is to blame. For them, bad management is to break one or more of 'ten commandments', so their ten commandments immediately become basic for *good* management. They are:[9]

There must be a strategy.
There must be controls, including cost control.
The board must participate actively.
No one-man rule.
Management must have depth.
Management must know of and respond to change.
The customer is king.
Avoid the misuse of computers.
Do not manipulate the accounts.
The organization structure must meet people's needs.

This list is commendable and very good advice, but it is by no means complete and many of their rules are interrelated. While some of the concepts can be said to be included in the culture concepts we have already looked at, they are all positive, whereas some of the Ross and Kami concepts are negative: no one-man rule, do not misuse computers, do not manipulate the accounts. That brings us back, perhaps, to one of the 'best company' concepts: do business straightforwardly and honestly. It was Barmish who, having considered a total of fifteen case histories in the business world, drew the dreadful conclusion that the basic cause of business disaster is greed: human greed, simple and unadulterated.[10] In most cases, he alleged, greed crossed over the line of propriety and became corruption. But let us be positive. Let us assert that the old adage is true and honesty is indeed the best policy and let us hope that all our readers are and will continue to pursue that policy, whatever else they do.

Is greed the 'lowest common denominator' when it comes to company failure? We hope not. A journalist, R. A. Smith, having analysed a number of company failures, concluded that the basic reasons for failure were:[10]

There was an autocrat.
There was resistance to change.
There was lack of control.

And then:

There was overdiversification.
There was bad luck.
There was too much decentralization.

We have separated his conclusions into two groups because not only are the reasons for failure given in the first group the most important in our view, but they are also reasons cited by Ross and Kami, though expressed in different wording, as listed earlier. While Smith cites these three aspects of company culture as the cause of failure, we do not think he is right. An autocrat can well have a role to play, some resistance to change may well be a good thing and a certain 'looseness' in control allows initiative to be exercised. So it is not those things as such that bring a company into difficulty, but having too much or too little of them. Troubles come, for instance, when the autocrat is too autocratic and he is both chairman *and* chief executive.

Man is management

Let us consult with one more expert before we end this review of the possible causes of company failure, in an attempt to see to what extent they are rooted in bad management, and could have been averted by good management. John Argenti, in his book *Corporate Collapse*, discloses a wide variety of causes for company failure, including lack of good leadership, an obsolete product, no sense of urgency and no understanding of cash flow.[11] Analysing his findings, he tries to pick out the recurring factors and gives what he

calls an 'interim list' of causes which, when put together, might solve
the problem as to *why* companies fail. The six major factors which he
elects for this role are:

1   Top management.
2   Accounting information.
3   Change
4   The manipulation of accounts.
5   Rapid expansion.
6   The economic cycle.

   The manipulation of accounts, listed above, may seem to be within
the legal framework, but it can be and often is designed to deceive. A
popular term for this type of accounting is 'creative accounting'. As
pointed out later in this chapter, an annual report is like a studio
portrait – and think of the 'dressing up' that can precede that!
Argenti goes on to list a number of other factors, including planning,
gearing, morale, shortage of capital and even bad luck as contributing to failure, but you will realize, we are sure, that they all
amount to mismanagement. Even 'luck', notwithstanding its meaning as given in the dictionary, is something that we feel can be
shaped and determined by management. It is this that leads us to the
conclusion that it is mismanagement that brings disaster, while it is
good management that will prevent it.

What is good management?

Yes, what is good management? Good management calls for good
managers. The system, the culture, cannot of itself bring success.
Since a company – any company – all companies – consist of a
number of people, from just a few to several hundred thousand,
then the good manager will always pay attention to his people.
Winters makes this point, saying that while managers require a
broad range of skills, above all they must have a highly developed
sensitivity to *personal* as well a business matters. [12] That broad range
of skills to which he refers should include, according to him, the
ability to make financial decisions, to perceive the needs of the
marketplace, to communicate well with his people and last, but by
no means least, to motivate his people in order that they, with him,
accomplish the company's goals.
   At the moment, we are talking about managers in general,

whatever their status within the company, but all that we have said applies pre-eminently to the chief executive, the person at the top. There always has to be someone at the top, a leader. Some companies fail because they lack just that and are run by a committee. There is a lot of difference between running a company by committee and running a company by consensus. The Japanese are past masters at the art of running a company using consensus, but their chief executive will always be a dominant personality. We shall be looking at one or two of them later. The successful chief executive in a major company will set up a team or a number of teams to look after various aspects of the company's activities, but it is inappropriate to refer to such teams as committees. We see a committee as a group of individuals called together from various places to consider a subject and report upon it, and we do not think much of them. Indeed, it is commonly said that whenever you don't wish to make a decision, the best thing to do is to relegate the subject to a committee, since then a decision will almost never be taken.

A management *team* is something very different. It consists of a group of individuals who will each have their specific role to play, there will be specific objectives and there will be a leader: we call such a leader a manager whether or not that happens to be his title in the organization. What sort of a person has he to be?

What makes a good manager

The more you read about management, the more complex it seems to get. It seems that many of the qualities demanded, said to make a good manager, are mutually exclusive. He is called upon to be highly intelligent, but not too clever. He must be forceful, yet remain sensitive to people's feelings. He must be dynamic and get things going, yet he has to exercise much patience. He must be a fluent communicator, yet a good listener. What a list of conflicting qualities – yet it seems there are quite a few such managers and even chief executives about. Not as many by far as there ought to be, but certainly there are some. We are going to look at the careers and the achievements of a few of the most outstanding of such characters shortly, in an attempt to see 'how it is done'.

Still searching for rules to guide us, particularly when we come to consider the chief executive, the one who has to carry the ultimate responsibility, we find that he should have the following qualities:

1   Ability to move between the past, present and future of the company.
2   Show his team a clear and convincing route to the company's objective.
3   Set an example to follow. Practise, not just preach.
4   Be a guide, counsellor and mentor to others in the company.
5   Put forward new ideas and get their acceptance.
6   Learn from success and also from failures – own and others.
7   Foresee technological change and set strategies accordingly.
8   Self-achiever and also achieve results through others.

The chief executive must continually be asking basic questions concerning his company, such as:

Where are we now?
How did we get here?
Where must we be tomorrow?
How do we get there?

As we turn to our case studies, we shall see our company 'doctors' asking these same questions, just as the GP asks patients questions when they come to consult him. We shall also see that if only these questions had been asked earlier, the 'doctor' need never have been called in at all. That is the task of 'preventive medicine'.

Coping with growth

It seems that the inability to cope with growth lies at the root of many company failures. How does management, and particularly the chief executive, cope with growth? Growth implies more and still more people who become management's concern: its greatest single asset and yet often presenting management with its greatest problems. Once again, we do well to look at those companies that have grown successfully. For instance, *Johnson & Johnson* is a US$5 billion company, but it in effect consists of 150 independent and separate companies each headed by its own chairman. The companies are divided into eight groups, the grouping being based upon product or geographical association. The central staff is small and there are no specialists, located at the company headquarters, travelling to individual companies to watch over their affairs or tell them what to do. They follow company policy, but are not supervised in detail.

This is typical of successful conglomerates and those who do not do this get into trouble.

The lesson is being learned. *ICI*, the leading UK chemical company, had over 2000 employees in its central organization barely five years ago, but has now trimmed this down to less than 200 in its battle to survive and succeed. This was thanks to their particular 'doctor', chairman Sir John Harvey-Jones. *Dana*, a US giant, with 35,000 employees, had a central corporate staff of 500 in 1970, but the doctor took a look, and that staff is now down to 100! Indeed, it looks as though once a corporation grows above a certain size, a central staff of about a hundred is the optimum, but we would not venture to make that finding an empirical law.

Seeing ourselves as others see us

All public companies present themselves to the outside world, first and foremost, through the annual report and accounts which they distribute to their shareholders. Such documents can be very revealing, especially when the results being achieved from year to year are compared, but unfortunately they sometimes hide far more than they reveal. That can be the result of what we have already referred to as 'creative accounting', and explains why it is so attractive to some. The balance sheet, an integral part of all such documents, is a snapshot: a picture of the company on the last day of its financial year. But snapshot is not really the right word: it is more a studio portrait, taken after a lot of careful preparation. You know what happens when one goes for a studio portrait. We dress up for the occasion and the photographer does his best to arrange us to advantage, often setting us against a very artificial, if not false background. It is much the same with a balance sheet, with creative accounting contributing to a picture that is better than reality. In some extreme cases it bears no resemblance at all to reality!

The company accounts have to be audited: that is a legal requirement. So the auditor is the outsider who comes closest to taking a careful look at the company. In most countries there is a legal requirement saying that company auditors can qualify the published accounts if they have any reservations regarding the status of the company. It is called the 'going concern qualification' in the UK and implies that the company is at risk. A survey of eighty-six publicly quoted independent industrial and distribution companies in the UK who were placed into receivership or went into voluntary liquidation or were wound up showed that three quarters of them had never been 'qualified'.[13] On the other hand it appears that the great majority of companies who receive the qualification do *not* fail. Surely this shows that their managements were alive to the danger and took steps to combat it, while those who ignored the danger or sought to conceal it were taking the very course that would lead them to disaster.

While the auditor is one very important onlooker, there is another: the bank manager. We are thinking now of the bank manager whose bank has a vested interest in a company, in that it has lent it money. The bank manager is the best placed of all those associated with a company to detect when trouble is looming ahead. However, while it appears that such banks do watch what is happening, in order to protect their interests, their approach is passive rather than active. It is a feature of banking practice to review the accounts of companies on a regular basis, which they process and analyse. From this data, they say, it is relatively easy to establish patterns within the accounts and watch for abnormalities. But what then? The bank takes up a self-protective role, refusing perhaps to advance more money. We, however, believe that the bank should adopt a positive role, advising the client that a problem seems to have arisen, and then seeking a satisfactory solution together with the directors of the company. There are signs that the major banks are making a move in this direction, but it is very slow in growing.

Summary

We have seen that good management is at the heart of any and every successful company and is essential if a company is to survive and succeed. It is as essential as breathing! While the literature on the subject is vast, and we have only been able to take the briefest of looks at the mountain of advice that is available, it has at least become clear that there are a few simple basic truths that need to be recognized and applied if success is to be achieved and failure averted.

References

1 Kharbanda, O. P. and Stallworthy, E. A., *Corporate Failure: Prediction, Panacea and Prevention*, McGraw-Hill, 1985.
2 Slatter, S., *Corporate Recovery: Successful Turnaround Strategies and their Implementation*, Penguin, 1984.

3   Kibel, H. R., *How to Turn Around a Financially Troubled Company*, McGraw-Hill, 1982.

4   Deal, T. E., and Kennedy A., *Corporate Cultures: The Rites and Rituals of Corporate Life*, Addison-Wesley, 1975.

5   Uttal, B., 'The corporate culture vultures', *Fortune*, no. 108, 17 October 1983, pp. 66–72.

6   Hayes, R. H. and Wheelwright S. C., *Restoring our Competitive Edge: Competing Through Manufacturing*, Wiley, 1984.

7   Donaldson, G. and Lorsch J. W., *Decision Making at the Top: The Shaping of Strategic Direction*, Basic Books, 1983.

8   Sobel, R., *IBM: Colossus in Transition*, Sidgwick and Jackson, 1984.

9   Ross, J. E. and Kami M. J., *Corporate Management in Crisis*, Prentice-Hall, 1973.

10 Smith, R. A., *Corporations in Crisis*, Doubleday, 1966.

11 Argenti, J., *Corporate Collapse: The Causes and Symptoms*, McGraw-Hill, 1976.

12 Winters, R. J., *It's Different When You Manage*, Lexington Books, 1975.

13 Taffler, R. J. and Tseung M., 'The audit going concern qualification in practice – exploding some myths', *The Accountants Magazine*, no. 88, July 1984, pp. 263–9.

3 The road to recovery

There is no single road to recovery, but many. If you wish to travel across country by car you will study a map and see that there are several possibilities: perhaps a scenic route, perhaps a fast but boring route, perhaps a route that will be the easiest to follow. If we belong to an automobile club we may well seek the advice of the experts and ask for a route map. The experts will not only know the best route, but they will have up-to-date information about the hazards on the way: roadworks, traffic jams, weather conditions. Eventually you select the route which you think is best suited to you at that point in time. It is the same with a company. In particular, if you want the best solution to the problem, you will call in the expert to diagnose. You yourself may well be too close to know the real problem, let alone the answer.

The diagnosis

When we think of the expert as the doctor, with the company his patient, there will still be more than one solution to the problem. The patient has symptoms. There is very evidently something wrong – but what? An experienced doctor examines the patient, his body, his eyes, his tongue. He taps here and there, asking a series of apparently naive questions, seeking to locate the real cause of the trouble. He may ask for a series of tests to be made to confirm his diagnosis although it is quite likely that he will start a course of treatment before the results of the tests are known, so sure is he that he knows what is wrong. But remember that the patient went to the doctor in the first place. With a company it can be just the same. The management will realize that there is something sadly wrong – it sees the symptoms. But *what* is wrong? What is the cause of the symptoms? All too often the company's own management is far too close to the situation to take a detached and impartial view. In addition, having been directly responsible for the situation, it has to question its own conduct and this is always a most difficult thing to do. There are very few people indeed who are good at 'self examination'. If they are wise they will call in an outsider to analyse the situation and recommend a course of action that will bring the company on the road to recovery. This is now being done often enough for a new breed of consultants (or managers) to have developed, often referred to as 'company doctors'. More often than not, it is not the company board that seeks help, but its creditors, in particular the banks, who insist on an outsider, the company doctor, taking charge. Sometimes, but less frequently, when crisis comes, the chief executive of the company himself or herself will face up to the situation and institute a strategy for recovery. But this is usually the exception.

In order to institute a strategy for recovery, one has first to make a diagnosis: ascertain what has gone wrong. We have just asserted (in Chapter 2) that when things go wrong with a company it is the management and in particular the chief executive who is at fault, and have also reviewed the literature on management seeking to establish what is good management practice. The specialist (the company 'doctor' who has done it before) will have had the necessary experience and will know what to look for and what to do, even although, as we have said, every company will be unique and require its own specific remedies, which have been summed up in the phrase 'turnaround strategy'. Without that experience, what does one do? The literature on turnarounds is of fairly recent origin. Serious study of corporation failure and collapse only began in the 1970s. Now the subject is no longer taboo and is publicly debated, although most of the attention has been given to techniques for the determination of companies at risk and likely to fail. While there has been quite a literature 'explosion' in this field, it has been largely directed at the potential investor, with the objective of warning him of danger ahead. In addition, many of the writers on the subject have adopted a completely academic approach, analysing the data and presenting us with complex formulae for the prediction of failure, but stopping right there. They seem to have entirely forgotten to ask: 'Why am I making this prediction?' and overlook entirely the fact that an answer is required to the next logical question: 'After prediction, then what?'

The academic approach

Altman is a leading exponent of the techniques that have been developed for the prediction of failure, but as you will see from the title of his book, *Corporate Financial Distress: A Complete Guide to Predicting, Avoiding and Dealing with Bankruptcy*, failure is equated with bankruptcy.[1] This is inevitable in that, as we have said earlier, the only statistics available are the bankruptcy statistics. They, however, are very detailed and comprehensive, providing a wealth of data for the researcher. However, one reviewer of Altman's book points out that Altman's subtitle is an overstatement.[2] His opinion must be considered authoritative, since he also reviewed Altman's earlier book on the subject, written in 1971.[3] It is certainly true that while 'avoiding and dealing' with bankruptcy are said to be two-thirds of the subject, they occupy a bare 10 per cent of the text. Nearly half the book is devoted either to prediction or to the legal and other aspects of bankruptcy. It is obviously helpful to know how to cope with bankruptcy when it comes, but we have no intention of entering into that subject at all. Why not? It is of course our hope that the examples to which we are going to turn, all showing that such a tragic end *can* be avoided, will be a source of strength, encouragement and guidance to managers such that they never even get into difficulty and need a turnaround strategy, let alone fail. No, the title to this chapter asserts that there *is* a road to recovery and it will be our objective to map it out.

Returning to the historical development of prediction techniques, the basic approach has been developed following the discovery that certain financial ratios, calculated from the data given in the annual accounts of a company, were different for failing companies, as compared with those companies that prospered. A milestone was reached in this research with the publication of the work that Beaver had done between 1966 and 1968.[4] Beaver established a relationship between ratio analysis and company failure, having examined some thirty ratios and testing each one for relative efficiency as an early indicator of business failure. This work of Beaver led on to the development of a specific technique, called multivariate analysis (MVA) or multiple discriminant analysis (MDA), whereby a specific combination of these ratios was used to discriminate between companies on the road to success and those heading for failure long before total failure, or bankruptcy, actually occurred. For an in-depth review of MDA and its financial applications we refer you to Altman *et al.*'s comprehensive book on the subject, *Application of Classification Techniques in Business*.[5] Today the number of formulae for the prediction of business failure is far too large for us to even begin to assess them all. In addition, their use has become a commercial activity, with companies such as Zeta Services Inc. in the US and Performance Analysis Services Limited (PAS) in the UK offering an advisory service based on proprietary formulae develop-ed from this academic research. The Zeta model is based on the work of Altman, while the PAS model is based on work done by Dr Taffler of the City University Business School in London. Both Dr Taffler and John Argenti have reviewed the work done by Altman and his co-workers, pointing out that his formulae relate to US companies and US conditions. They have then gone on to demonstrate that the formulae need to be modified for other countries, such as the UK. The data published by Dr Taffler relates to UK conditions while Argenti went a step further, encouraging us to look at management and the man rather than the figures from the annual reports of a company.[6] This, of course, is what we have done and will continue to do. So, while these techniques have a place, particularly in providing early warning of impending disaster, they offer no ready route to recovery.[7]

Companies in crisis

The title of an article caught our eye and we thought it could be very relevant once we started thinking about companies in crisis and the road that they would have to take to recovery. The article invited us to 'turn a crisis into an opportunity'.[8] In a sense that is what should happen when crisis comes, since the objective is to do far more than just get out of trouble. The objective is to get back on the road, the road to recovery. The article dealt with a wide range of crises, from a train derailment to a terrorist attack, but it demonstrated that there were certain common traits in every crisis. Crisis, through proper management, can be turned into an opportunity! Crisis comes suddenly, creates a sense of urgency and demands instant action. Crisis is highly visible and *has* to be dealt with. This means that not only the chief executive and his co-directors are aware, but also all the employees. A crisis focuses *everyone's* attention on what has happened and cries out for cooperation. It also gives individuals chance to demonstrate their capabilities: the occasion brings the man. Sometimes that man is the chief executive and that is the best outcome of all. It was Samuel Johnson, made famous by Boswell as one who was always pointing out the obvious, who said that when a man knows he is going to be hanged in a fortnight, he concentrates his mind extremely well. This is in fact what happens in a crisis, bringing people to do things and achieve results they never dreamt that they were capable of achieving.

Attempts have been made to formulate what should be the proper reaction to a crisis situation, but this will not work. Each crisis is unique, just as each company is unique, just as each human body has its own unique 'chemistry'. It is therefore not possible to set out beforehand what should be done. The crisis itself produces the answer, in that, as Samuel Johnson said, 'it concentrates the mind'. To illustrate, one paper, defining crisis as some external, critical event, sought to establish through surveys the appropriate strategy in the face of financial crisis from among a group of possibilities.[9] The alternatives that were open were said to be:

- Develop an aggressive marketing strategy to increase sales.
- Seek cuts in operating budgets of all divisions and departments.
- Impose across-the-board cuts in operating budgets.
- Enlist support of unions – for jointly improving productivity.
- Staff should be reduced
- Eliminate new products that are still only marginally profitable.
- Increase capital expenditure, to provide more efficient equipment.

These were supposed to be rated in order of importance, but we will go no further because this will never be the way a crisis is handled and we know from the responses we ourselves have made to surveys of this type how superficial the response can actually be. At the moment of crisis the immediate need is always obvious. It may take courage and resolution to implement the necessary action, but the crisis situation seems to call forth the qualities required – not always, but quite frequently, as some of our case studies will demonstrate. Not always, because companies fail and will go on failing despite all the good advice that is offered.

Bankruptcy as a management tool!

It is possible in certain circumstances for a company to cope with crisis by resorting to bankruptcy. In the US the bankruptcy laws have a provision, commonly referred to as 'Chapter 11', whereby a company may stop paying its debts while it reorganizes its finances. There is no compulsion on the existing directors or the chief executive to resign, with a receiver taking over, nor is there any time limit. The major countries in Western Europe, Germany, France, Italy and the UK are in the process of rewriting their bankruptcy laws and while doing so are looking closely at the American procedures.[10] The main dilemma is the course that should be taken when the assets are greater than the debts. Should the creditors be helped to get their money back as quickly as possible (it is there) or should the company be helped to recover. In that case the creditors will have to wait for their money and there is always the chance that if the turnaround is not successful they will never get it. The current trend is to design the law so that the company in trouble is helped to survive, because of the social implications. Chapter 11 in the US provides for this alternative very neatly, but it now seems that it is being abused.

In the US firms that get into difficulty can take legal shelter not only from their creditors but from court claimants and the unions. Until 1982, Chapter 11 was used mainly by companies in financial trouble, but the Manville Corporation, facing massive liability suits as a consequence of the use of their asbestos products, used Chapter 11 in a novel way.[11] The company can carry on under the existing directorship, so it was split into two, one carrying the entire liability but few assets, while the other carries on with the day-to-day manufacturing business of the company. After meeting operating expenses, that company would transfer all residual cash to the company carrying the liability for claims, to assist it in meeting those claims. But the settlement of claims would just have to wait until the money was there: the company could not be liquidated to furnish the funds. Manville now has imitators. The company A. H. Robins, manufacturers of the *Dalkon Shield*, a contraceptive device, now facing claims from women the world over, has adopted a similar procedure. Union Carbide, if only to survive in the face of the Bhopal disaster, may well have to follow suit. On the other hand, both Wilson Foods and Continental Airlines have used Chapter 11 in order to break labour contracts. The companies survive, but the question remains: are these acceptable roads to recovery?[12]

Part of the problem lies hidden, because when a company gets on the road to failure this is due, as we have said, to mismanagement. But at what point does mismanagement become wrongful trading or fraud? Most countries have criminal penalties for fraud and the new bankruptcy law introduced in the UK in April 1986 makes directors personally financially liable in certain circumstances. But of course their liability would have to be established in the courts in accordance with the law.

Delegation as a management tool

We have said and we shall later demonstrate by example, that the chief executive is *the* most important person in the company, since it is upon his abilities that success depends. It is the chief executive who will have led a company down the road to failure and it is a chief executive who will have to lead a company up the road to recovery. Chief executives do not live for ever and the day comes when a successor has to be appointed. It is said that picking a successor is the most important and at the same time the toughest decision that a chief executive and his co-directors will ever have to make.[13] It is also, it seems, often the worst decision that they make. The magazine *Fortune* regularly publishes a list of the top 500 companies in the US and the longest-reigning chief executive among the companies so listed, J. Peter Grace of the company W. R. Grace, when thinking of his retirement and his inevitable replacement, said that a lot of wrong people are selected. It is a growing problem, but what guides the choice? Those with experience highlight the problem. Ben Heineman proclaims his experience and expounds the problem when he says:

> At Northwest Industries we operate a large number of companies and I have not always taken the recommendation of the retiring chief executive. I thought I knew better and I had to live with the decision. It's the biggest guessing game, a gamble, for there is 'no rung on the way up the corporate ladder that prepared you for the last one'.

There is, however, one interesting rule of thumb: 'it helps to have been knocked down on the upward climb'. You will see later how many of the company 'doctors' whose experiences we review were indeed knocked down as they sought to climb upward.

Age is also significant, although some of our 'doctors' have been young enough when they got started in the role. Michael Edwardes (later Sir Michael) received the *Guardian* 'Young Businessman of the Year' award in 1975, and two years later he was invited to take on the awesome task of bringing about the recovery of British Leyland. But in general it seems that an older man would be preferred. James H. Evans, the chairman of Union Pacific, is reported as saying: 'I'd always go with the guy 55 over the guy 45. He's had ten more years experience and has been roughed up in the fray'. The general expectation is that there should be an 'heir apparent', groomed to take over at the appropriate time and this is obviously the way in which the problem should be approached. But it seems that there is a great dearth of 'heirs apparent'.

To illustrate, a prominent advertisement in the national press (in India) caught our eye. Its headline: 'Wanted: Chief Executive'. The company issuing the advertisement was a large, successful, internationally known trading company so we wondered how such a company could get into such a position, with no one ready to step into the chief executive's office. Was this the exception or the rule? It was not an exception, since there had been similar advertisements, also issued by well-known and highly respected companies, in times past. Checking with our friends in the 'head hunting' business, we got confirmation that this was indeed nothing unusual. But why? What was wrong? Surely it was self-evident that a time would come when a new chief executive would have to take over and there would normally be plenty of time to groom someone within the organization to take over. Sudden illness or death might precipitate a crisis, but that was not the cause.

Afraid to delegate

We have come to the conclusion that while managers profess to understand and apply the principle of delegation, in practice they know nothing about it. Delegation is an art that has to be learnt on the job – the hard way. To delegate is to entrust part of the work to another person and the dictionary describes it thus:

To entrust to another.
To appoint as one's representative.
To assign responsibility and authority.
Act of empowering to act for another.

This not only makes very clear what delegation is, but also tells us that the responsibility that is being delegated must be accompanied by the appropriate authority and it is this element that is so often ignored. Peter Drucker once defined a manager as 'one who accomplishes tasks through others', but it looks as though that definition needs revision since in an interview with the *Boardroom Reports* in 1984 he is reported as saying that the most common mistake that managers make is to 'think that they are supposed to delegate part of *their* job. . .the purpose of delegation is to enable the manager to concentrate on his *own* job, not to delegate it away'. What he must do, however, is to properly and fully delegate to others all the jobs which he need not do.

When you see an overburdened manager, working long hours, taking work home, assess whether he should really be doing that. A manager should learn to work skilfully, but not necessarily intensively. Long hours are often an indication that he is not delegating as he should. Efficient managers constantly evaluate their workload to see what they can delegate to others. Andrew Carnegie considered delegation to be so important that he said that 'When a man realizes he can call others in to help him to do a job better than he can do it alone, he has taken a big step in his life'. Our case studies will bring us more than one example of that: we leave you to see which they are. But why are managers so slow, so reluctant to delegate? Here are some of the reasons:

They believe that they alone are capable of doing the job.
They are afraid to make a mistake in choosing the delegatee.
They have a feeling of job insecurity.
They are unable to communicate properly.
They are not clear about their own authority.
They can do the job faster themselves.
They prefer fire fighting to fire prevention.

What we are trying to do here is to institute a process of self-examination. Our readers will have picked up this book because they are interested in management matters and in all probability they will be holding down a job as a manager – there are really few of us who are not 'managers' these days! To help in this process of self-examination, let us conclude this brief examination of the principle of delegation, crucial as it is to success, by asserting that *you* cannot delegate if:

You take yourself too seriously.
You have no trust and confidence in your subordinates.

You never take a day off.
You take work home every night and weekends.
You have no hobby or interest other than the office.
You rarely read for recreation.
You worry about details.
You are always overruling your subordinates.
You rarely have time to discuss details.

Normally we get to know little about the private lives of the leaders of industry and you will see that is true of the turnaround managers and company doctors whom we are now going to learn from. We shall see, however, that they successfully delegate much to others, getting them to work with them, so they will not be committing the mistakes we have just listed. While some of them, if not all, get to work early and stay late, that is not of necessity but of choice.

Using consultants

Continuing the analogy, and having stated that there *is* a road to recovery, not all of us, when disaster looms, would wish to take the much-publicized option of appointing a new chief executive as a turnaround manager. There is an alternative these days which can be quite effective, although it is not an alternative that we shall enlarge upon once we have introduced it to you, because it hardly harmonizes with our present theme. Once it is recognized that there is a need for positive action, one course is to call in a consultant. But it must be appreciated that to be effective, he has to be allowed to play a most intimate role. The consultant, during the period of his assignment, has to be treated very much as an 'insider'. He must have all your confidence and nothing must be withheld from him. Their role is usually that of a 'catalyst'. They initiate and speed up the reaction without taking part. The preface to a book on the subject identifies the role a consultant should play thus: [14]

> Management consultants often have a talent, knack, skill, flair, call it what you will, of adjusting the pieces of a mental jigsaw into an order which creates a clear picture.

But the consultant cannot guarantee success. The consultant can only bring about change if his client is willing to listen and since his advice is likely to be unpalatable, it may be difficult indeed to get the client to listen. Indeed, we should go so far as to say that a consultant should not be called in unless the client has already made a firm resolve to act upon such advice as may be tendered to him. Unfortunately, many of the benefits that result from the employment of a consultant never see the light of day, because they are normally extremely confidential. Also, since to call in a consultant amounts to a confession of failure on the part of management, secrecy is once again the order of the day.

A common cause of trouble is what we call the 'pet project', as you will see when we come to our case studies. Pet projects have been the death of many a company and the book to which we have just referred gives us a most interesting example.[14] The story is anonymous, but the lesson is clear. To quote:

> A client (a technical enthusiast) in electrical and electronic engineering. . .saw that much of his electrical products were becoming obsolete with the trend for newer electronic technology. Of course, change to electronics. . .is a formidable and expensive task. My contribution was to curtail my client's enthusiasm – to point out that there was still several years' life in the old products and that he should not get bored with them too soon – particularly as some of his competitors with an equal eye to the future were getting out of the obsolescent market – leaving a greater share of it to my client.

As we said right at the beginning of this chapter, there are more roads than one to recovery and success and it is not a bad idea to choose a road no one else is going along. Free of the crowd, you can get on better!

In view of its importance one would have thought that turnaround strategies and their implementation would provide a most lucrative career for consultants, but that does not seem to happen. Perhaps this comes about because reform has to come from within, so that the consultant who develops the necessary skills turns into a chief executive. What *is* very clear is that prevention is always better than cure. Prevention involves discovering and unearthing trouble *before* it turns into a crisis. Above all, don't get the idea that there is any special 'magic' involved. All that is required, most of the time, is common sense. Don't be awed by the size of companies and so be led into thinking that those who run them have very special attributes. They really have not. There is a book with a very dramatic title, *Life and Death on the Corporate Battlefield* which is well worth reading in this context.[15] Written by two enthusiastic journalists, it highlights and explodes a number of myths, such as the idea that in big business the executives know exactly what they are doing. They don't! Harold Geneen, who ran the world-famous company ITT for seventeen years, up to his retirement, propelling that company to near the top among the multinationals, was prepared to say that 'most chief executive officers today *don't know* how to handle their jobs'.[16] Senior executives, even in the biggest of companies, are neither omniscient nor omnipotent. They are very human, so human indeed that at a time of crisis they are quite likely to put their own interest, such as the preservation of their position, before the interests of their company. Please don't do that.

Summary

We trust that the illustrations and examples we have brought to you so far have brought a conviction that whatever the crisis, there is no need for despair. There is *always* a road to recovery: the problem is to find it. It seems that the relevant knowledge rests with the few rather than the many. Perhaps this is because the best teacher is experience and one has to have had experience – the bitter experience – of having been personally involved in a crisis in order to learn how to cope. It is also true that such knowledge is extremely valuable, and can result in a very lucrative career for those who make a business of company turnaround, as is also demonstrated by some of the case studies to which we shall come.

References

1   Altman, E. I., *Corporate Financial Distress. A Complete Guide to Predicting, Avoiding, and Dealing with Bankruptcy*, Wiley, 1983.
2   Wilcox, J. W., Book Review, *Journal of Banking and Finance*, no. 8, March 1984, pp. 142–4.
3   Altman, E. I., *Corporate Bankruptcy in America*, D. C. Heath, Lexington, 1971.
4   Beaver W. H., 'Financial ratios as predictors of failure', *Empirical Research in Accounting: Selected Studies*, supplement to *Journal of Accounting Research*, January 1967, pp. 71–111. Beaver, W. H., 'Alternative accounting measures as predictors of failure', *Accounting Review*, January 1968, pp. 113–22.
5   Altman, E. I., Avery R., Eisenbeis R., and Sinkey J., *Application of Classification Techniques in Business, Banking and Finance*, JAI Press, 1981.

6   Argenti, J., 'Company failure – long-range prediction is not enough', *Accountancy*, August 1977, pp. 46–52.

7   Kharbanda, O. P. and Stallworthy E. A., *Corporate Failure: Prediction, Panacea and Prevention*, McGraw-Hill, 1985.

8   Stephenson, D. R., 'Turning a crisis into an opportunity', *Manage*, no. 35, March 1983, pp. 28–9.

9   Smart, C. and Vertinsky I., 'Strategy and the environment – a study of corporate responses to crisis', *Strategic Management Journal*, No. 5, July-September 1984, pp. 199–213.

10 'Europe's bankruptcy laws take a leaf out of Chapter 11', *Economist*, no. 293, 15 December 1984, pp. 87–8.

11 'Manville reorganisation plan resolves nothing', *Business Week*, 5 December 1983, pp. 72–3.

12 'Companies going bust – New ways to keep out of Carey Street', *Economist*, no. 299, 26 April 1986, pp. 77–8.

13 Rowan, R., 'The tricky task of picking an heir apparent', *Fortune*, no. 107, 2 May 1983, pp. 56–64.

14 Tisdall, P., *Agents of Change: The Developments and Practice of Management Consultancy*, Heinemann, 1982.

15 Solman, P. and Friedman T., *Life and Death on the Corporate Battlefield: How Companies Win, Lose and Survive*, Simon & Schuster, 1983.

16 Lubar, R., in a review of H. Geneen and A. Moscow, *Managing*, Doubleday, 1984, published in *Fortune*, no. 110, 29 October 1984.

4 One man can make the difference

While management as a whole has a most important role to play, there seems to be no doubt at all that the quality of the man (or woman) at the very top is crucial. What is more, an outstanding personality *below* the top cannot bring success: that seems more a recipe for disaster. A typical example of this is Iacocca, whose work we examine in detail in Chapter 10. At Ford, where he rose meteorically, there was a personality clash, and he had to go right to the top – at Chrysler – before his very special abilities could bring dramatic results.

Why *do* companies fail?

There is no doubt, as we shall be demonstrating with a multitude of examples, that the chief executive, more than any other single person, can make or break a company. Thus, when assessing the status and quality of a company, it is vital to take a good, clear look at the chief executive. Among the possible causes of corporate collapse the most significant is undoubtedly the quality (or rather, lack of quality) of the chief executive.[1] Companies in trouble have been found to have very similar symptoms, such as:

- Lack of good leadership.
- An obsolete product.
- No sense of urgency.
- No understanding of cash flow.

Six major factors have been identified as being at the root of business failure. They were:

1 Top management.
2 Accounting information.
3 Change.
4 The manipulation of accounts.
5 Rapid expansion.
6 The economic cycle.

Notice that both lists are in effect headed by the same cause, for it is the top management which alone can ensure good leadership.

A system based on these concepts has been developed that enables one to assess the viability of a company.[2] It assesses various aspects of management performance, as set out in Table 2. Failure is seen as the culmination of a sequence starting with management defects that bring mistakes, which in turn produce symptoms. These symptoms, with their proposed scores, are presented in Table 2. The important point for us at the moment is the weighting given to the chief executive and his influence on the conduct of the company. The scores set out in Table 2 are all bad marks, so the higher the score, the worse the state of the company. There is said to be a probability of failure if the score is 25 or higher, while if it reaches 35 failure was certain. Notice that the chief executive can contribute more than half to possible 'failure' (25) all by himself (8+4+2). So top management gets – and deserves – very substantial weighting in this assessment. If top management was failing in management ability, then the company was almost inevitably on the road to failure.

Table 2 *The Argenti sequence. This table presents the weighting given by Argenti to the various aspects of management performance in order to assess a company's viability. Note in particular that the higher the score, the worse the state of the company*

Defects	In management:
	8 The chief executive is an autocrat.
	4 He is also the chairman.
	2 Passive board – an autocrat will see to that.
	2 Unbalanced board – too many engineers or too many finance types.
	2 Weak finance director.
	1 Poor management depth.

In accountancy:

3   No budgets or budgetary controls (to assess variances, etc.).

3   No cash flow plans, or ones that are not updated.

3   No costing system. Cost and contribution of each product unknown.

15   Poor response to change, old-fashioned product, obsolete factory, old directors, out-of-date marketing.

Total defects   43   *Pass*   10
mistakes

15   High leverage, firm could get into trouble by a stroke of bad luck.

15   Overtrading. Company expanding faster than its funding. Capital base too small or unbalanced for the size and type of business.

15   Big project, gone wrong. Or any obligation which they cannot meet if something goes wrong.

Total mistakes   45   *Pass*   15
symptoms

4   Financial signs, sugh as Z-score. Appears near failure time.

4   Creative accounting. Chief executive is the first to see signs of failure, and in an attempt to hide it from creditors and the banks, accounts are 'glossed over' by, for instance, overvaluing stocks using lower depreciation, etc. Skilled observers can spot these things.

3   Non-financial signs, such as untidy offices, frozen salaries, chief executive 'ill', high staff turnover, low morale, rumours.

1   Terminal signs.

Total symptoms   12

Total possible score   100   *Pass*   25

So important, then, is the chief executive. But what does a chief executive have to be and to do, to lead a company to success? That is a most difficult question to answer, as you will see as we go on to look at a few, but very diverse, examples. They seem to be as different from one another as chalk is from cheese, yet each guided a company – and some many companies – to success. Are there any constant qualities which we can identify? Well, let us see. The men we have chosen to look at have at least one thing in common: they are company 'doctors'. That is, they have turned around, or 'cured' not one but many companies in their time. But their techniques seem to be drastically different the one from the other. Let us start in Japan.

Umeo Oyama

A disco dancer at seventy-four, Umeo Oyama is best known for the one big turnaround that he refused to take on, the salvation of the Riccar Company, a sewing machine manufacturer. At seventy-four he had already 'doctored' nineteen ailing companies of various sizes, most of which have survived and gone on from strength to strength. He is a wisecracking, nonstop talker, hasn't caught a cold for thirty years, eats green vegetables like a rabbit, has a good sense of humour, and asserts that he has many rescue missions still to come.

His formula for success is to save money, in particular by exercising rigid control of all the outgoings, in harmony with an ancient Japanese proverb:

Chiri mo tsumoreba yama to naru.

which when translated means, in effect:

Look after the pennies and the pounds will look after themselves.

This proverbial approach may seem to run contrary to another well-known proverb, 'penny wise, pound foolish', but it all depends upon the context. Umeo Oyama was looking at the production facilities. When it comes to the spending of money on research and development, the wisdom of the second proverb should indeed hold sway.

Looking after the pennies

How does Umeo Oyama look after the pennies? He personally checks expenses as little as a hundred yen (about 40 US cents), and spends hours every day approving hundreds of invoices. He is particularly allergic to entertainment expenses. He temporarily reduces salaries, presses older employees to take early retirement, asks lenders to reduce their interest rates and suppliers to reduce their prices. . .while the turnaround is being accomplished. He draws no salary but acquires stock in the company 'for a song': easy enough because it is a failing company. He then reaps a major financial reward when the stock recovers in response to his efforts within the company.

The Ikegai Corporation and the oldest machine tool manufacturer in Japan, is but one example of his work. Its bankers, the Industrial Bank of Japan, requested Umeo Oyama to take over in 1984. While it was indeed a bad time for the machine tool industry, the Ikegai Corporation had developed 'hardened arteries'. It had already lost a third of its workforce through various economy schemes before Umeo Oyama arrived on the scene. As usual, he cut expenses to the bone. He eliminated the 3 per cent discount offered to distributors and even got the bank who had called him in to reduce their rate of interest on their loans from 8 per cent to 4 per cent. Within two years the company was paying its first dividend in thirteen years, and Umeo Oyama will start drawing a salary. Meanwhile, he had taken a block of a million shares in the company at 350 yen, which over the same period had risen to 450 yen.

He discovered that the management had been extremely in-efficient. Many workers were drinking on the job, since the management had been trying to gain their goodwill through alcohol. Umeo Oyama greeted them all in the morning, and then made sure to shake hands with every one as they left in the evening, smelling their breath at the same time to confirm that they were sober! The workers themselves were anxious for improvement: to illustrate the impact of the deplorable state of affairs on them there is the story of the son of an employee who was refused marriage by his fiancee's family because the firm was thought to be going bankrupt. Umeo Oyama cut costs to such an extent that a running loss was turned to a profit within a month. He found that entertainment costs were 7 per cent of sales, whereas the average in Japan was 0.5 per cent, so that was another area for attack. He achieved a most remarkable turnaround, and the company now has an excellent financial rating even though the steel industry is still a depressed industry.

An even tougher commitment was Tsugami, manufacturers of high quality measuring instruments and machine tools. The company had obsolete manufacturing methods and outmoded technology, tough in-house labour unions, and the recession to contend with. Salaries were being paid more than two months late, those on pension were not getting their pension, payments to subcontractors and suppliers were late: even the employees' tax and social welfare deductions were not being paid. And, of course, the company was massively in debt to the banks. Umeo Oyama began by meeting all the employees to assess their mood and ask for ideas. The union agreed to cost cuts to prevent layoffs, so that some 450 out of 1800 employees took early retirement and the rest accepted a 10 per cent cut in wages. He eliminated a very expensive practice in the works, whereby every part of the tools they were producing was polished, by simply asking the workers a naive and somewhat stupid question: 'Does your wife powder her hip?' This did the trick, because it made them reflect upon the effectiveness and purpose of what they had been doing. He was successful in transforming the company and now his son Ryuichi is a vice-president.

Seeing Umeo Oyama seems able to accomplish the impossible, why did he refuse to help Riccar in 1984? Riccar was the third largest sewing machine manufacturer in the world and it would have been quite a feather in his cap. Various reasons have been given. Initially he agreed and this was hailed with relief by both the company's banks and its employees, and it was said that he then turned the job down because his masseuse told him that the company failed to repair her sewing machine despite repeated requests. Another reason given was that the company had sought legal protection under Japan's corporate rehabilitation laws, whereby all its debts would be written off. Umeo Oyama's reaction: 'The law shouldn't protect such companies'. But we suspect a much more prosaic reason, namely that he was unable to buy stock in the company at an advantageous price. At all events, the company went bankrupt with debts of US$385 million, the fourth biggest crash in post-war Japan, and Umeo Oyama lost some of his credibility. In a poll later conducted by *Nikkeie Business* he figured not only in their popularity list but also in their unpopularity list.

But how do others really see him? Some see him as practical, impatient with sloppiness and waste, with a unique blend of charm and fury. He gets angry and shouts a lot. . .perhaps the end justifies the means? Others, however, describe his methods as crude, suspect his motives and see him as a publicity seeker, only in the business for the money. He seems to have no set pattern in his rescue work, and even his son Ryuichi says 'We don't know exactly what is going on in his mind'. He has certainly enabled the companies he has served make money, though he himself has also made money in the process – he owns a Rolls Royce and lives in a mansion in Central Tokyo, where the land alone is said to be worth US$10 million.[3]

It takes all sorts

By way of contrast – and it *is* a contrast – let us now look at a company 'doctor' in the UK, Sir John Cuckney, currently chairman of Westland Helicopters, a company at the centre of a political storm in the recent past, mentioned briefly in Chapter 15. Sir John actually aspired to be a medical doctor, we are told.[4] Instead he has become Britain's most celebrated 'company doctor'. His most recent success was to avert bankruptcy at Westland, a task given to him by the Bank of England in the summer of 1985. Sir John has long been well-known in financial circles in the City. He is a typical Englishman, calm, having dignity under pressure. Son of a pioneering aviator, he served in the Royal Northumberland Fusiliers, whose motto is:

Whither the fates call.

Fate called him to history and economics, rather than medicine, eight years at the War Office and then stockbroking. He became a director of Lazard Brothers, a 'blue-blooded' merchant bank, going on to buy his own small merchant bank. At the same time he was called in to sort out a financial crisis at the Mersey Docks and Harbour Board in North West England, and from then on this became his speciality. He seemed to pick up directorships and chairmanships galore. He was chairman of Brooke Bond, the internationally famous tea and food processing company, where he first learnt to cope with hostile shareholders: in this case questioning the living conditions of company employees in India and Africa. He was also chairman of John Brown, an engineering company he was at the same time salvaging, being chairman of its major shareholder, the Midland Bank. He was also chairman of Royal Insurance and Thomas Cook, the travel agents. Notice the diverse nature of the companies in which he is involved. Umeo Oyama largely confined himself to the machine tool industry, in which presumably he feels himself knowledgeable, but the nature of the company seems immaterial to Sir John, presumably because he is fundamentally a financial man and it is the financial aspects of the company which he deals with, rather than the technical aspects.

Looking at him as a man, he is known to 'juggle' many different and very separate jobs simultaneously through the most efficient use of his time. He sticks to the main points at business meetings and refuses to deal with side issues which, if necessary, he delegates to others. A most public example of this approach of his came in the struggle for the destiny of Westland Helicopters. At a shareholders' meeting in the middle of the crisis, Alan Bristow, who supported the offer being made by the European Consortium, insisted that Sir John had privately given him the breakeven point (in numbers) for the Black Hawk helicopters that would be manufactured at Westland under the alternative proposal being put forward by Sikorsky-Fiat. Sir John denied that he had given Mr Bristow any information not available to all the other Westland shareholders. When pressed, with Mr Bristow asserting that he was evading the issue, Sir John replied:

It might be evading the issue. . .but it is not relevant to this meeting.

Shareholders present cheered boisterously and Mr Bristow had to shut up and sit down. As one admiring banker commented: 'He never gets depressed or overelated. He always keeps his cool.' Thus far Sir John, a very different character to Umeo Oyama, but equally effective when it comes to rescuing troubled companies.

John Willis – the French expert

John Willis, an Englishman living in Paris, has seen and satisfied a need in relation to the operation of foreign-held companies in France. He is an accomplished balloonist, but he keeps his feet firmly on the ground when it comes to business. His speciality is 'doctoring' small- and medium-sized French-based companies facing difficulty. Born in India, but educated at Marlborough College in the UK, he never went on to university, first starting work as an apprentice with the British Aircraft Corporation and becoming an electronics engineer, then a missile salesman for that company. Thereafter he was with Univac for a short while and it was their contract with Air France that took him to Paris, where he has lived ever since. Once there he had eight different bosses in eighteen months, but finally set himself up as an investment advisor with his own company *Rule Conseil*. This company, which advises foreign-based internationals on the complexities of French business practice and its legal codes, has a staff with special strength in law, accountancy and government legislation. The company concentrates on turnarounds, with John Willis taking over for a year or two, his fee being either in cash or in kind (shares). He concentrates on the 'bottom line' and he always looks at five main areas:

- Currency control.
- Documentation.
- Trade union relationships.
- Finance.
- Debt responsibility.

In these areas he highlights those aspects that are peculiar to the French system of things and shows how they should be handled. For instance, the Comite d'Enterprise, the local trade union committee, has a very important role in law and their support in a turnaround, where labour could well have to go, is a must. Another peculiarity of French law is that a lender to an ailing company is liable if the company goes bankrupt. Even the personal fortunes of managers and directors can be forfeited. Willis himself would be personally liable if his turnaround failed and the company with which he was involved went bankrupt.[5]

The story goes that Willis discovered and developed his present business almost by accident, noticing that the failure of British companies to understand the complex French practices was a frequent cause of disaster. He first went into partnership with two British accountants, but was soon on his own. It appears that the 'doctoring' began when an investor asked him to help a nudist village, *Aphrodite*, being established in the South of France. Founded in 1975, the aim of the company was to sell 550 apartments but in two years had sold a mere fifty. Willis knew nothing about real estate, but he analysed the problem. The business was not being run professionally. So he went out and recruited professionals to run it and by 1979 sales had increased to nearly a hundred a year, four times the previous rate, despite a recession in real estate in France. Thus the company continues to flourish.[6]

It seems that French business practice is most complicated, with a continual demand for paperwork. Hiring and firing is complex, collective agreement formalities formidable and the accounting rules a nightmare. Willis warns that in France 'paper comes out of your ears' and it is completely impossible to do business without going through all the necessary formalities in precise detail. There was, for instance, the case of a British company proposing to install fruit machines at Calais Hoverport. Willis warned the company not to go ahead without formal permission. The Calais local authorities gave verbal permission and the company went ahead, but before installation all the machines had to go back. The paperwork *must* be there!

What is the Willis approach? He insists that authority must go with responsibility. He gets the authority and then brings in his own personal incentive by taking a stake in the company, *à la* Umeo Oyama. What do his clients think of him? One said of him: 'He displays an enormous amount of tenacity, both financial and economic'. The director of another company, this time from Ireland, said: 'Had it not been for his help, we would have been sunk'.

It seems that Willis has succeeded where so many others have failed primarily by careful attention to detail. In that sense too he reminds us somewhat of Umeo Oyama – have we found a 'common chord' in 'company doctors'? Let us see.

Seeking an expert opinion

The magazine *Fortune* instituted some research into potential chief executives, eventually publishing the results as a cover story.[7] A dozen executive search firms were asked to review their 'star' file or secret 'hot list' to nominate the best person they had on their books to be chief executive in ten separate industries. Some recruitment companies named two or three people for one particular industry, while others had nobody on their list for some industries. The result of this enquiry was to produce a list of 150 names in all. Then four of the search firms were asked to rate the persons nominated, without disclosing their source. This produced a short list of thirty, three for each industry. The top ten were publicized in the magazine, each with a half-page description. It certainly must have brought an immediate raise in salary for all those fortunate enough to have had their names blazoned abroad in this way.

We were interested, not in the names, but in the principles guiding the selectors. Here are some of the things they said:

- The prospective chief executive has to be action-orientated. You find a lot of planners who can't act.
- We look for somebody who has effectively managed change. If you are looking outside for a new leader, you are saying things have to be altered.
- I look for the ability to build a sense of shared values. An outsider

coming in as chief executive officer must still be able to motivate and generate loyalty.
- I think the key is judgment . . . a vision of where the enterprise should be heading.

Yet another expert in the field says that he looks for commitment: a willingness to pay the price, including family and personal sacrifice. If you meditate upon the qualities and attributes of the 'company doctors' we have just been looking at we think you will see all these several qualities coming through – and as we go through our case studies this remains true. The qualities highlighted above *are* important. The 'company doctor' has to be a man of action, he has to manage change, he has to take the employees along with him, and he has to have a clear vision as to the way he wants the company to go.

Summary

The principle has been established that it is the chief executive, more than any other single individual in a company, who can make or break that company. So vital is this one man to success. It is for this reason that the chief executive must figure prominently in any qualitative assessment of the 'health' of a company. Of course, the chief executive does not conform to any standard pattern, nor would we expect him (or her) to. By taking a brief look at some chief executives who have had substantial experience in restoring the 'health' of companies, and so can be classed as 'company doctors', such as Umeo Oyama, Sir John Cuckney and John Willis, we have seen that despite their very different approaches, they have things in common. They have successfully 'doctored' a number of companies and it seems that they thrive on challenge.

While each 'doctor' is of course unique, certain common characteristics are beginning to emerge and we shall build on these as we now go on to look at many more 'doctors' and see how they went about their 'doctoring'.

References

1   Argenti, J., *Corporate Collapse: The Causes and the Symptoms*, McGraw-Hill, 1976.
2   Argenti, J., 'Company failure – long-range prediction is not enough', *Accountancy*, August 1977, pp. 46–52.

3   Hann, P., 'Umeo Oyama: this corporate doctor with homespun remedies is no quack', *International Management*, May 1985, p. 53.

4   Hagerty, R., 'For "Company Doctor" rescue cases are routine', *International Herald Tribune*, 15–16 February 1986. (A business profile of Sir John Cuckney, chairman of Westland Helicopters.)

5   'John Willis: threading a path through the French way of doing business', *International Management*, November 1984, p. 45.

6   Betts, P., 'Company doctor – To the rescue in France, *Financial Times*, 10 September 1985, p. 10.

7   Rowan, R., 'America's most wanted managers', *Fortune*, no. 113, 3 February 1986, pp. 18–25.

Part Two

Typical turnarounds

5   Steel and the Americans

Steel is basic to any economy: this remains true despite the several substitutes that are now available. Both metals and plastics have been increasingly used as substitutes for steel since the Second World War, with the result that there has been a decline in the steel industry worldwide, but more particularly in the developed world, where the industry had been established for a century or more and had long reached the stage of maturity. The developed world has been the more severely hit because there have been major new entrants manufacturing steel and steel products on a major scale: India, Japan and Korea are typical. So not only is the worldwide market in decline, but there are many more companies competing in that market than there were. Does this mean that all is lost? Not necessarily: even in such adverse conditions it is possible for companies not only to survive but thrive. We are going to take two illustrations, one from the US and the other from the UK, but in both cases it has been an American who has accomplished the turnaround. But let us begin by looking at the industry as a whole to see the scale of the problem.

The background

Going back, first of all, to the 1950s, world production of steel was then some 300 million tonnes, of which the US made some 40 per cent. By 1982, although world production had more than doubled, to some 650 million tonnes, the US share of that market had dropped to some 10 per cent. If you do the sums you will see that despite the worldwide increase, tonnage production in the US had actually halved over the period. The situation climaxed in 1982, with the US industry losing some US$3.4 billion in that year and shipments dropping by some 30 per cent over the year before.[1] In a desperate bid to survive, excess capacity to the tune of some 20 million tonnes was closed down and 150,000 workers in the industry lost their jobs. Suffering from cheap imports, chiefly from Korea, the industry asked Washington to help by restricting imports into the US. This was done, although there were strong protests, particularly from the European countries, whose steel industries were in the same difficulty and had sought a measure of relief by exporting to the US market. Despite the protective measures taken, the steel companies were still losing some US$20 on every tonne produced and many major companies were in serious difficulty. The Wheeler-Pittsburg Steel Corporation filed for bankruptcy, while Armco have been busy restructuring the company in order to avoid bankruptcy. Table 3 illustrates how the major American steelmakers with union contracts fared over the past two years. It is not a happy picture. The continuing question is: Where do we go from here? Import restrictions would help to increase domestic sales and if maintained for some five years would give the industry a chance to modernize and become competitive on the world market, but some experts have

Table 3 *Major American steelmakers. This table lets us see how the major American steelmakers with union contracts have been faring. Things are getting better, but they still have a long way to go*

	1985		1984	
	Sales US$ billion	Net income US$ million	Sales US$ billion	Net income US$ million
US Steel*	6.6	27	6.5	142
LTV*	5.4	(227)	4.5	(217)
Bethelem	5.1	(196)	5.4	(113)
Inland	3.0	(178)	3.1	(41)
Armco	3.7	(55)	4.0	(295)
National	2.1	(88)	2.3	(21)

Notes:
* Operating income from steel production only.
( ) indicates a loss.

pointed out that import restraint is not necessarily the solution. Indeed, that particular policy can backfire. To quote John C. Tumazos, an analyst with Opperheimer & Company:[1]

Steel prices in this country are already 30 per cent higher than in Europe or the Far East, and the quota program can cause that to continue . . . .It forces manufacturers to relocate their facilities abroad. It encourages work on plastic cars and it accelerates substitution to aluminium . . . .Long term, quotas are the worst possible strategy the steel industry can pursue. They're accelerating the decline in steel volumes.

Nor should one underestimate the resourceful importer, according to Robert W. Crandall, an analyst with the Brookings Institution. He points out:[1]

If you put limits on steel sheet, then companies will import body stampings. If you limit steel stampings, then companies will import the next fabricated product.

The unions pose their own threat. The unions in the steel industry are not only strong and powerful, but knowledgeable. An advertisement by the United Steelworkers Union on the eve of negotiating new labour contracts proclaimed:[2]

America's economy is like a row of dominoes . . . if the steel dominoe falls, others will also fall.

Nevertheless, the union is being realistic. With jobs continuously threatened, they agreed in January 1986 to cuts in pay at the weaker of the six major producers. US Steel is not included, so that particular company is likely to face confrontation with the unions and a possible strike. If that happens it will be the first since 1959.[3] In a report commissioned by the union, a New York consulting group was asked to help devise strategies for the crucial negotiations. Such an assignment is almost unthinkable anywhere else in the world. The 76–page report, appropriately entitled *Confronting the crisis*, warned of a grim future for the industry, with employment levels unlikely to recover and there being no alternative to wage cuts. So the union decided to cooperate. In return for their cooperation the unions have demanded and secured much more control in the way the companies were being run, and looked for compensation in terms of cash bonuses from profits or shares. This is the pattern of things as already established with Wheeler-Pittsburg, now operating under court protection. Wage cuts were taken, but the union got a seat on the board and monthly meetings between the top executives in the company and union officials. This has resulted in a marked improvement in labour relations. The unions are now beginning to claim that they have already played their part, since 70 per cent of the cost savings achieved so far have been at their expense, by way of wage cuts and layoffs since 1982, when the industry went into deep decline. Employment in the industry has halved over the past ten years: some 450,000 in 1977, it is now less than 200,000. But none of this can bring a lasting solution. That has to be sought elsewhere, as we shall now see.

There is salvation in diversification

David Roderick is a quiet accountant who took charge of US Steel in 1979. At sixty-two he hardly looks like a 'ruthless company doctor and corporate hatchet man', but he has shaken up this steel, coal and shipping conglomerate more than anyone else since the legendary Andrew Carnegie and J. P. Morgan first put the company together at the beginning of the century.[4] Roderick bought Marathon Oil for US$6.4 billion, an acquisition which caused US Steel to be listed in the oil section of the *Fortune 500* and he has now acquired Texas Oil & Gas, one of the most successful gas exploration and distribution companies in the US. He seems to expect the young and entrepreneural management of this company to play a key role in the management of US Steel and such a transformation of its management could well be its salvation.

This diversification into oil and gas has been associated with the most comprehensive retrenchment ever accomplished in a company in the US. It is Roderick's prescription, designed to revive an ageing bureaucratic organization. Michele Applebaum, an analyst with Solomon Brothers, seems to agree with his approach:[4]

> As the chief architect of the 'new' US Steel, Roderick's goal has been to turn the company from a money-losing behemoth . . . into a profitable, streamlined, natural resources company with two major divisions – steel and oil.

Since Roderick took over in 1979 the steel-making capacity has been slashed from 38 million tonnes to 26 million tonnes, some US$3 billion worth of assets have been sold, bringing in cash that has helped to keep the company in being during one of the worst slumps ever met in the industry. All the company's cement works, a large part of its shipping and barge fleet, a great chunk of its forests and a substantial slice of its coal mining activities have gone. Old, inefficient steelmaking plants have been scrapped, for Roderick had no sentimental attachment to steel as had his predecessor, a production man. Capital assets written off in 1981 totalled US$650 million: in 1983 they peaked at US$1.5 billion. He took a similar unsentimental approach to reductions in the labour force. Employment peaked at 172,000 in 1979, but it has now been halved to 88,000, and this includes some 20,000 employed by Marathon, not there at all in 1979.

This drastic pruning, associated with diversification into gas and oil, is a defensive strategy designed to protect the company against the continuing uncertain future in the steel industry. The Marathon acquisition has indeed proved a perfect match for the slumping steel giant. Big enough to make a real impact – some 25 per cent of the labour force now work for Marathon – its steady if not spectacular earnings have cushioned the balance sheet against the major write-offs we have just described. The acquisition of Texas Oil & Gas could provide additional support. Marathon's sizeable operating profits, running at some US$1.2 billion a year, have more than offset the losses still being made in the steel business. As a result, while most of the steel companies are still passing their dividends, US Steel is confident that it is going to start paying dividends once again. While its market share has fallen, the steel side not only survives but thrives. Ruthless pruning has increased productivity, now five hours per tonne of steel, less than half what it was a few years ago. Operating costs in 1985 were some US$10 per tonne less than those of its competitors and over US$100 per tonne less than they were only three years ago – and this progress is still expected to continue.

As explained above, the situation on the labour front does not look too promising. There has been an industry-wide 'no strike' agreement that has staved off a major strike for some twenty-five years, but this is now lapsing and walkouts are threatened.[5] Their diversification into the oil and gas field would ward off damage from even a lengthy strike in the steel plants, while at the same time offering protection against a hostile takeover, by 'getting into bed with a large and friendly partner'. However, Roderick's objective appears to be a little different. He says:

We did not buy the company [Texas Oil & Gas] for what it is doing in 1986 or 1987 or 1990 – we bought the company because we are satisfied that it is the premier natural gas finder, gatherer and distributor, and has a tremendous future.

The breakdown in coordinated negotiations with the union after more than thirty years could prove a nightmare for the steel industry, since separate negotiations with the various companies in the industry could well result in each company pushing hard to match or exceed the concessions given by its competitors. Nevertheless, Roderick remains confident.[6] He says that US Steel now has some of the newest capacity in the industry: 'we can give anyone a run for his money.' There is continuing upgrading of the finishing facilities, with careful assessment of the viability of individual products. Work practices and employment costs are being kept competitive, at least in the American context. The American wage cannot match the Korean, and at the same time the steelworkers wage has to be kept in line with that of other blue collar workers in the US. Back in 1980 the steel worker was one of the best paid, getting some 90 per cent over the average, but that situation cannot be sustained. The industry can no longer afford such wages. It has shrunk and is still declining, but US Steel is well on the road to recovery. And this recovery is a result of diversification so drastic that the company has been given the nickname *US Oil* by the media.[7] It is certainly justified, in that there has been a complete change in its revenue portfolio, as is demonstrated below:

Percentage revenue from:	Steel %	Oil and gas %	Chemicals %	Others %
1979:	73·1	–	9·3	17·6
1984:	32·0	53·0	7·0	8·0

Announcing the acquisition of the Texas Oil & Gas Corporation in 1985, Roderick undoubtedly had his eyes on the future. He now has two 'legs', steel and energy, but he may well look for a third, using acquisition once again. Indeed, it has been suggested that he might be prepared to spend up to US$5 billion on such an acquisition, in order to reduce steel to less than 25 per cent, rather than the 32 per cent indicated above.

Although the diversification we have outlined has helped US Steel

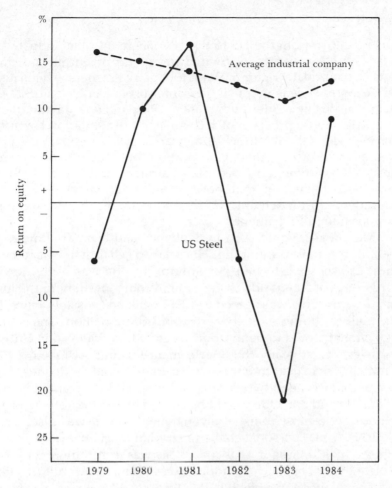

Figure 2 *US Steel is still below average. This comparison between the return on equity for US Steel and the average for industrial companies in the US shows that the company still has some way to go.*

to a turnaround, the company's return on equity is still below average for an American industrial company, as is illustrated in Figure 2. In order to solve the continuing problem, Roderick could even sell off his ailing steel division, but that would be radical surgery. It looks as though Roderick is ending up a 'surgeon' rather than a steelman.

British Steel

Let us now turn from the US to the UK. There the steel industry is almost entirely government owned: there are practically no producers in the private sector and not too many finishers. The British Steel Corporation was in much the same sort of trouble as US Steel back in 1980: losing money at the rate of US$4 million a day, markets contracting and no prospect of recovery. But the situation has now been reversed – thanks to an American, Ian MacGregor. He had retired as head of the Amax Corporation, but was invited by Her Majesty's Government to become chairman of the British Steel Corporation, taking up that position on 1 July 1980. It was an unprecedented arrangement, which came in for much criticism from the opposition in Parliament.

Ian MacGregor, while born in Scotland, had been an American citizen for most of his adult life. His salary as chairman was to be a modest £48,500 (US$70,000) per annum, but he was a partner in Lazard Freres of New York, who required compensation for the loss of his services. This was agreed at US$1·2 billion, possibly rising to US$3·3 billion, but was finally agreed at US$2·2 million. The actual final payment would depend upon what he had achieved in British Steel over three years, his performance being assessed by a committee of five, in accordance with certain agreed guidelines. The committee consisted of two Lazard nominees, two appointed by the government and one who would be chosen by the four others. This was not only a most unusual arrangement, but it was also, very obviously, a great personal challenge for Ian MacGregor.

When Ian MacGregor took over, he was confronted with an organization that had a tremendous excess of manpower: it was like a fat man with heart trouble. It had to lose weight fast just in order to survive. Productivity was miserable: there were 'archaic featherbedding rules – change them if you can!' He was immediately faced with a bitter three month long strike, which brought no relief for either management or workers. The domestic market share was being steadily lost to imports from the European steelmakers. Since the government was the sole shareholder, Ian MacGregor was always answerable to the politicians, with all the problems that it inevitably brings. Thus far the problem: what were his credentials? Why was he chosen? He was an expert in steel technology, a metallurgist specializing in tank armour, first going to the US in 1940 on a British procurement mission in that context. He had behind him ten years' successful stewardship of Amax, a decade of expansion and growth. Not only had he a technical background, but he was an investment banker who had engineered successful mergers in the steel industry. He had also had some exposure to a state-owned enterprise, since he was for a time deputy chairman of British Leyland Limited, the government-owned car and truck manufacturer. An incessant traveller, well versed in politics, he seemed to have a great talent for making friends in high places. It was this latter attribute, perhaps, that above all caused Lazard's to put such a high price on him when they let him go!

But Ian MacGregor was sixty-seven when he took the job on and would have turned seventy before it was completed. Why did he take up such a challenge, putting both his reputation and his health at risk? In retrospect (a year after taking office) Ian MacGregor expressed his feelings about the job thus:

> I had the feeling there was work to be done over there, and I was convinced that the government was going to make a try at improving the productivity of the British workforce.

He saw it as a most interesting assignment and while he would be working at fairly long odds he felt that 'people were inherently good and reasonably susceptible to changing their practices to achieve success'. At the end of the day he found no reason for regret. He seemed to thrive on work, maintaining a rigorous schedule, with the very un-British habit of arriving at the office at 8.00 a.m. and often not leaving until after a working dinner. He did not seem to tire, but maintained 'youthful grace and bounce'. He certainly made the position as he saw it very clear to all his staff, telling them that their jobs were in danger if production did not rise. In the end, it seems, he even gained the admiration of the union. The general secretary of the Blast Furnacemen's Union was quoted as saying:

> I want to put on record the respect and admiration I feel for the tremendous efforts that Mr MacGregor has made to get the corporation back on its feet.

One union member echoed the feelings of many when he said:

> Many of the critics who opposed his appointment are having second thoughts today. I think we are in a far better position than we were a few months ago when we were a totally demoralized force.

Ian MacGregor's objective when he took over was to halve the current losses by the year ending March 1982 and break even within the next two years. He approached the task with a degree of caution, saying:

> It took careful work by a large number of destructive people to get the British Steel Corporation to its present appalling position. It will take some time to get us back.

As we see later, MacGregor was nearly on target, since British Steel made a profit in the year 1985–6, an operating profit having been achieved a year earlier.

How the mighty fell

Britain's steel industry made a heroic contribution to success in the Second World War, but by the end of the war it was crying out for modernization. Instead it got nationalization, with a Labour Government coming into power immediately after the war. Come 1951 the Conservatives won power and the industry was privatized once again, but for the next fifteen years was 'in limbo', no modernization being carried out for fear of re-nationalization, if ever the Labour Party got back into power. This finally happened in 1967, with the fourteen largest companies, manufacturing some 90 per cent of the total output in the UK, being 'smelted' into a government-owned British Steel Corporation (BSC). This was not in response to popular clamour, nor were there any convincing commercial arguments for the re-nationalization. It was an act of pure dogma, favoured by the unions because they saw it as bringing them job security, as indeed it did. This grand merger created the third largest steel company in the world at the time, after US Steel and Bethlehem, both US companies. Now it was the task of the government to fund modernization and to finance the losses, so politics took over. Instead of pruning and integrating the separate companies forming the group, and so consolidating the merger, the government took the easy route. It embarked on a spending spree of expansion. Annual installed capacity in 1973 was 27 million tonnes. By 1980 it had risen to 35 million tonnes and it was projected to peak 38 million tonnes in 1985. The world market situation was completely ignored. At the same time there was worldwide expansion, with new countries, such as Korea, entering manufacturing. This when the major markets for steel, car and ship manufacture, were in decline, so British Steel's plans for the future had to remain on paper.

There was a change of course in 1977, when Sir Charles Villiers became chairman. He closed twelve obsolete plants and cut production back drastically: to 15 million tonnes per annum. But that was all he did, with the result that BSC became a money drain, uncompetitive and with ever-mounting losses. When the Conservative (Thatcher) Government took over in 1979 BSC was, in effect, bankrupt, although it still rolled merrily on with government funding. The Thatcher Government was keen to privatize once again, but realized that the first thing to do was to make the company solvent. There was indeed a huge drain on the Treasury, but there was much more to it than that in the eyes of the incoming government. In the words of Sir Geoffrey Howe, then Chancellor of the Exchequer: 'It's more than money on the books. Its the erosion of authority and credibility of management'.[8] Since Sir Charles Villiers' term of office was coming to an end, there was a 'head hunt' to replace him. It was said of him that while he was a good merchant banker he 'lacked the force and finesse required'. His clumsy tactics when negotiating with the unions had brought another disastrous strike in 1980. The search for his successor ended with the location of Ian MacGregor.

Ian MacGregor takes over

Ian MacGregor saw his first task, when he became chairman of BSC, to restore morale. He saw it as very important for the 'top person to figure out how to motivate'. He was severely handicapped at this point, because the best motivation of all is financial incentive, something which only profitable companies can offer. So he turned to another motivating factor: he offered the employees independence and responsibility. He said of government-owned and controlled companies that they become organized like the government itself, operating in a bureaucratic mode with centralized decision-making. He thought that if he could 'decentralize' the organization he would see some improvement in performance. He was actually following the classic route taken by all 'turnaround managers' (or company 'doctors' as we keep on calling them) when confronted with a massive hidebound organization, whether he saw himself in that role or not.

So, with help from Roger Morrison, the head of the London office of the world-famous management consultants McKinsey & Co., he broke BSC up into separate units along product lines and the managers of these several units were given responsibility for everything within their unit, from the procurement of the raw materials to the marketing of their products. For instance, to take an extreme case, while BSC manufactured steel slab, they were free to purchase it outside the company if they could do a better deal. This approach to management gave them a measure of independence, authority and responsibility. It was also possible to give them targets for which they could be held responsible. Labour relations were also decentralized, so that issues could be settled at the local level, instead of every minor dispute flaring up into a national crisis. At the same time, the Villiers plant closure programme was urged ahead, resulting in the elimination of some 70,000 jobs in seventy weeks, leaving 110,000 on the payroll, of which 40,000 were employed in BSC's non-steel making activities. This was a very painful procedure, with unemployment nationwide running at some 10 per cent, but the blow was softened by giving very generous redundancy payments. These averaged US$12,000, but were as high as US$40,000 for the highly skilled who had to be laid off. Simultaneously, as a socio-economic measure, the company set up an organization to attract new industry to the steel towns, which were becoming industrial deserts, and Ian MacGregor invited Sir Charles Villiers to stay on to run this project.

The other major and very obvious task was to improve productivity. But how does one improve labour efficiency in an industry where 'featherbedding' was notorious? There was a tangle of craft unions to deal with, each strenuously guarding its special privileges. There were in all sixteen unions operating within the company, with a systematic system of job specialization and job demarcation that had been developed by the unions over the years. There was continual pressure from the shop stewards to maintain this system and it was very difficult for management to resist it. In this climate it was a major accomplishment for Ian MacGregor to persuade both the workers and their unions to accept a 'more efficient deployment of manpower'. To bring this about he spent a lot of time on the shop floor: it seems he likes very much to talk to people at that level. He introduced a system of bonus payments for performance above agreed norms, the punishment for failure being job losses. One consequence of the 1980 strike had been that the resultant imports had clearly demonstrated to the workers that they had no longer any monopoly in the British steel market and this was a point that Ian MacGregor drove home relentlessly. He told them that unless they were competitive, BSC could not and would not survive. Ian

MacGregor was able to carry all the unions along with him on this except for the Iron and Steel Trades Confederation (ISTC), which represented some 40 per cent of the BSC employees. Its general secretary, Bill Sirs, saw Ian MacGregor as a 'hard-headed American businessman who had no regard for social consequences and hates the unions'. But Sirs, unlike most of the other union leaders, was no dogmatist. He sought to substantiate his stand with figures developed by his research staff. He recognized that production costs must be controlled and he has even written a book about that. He also felt that Ian MacGregor had gone too far with capacity reduction by bringing it below the current domestic requirement. He led and lost the 1980 strike. He also opposed Ian MacGregor's corporate plan for the short-term future of the company, whereby annual capacity would be cut by a further 14 million tonnes and the annual wage increase was to be postponed from the January to the July. Sirs insisted on polling his members on this issue, whereas Ian MacGregor wanted *all* the BSC employees to be polled. The end result was that 65 per cent of the employees voted on the issue, and a majority, 78 per cent, favoured the plan. So Ian MacGregor had his way.

There is improvement all round

The end result of these drastic changes was that productivity, which had lagged far behind that of the French and German steelmakers, began to improve. Two Welsh mills, which had been marked for closure, became as productive as any in Europe. Costs became competitive, but unfortunately there were too few buyers. BSC was operating in a declining market. While BSC's share of the home market, reduced by the 1980 strike from 54 per cent to 48 per cent, bounced back to 50 per cent, that market had shrunk to its lowest level since 1951, being only some 12 million tonnes. The losses for the year 1980–1 was a record US$1·6 billion, increased to US$2·4 billion when one-time expenses, such as severance pay, redundancy payments and plant write-offs were taken into account.

Ian MacGregor used his skill at salesmanship to get a bigger share of the North Sea pipeline business and flew to Tokyo to persuade the steelmakers there to be less aggressive in their marketing. To quote him:[9]

> I talked gently to them pointing out that it seemed prudent for them to be sure we're happy. They're old friends of mine: they understand.

In an endeavour to further enlarge his market, Ian MacGregor promoted the road/rail link across the English Channel, which would of course use vast quantities of steel. Due to excess capacity there was severe price competition, with European producers selling steel in their home markets up to 15 per cent below the prevailing prices in the American and Japanese markets. Much against the wishes of Ian MacGregor and his 'overseer', the Minister for Industry, the European steel manufacturers sought to form what was in effect a cartel system to protect their sales. However, it proved impractical, since they could not reach agreement on their respective quotas. Ian MacGregor even played a diplomatic role in this context, telling his friends on the Continent some of the 'facts of life'. One report concludes that indirect subsidies paid by European governments to their steel industries are larger than those paid to British Steel and that these subsidies form a major element in their marginal profits. In quantitative terms the subsidies in France, Italy and West Germany may reduce costs by some £6-8 per tonne, while the corresponding figure in the UK is a mere £1 per tonne. While these figures are small when set against total production costs of some £300 per tonne, they are very significant when the average profit being made by the Europeans is only £5 per tonne.

BSC had not only to face stiff competition abroad, but also at home. The companies still operating in the steel industry in the UK (not taken over when the industry was re-nationalized) grew vigorously, finding profitable 'niches' that BSC could not reach. By the early 1970s their market share had grown to some 25 per cent, and while it has fallen since then they managed to thrive under BSC's high cost 'umbrella' until Ian MacGregor arrived and BSC became leaner and more competitive.

What does the future hold for BSC?

Ian MacGregor has now left BSC, moving on to become chairman of the National Coal Board. Despite the year-long strike in that industry (1984–5) – a tale we have told elsewhere[10] – which had a severe impact, the 1984–5 operating results were the best for ten years. The accounts showed that production as such had been profitable, a net loss being incurred only because of interest charges and certain exceptional costs. The loss of supplies due to the coal strike was a great setback, Sir Robert Haslam, Ian MacGregor's successor, quantifying that damage alone at some £180 million. Now the 1985-6 results are in and BSC have made a net profit of £38 million – the first time that it has been in the black for eleven years.[11] BSC has won through at last, in line with MacGregor's expectations, and that without any government subsidy. Mr Bob Scholey, current chairman of BSC, has described this recovery as 'most spectacular'. While, at £38 million, the profit is modest, it is a major milestone seeing that the company has consumed some £7,000 million in state aid over the past seven years, the workforce being reduced from 225,000 to 54,000 over the eleven-year period. The turnaround is massive, since BSC had lost £385 million the previous year of which £180 million only, as we have just said, could be attributed to the coal strike. The corporation is now reviewing its export priorities and plans to increase its share of the European markets, where it has only a 2 per cent share at present. Success at last!

Perhaps it is appropriate, before we leave Mr Macgregor, to mention what he has accomplished at British Coal, where he has now completed his three-year stint. Although the oil price collapse has hit his hopes of breaking even, British Coal made an operating profit in 1985–6 of £500 million, the first time a profit had been made for a great many years. Productivity and earnings per man are at record levels, with sales and coal consumption on the increase. Although there was a loss of £50 million when interest and other charges were taken in, this has to be set against a loss of £1,200 million the previous year, the year of the miner's strike. Sir Robert Haslam, who has taken over as chairman, does not expect the industry to be profitable before 1988–9, though much depends on the price of oil. Sir Ian MacGregor, as he now is, has written a book which will be published, he said, 'after I have safely left the country'.[13] He leaves having put British Steel on the road to profitability and British Coal on the path to viability.

Another way to do it

Having looked at two major companies in the steel industry and all the problems they have faced and continue to face, we thought it would strike a happier note to conclude by looking at what we might call a 'new concept in steelmaking'. It demonstrates that even in such a mature industry as steel it is possible to innovate and achieve quite remarkable results. The story sounds almost too good to be true, but it is brought to us by a very respectable and credible source.[12] Our chapter theme is 'Steel and the Americans' and this is an American company in Texas: *Chaparral Steel Mill*. The company has an enviable record in terms of productivity and the quick adoption of new technology. The organization is lean and flexible and there are no barriers between the laboratory and the production floor. Research as a separate function is considered wasteful, so research is carried out right on the production floor, with workers as well as the technicians knowing just what is going on. Even functions such as safety, training and employment of new staff are line functions, not separated from the production activity as separate office disciplines. Everyone in the company meets the customer, including the production personnel and as a consequence come up with ideas for improving the product.

It really is amazing what people can do when you let them. The security guards don't get bored: they enter data into the computer in the middle of the night, run the ambulance check and fill up the fire extinguishers. They even do production checks and learn accounting, thus upgrading their job and their salary. The company is nothing exceptional in terms of size, with an output of some 1.5 million tonnes a year and a total workforce just under a thousand. Despite its relatively small size, the labour costs are some 10 per cent of selling cost, practically half the conventional figure in the industry. So it *can* be done!

Summary

So all the hard work put in by David Roderick and Ian MacGregor has finally paid off. Both are seen as quiet men, calm and resolute, and with very clear objectives. The actions they have taken are very similar, because they faced similar problems. Productivity had to be increased and the workforce pruned, an unpleasant but essential task. But the similarity ends there. MacGregor operated under government direction, and had no option open to him such as diversification. BSC had to be made profitable *as a steel company* and in view of the state of the steel industry worldwide that took a long time. Roderick had a much freer hand and was able to take a quicker route to recovery, through diversification. So he achieved turnaround for his company much more quickly. However, the example of MacGregor demonstrated that there is a road to salvation, even in as mature an industry as steelmaking.

Success at BSC seems to have come too late for the Thatcher Government, who now seem to be bringing their privatization programme to an end in order to prepare for the next election. It will be interesting to see what happens when that has taken place and a government with a new five-year term ahead of it comes into power.

References

1 Greenhouse, S., 'Economic Scene – the Struggling Steel Industry', *New York Times*, 17 May 1985.

2 'Steelworkers – Bend and Bow', *Economist*, no. 296, 29 March 1986, pp. 33–4.

3 Risen, J., 'US Steel, key union at odds on job concessions', *International Herald Tribune*, 10 June 1986.

4 Dodsworth, T. and Hall, W., 'US Steel in Transition – Stepping on the Gas', *Financial Times*, 11 December 1985, p. 12.

5 Perl, P., 'Us Steel Firms Fate Rests on Talks – Unions Forced to Negotiate Separate Pacts', *International Herald Tribune*, 14 March 1986, p. 6.

6 'Time runs out for steel – with 199 units closed, a quest is on for massive federal aid', *Business Week*, 13 June 1983, pp. 48–51.

7 Symonds, W. C., 'The toughest job in business – how they're remaking US Steel', *Business Week*, 25 February 1985, pp. 42–8.

8 Lubar, R., 'An American Leads British Steel Back from the Brink', *Fortune*, no. 104, 21 September 1981, p. 88.

9 Article: 'Steel industries Stinking of roses', *Economist*, no. 296, 20 July 1985, pp. 48–50.

10 Kharbanda, O. P. and Stallworthy, E. A., *Management Disasters*, Gower, 1986.

11 Gribben, R., 'Steel nets a profit of £38m', *Daily Telegraph* (London), 9 July 1986, p. 1.

12 Forward, G. E., 'Wide open management at Chaparral Steel', *Harvard Business Review*, no. 64, May-June 1986, pp. 96–102.

13 MacGregor, Ian and Tyler, Rodney, *The Enemies Within: The story of the miners' strike 1984–5*, Collins, 1985.

6 Examples from the public sector

Bureaucracy is equated in the public eye with inefficiency, delays and completely unimaginative handling of business and people. This thinking is even embodied in the dictionary definition of a bureaucrat, which reads '(especially *unimaginative*) official in bureaucracy'. All government is built on bureaucrats and built by bureaucrats and it is automatically assumed that an effective business can never be run by a bureaucrat. Peter Drucker, styled by many as a 'management guru', is convinced that government – any government – is totally and utterly incompetent as an industrial manager. In his more recent writing he has some advice for governments running industrial activities.[1] He had a three-point formula:

1 Clear and specific goals.
2 Set priorities.
3 Abandonment.

He adds movingly, from his own personal experience, that the last of the three, while novel, is the most important and the most difficult to implement. Abandonment is the closing down of inefficient, ineffective or outmoded enterprises. Despite Peter Drucker's pessimism, bureaucrats can run an enterprise efficiently, if we see the term 'bureaucrat' as the description of a government employee. But now a government employee who is *not* unimaginative, but full of inspiration, implementing the principles enunciated by Drucker.

By way of illustration we are going to India, whose government is considered by many to be an extreme example of bureaucracy in action. To some extent this is to be expected, if only because of the sheer size of the country. We once ventured to describe India as the 'world's largest democracy'.[2] 'Guess what country that is? India!', wrote an American reviewer, but despite his astonishment it is true. India, in terms of population, is three times the size of the US, and it *is* a democracy. It is now nearly forty years since India secured its independence and the country is seeing a spectacular boom in almost every product from steel to electronics. To quote an English journalist comparing India with the UK:[3]

> It is a startling success story. Her gross domestic product is the fourteenth highest in the world. Exports have grown five-fold in ten years. While Britain's manufacturing workforce is contracting daily, India has leapt from five million to seven million in a decade.

At least some of this success can be attributed to 'bureaucrats', bureaucrats who became 'turnaround managers'. We propose to bring two outstanding examples before you. We shall see that even within the bureaucratic system, of which any government-controlled company or corporation is inevitably a part, one man can still make all the difference, a fact that we find ourselves meeting time and again as we go through our case studies. But do not let us get ahead of our story: let us start at the beginning. For our first case study we take a look at the Neyveli Lignite Corporation.

The Neyveli Lignite Corporation

The Neyveli Lignite Corporation (NLC) was conceived in the 1950s as a large integrated industrial complex based on lignite (commonly called brown coal). The complex was to consist of:

1 Lignite mine, with a capacity of 6·5 million tonnes per year.
2 Briquetting and carbonization plant.
3 Thermal power station, 600 MW.
4 Urea fertilizer plant, capacity 450 tonnes per day.

With hindsight one can say that the project got off to a bad start. The original British consultants appointed to the project had very little experience of open cast mining, yet that was the crux of the entire project.[4] Any shortfall in the quantity of lignite mined had immediate repercussions on the dependent plants, since lignite was the basic feedstock for the entire complex. A low output of lignite meant poor capacity utilization of all the plants downstream.

Striving for capacity utilization

The Neyveli lignite has a fairly high calorific value (2200 to 2800 cal./ gram) and a very low ash content (3–6 per cent) and is thus superior to the brown coal found in Germany. However, the mining conditions are extremely difficult, the main problems being:

1   Enormous quantity of water (15–20 tonnes per tonne of lignite) to be removed.
2   The mining area gets flooded with water, being in the cyclonic rain belt.
3   Hard and abrasive sandstone is present, which damages the teeth of the excavators.
4   Very thick overburden, about six cubic metres per tonne of lignite.

These four problems proved a very serious hindrance to developing full output and were apparently not anticipated by the British consultants at the conceptual design stage. Their solution took a long time and called for some very hard decisions and resolute action. Even as late as 1972 only 2·3 million tonnes a year of lignite was being mined, just one third of the original design capacity. The immediate and obvious result of this shortfall was that both the power generation and the fertilizer production fell far short of their respective targets year after year. By the financial year 1975–6 the cumulative losses were some Rs840 million. Apparently a hopeless position. To help our readers assess the implications of the figures we give in Indian rupees we would mention that there are roughly 10 Indian rupees to the US dollar. This approximation makes calculation and assessment fairly simple.

   The realization by the management that capacity utilization was the key to the solution of their problems was, however, taken to heart and the actions which they took as a consequence started a process of turnaround. This resulted in such a transformation that by the year 1976–7 NLC earned a profit of Rs120 million on a turnover of Rs790 million. Thereafter the capacity utilization and hence both the turnover and the profits continued to grow steadily, with the result that the total cumulative losses had been wiped out by the year 1981–2 and there was even a credit balance of Rs30 million. All this is demonstrated in Table 4 and there is no doubt that the figures speak for themselves.

Table 4 *The growth in profits and capacity utilization at the Neyveli Lignite Corporation. This table illustrates the steady growth that was achieved over the years, once a 'breakthrough' had been achieved*

	1979–80	1980–1	1981–2	1982–3	1983–4
Lignite mined (million tonnes)	2.9	4.8	5.9	6.4	6.6
Power exported (megawatts)	1768	2454	2686	3073	3027
Urea (thousand tonnes)	105	135	99	101	124
Thermal power (load factor, %)	45	60	65	73	74
Mining capacity utilization (%)	45	74	90	99	102
Profit, Rs mill.	5	171	379	474	630
Internally generated funds (Rs mill.)	149	305	567	765	855

Source: The Centre for Monitoring the Indian Economy, Bombay.

So far a most remarkable turnaround, but the NLC management has not rested on its laurels. Along with its development of the capacity of the installation, which was finally brought in some cases above the original design capacity, particular attention was being paid to maintenance. It was found that preventive maintenance was a crucial factor if a high level of capacity utilization was to be achieved. In order to maintain capacity at near 100 per cent it was essential to achieve 4000 hours of trouble-free operation per year with the mining machinery. This was possible by setting up a regular and most meticulous maintenance schedule.

However, capacity utilization, despite its importance, is not the complete answer. Even more important is to sell the product at a rewarding price. The Tamil Nadu Electricity Board (TNEB) was the only customer for the power generated at the plant, but that corporation accepted the principle that there should be a reasonable rate of return on the investment that had been made. The rates are subject to mutual negotiation from time to time, and TNEB has recognized and accepted that the rate agreed should be remunerative enough not only to allow NLC to sustain its operations but to generate sufficient internal cash for expansion. The acceptance of this principle was the second major contributory factor towards achieving a turnaround.

A 'showpiece of the nation'

It was in these terms that the Vice-President of India, Mr R. Venkataraman referred to NLC and its achievements. The bouquet was well deserved judging by what it achieved in the year 1984–5:

- Best Performance Award for the highest (74·2 per cent) plant load factor among all the power stations in the country.
- Best Performance Award from the National Productivity Council.
- First Prize and Gold Medal for mine safety record.
- Cash incentive award of Rs30 million from the Government of India's Department of Power for exceeding the 65 per cent load factor.

Those last two awards are particularly significant. The safety award demonstrates that output had not been achieved at the expense of safety, by taking risks, while the degree of achievement in sustaining a load factor of nearly 75 per cent is seen when one is made aware that the average for all India is a mere 48·6 per cent.

Further, the quantity of lignite mined reached a new peak in that year of 71 million tonnes, plant utilization reaching a record 107 per cent. Thermal power generation capacity utilization peaked at 118·7 per cent, with a load factor of 77·2 per cent. No wonder then, that in terms of absolute profits NLC climbed to fifth among all the public sector corporations in the year 1983–4 and improved its ranking by three places in 1984–5, coming second. Such an excellent performance can only come through the hard work and complete dedication of the corporation's 20,000 employees. They had been led to success by their chairman and managing director, Mr. G. L. Tandon. The momentum initiated by him has been more than maintained by his relatively young (fifty-two years old) successor, Mr. N. P. Narayanan.

Is there any limit?

There is no doubt that the strength of the corporation lies in the three Ms: money, machines and men. Of these, the last – men – is undoubtedly by far the most important. The excellent results achieved by NLC have been achieved by putting men to work. There has been a dedicated team effort. Some of the laurels awarded to NLC have been listed above: another is AIMO's (All India Manufacturers Organization) coveted award for industrial relations and participative management.

Where does NLC go from here? We are sure that it is only upwards! Management has confidence and faith in their workforce and this lies at the heart of its ambitious plans through this present decade and beyond. Its strategic planning is effectively demonstrated by the figures given in Table 5. Not only has it a plan, but it is keeping to it, since Phase 2A is on schedule and Phase 2 well in hand.[5] It is clear that when these developments are reflected in the balance sheet the financial position of the corporation will be even further transformed. The complex will then fulfil Jawaharlal Nehru's dream, expressed by him in May 1957 while inaugurating this project:

> This type of project . . . is a symbol and witness to the developments to follow . . . a kind of catalyst which may lead to a very considerable development industrially. This lignite project promises to give the push to industrial development . . . .

That it most certainly has done and more, as we realize when we

Table 5 *The NLC strategic plan. Phase 1 was the original project, Phase 2A being completed as part of the sixth plan (1980–5), while Phase 2B is part of the seventh plan (1986–91). Phase 3 is foreseen in the eighth and ninth plans*

Phase	Lignite mT/year	Power MW	Project cost Rs million	Completion Year
1	6.5	600	2,500	1957
2A	4.7	630	7,500	1986[1]
2B	5.8	840	19,500	1990[2]
3	11.0	1500	40,000	1995[3]
Total	32.0	3990		2000[4]

Notes:
1 On schedule.
2 Main equipment ordered.
3 In conceptual stage.
4 Through expansion of earlier phases.

Source: Centre for Monitoring the Indian Economy, Bombay.

come across a feature article with the banner headline: NLC – a perennial source of thermal power.[6]

The present position

NLC has now become a major source of power supply for the ever growing needs of both industry and agriculture in Tamil Nadu, contributing nearly a third of that state's total requirements. This sustained performance has been largely responsible for averting a power crisis in the south in recent years, unfortunately till now a common experience in India. This 'perennial source' of power also has the unique distinction of running with the forced outage of a mere 5 to 7 per cent. This compares with the internationally accepted figure of 13 per cent and an all-India average of 17 per cent. This notable achievement by NLC is rightly attributed to its well-organized maintenance, constant monitoring and continuing improvements in operating procedures. The workforce never lets up: it is not only dedicated, but well trained. One hopes that the lessons learnt by NLC over the past twenty years are not only etched in the minds of the workers now there, but will be passed on to succeeding generations of workers. This is of course the task of management, so the management, too, must maintain its traditions. This is referred to as the 'company culture'. A sound company culture is an essential part of every successful company.

As was pointed out at the outset, the mining operation is at the heart of the entire complex and unless the output of lignite is continually sustained, the downstream units will inevitably suffer. The corporation is now completing Phase 2A and Phase 2B is well in hand. But is there enough lignite to cater for the entire master plan running up to the end of the present century? NLC is fortunate indeed: the lignite deposits in and around Neyveli, comprising the South Arcot district of Tamil Nadu are probably the largest in Asia. The total estimated reserves extend over an area of some 400 square kilometres and are estimated at around 3300 million tonnes. With the proposed expansions and extensions to the turn of the century, the quantity of lignite mined annually would be some 32 million tonnes per year. At that rate, the proposed scale of operations could be sustained for more than a hundred years. This assessment relates to proven deposits: there is always the possibility of further deposits being discovered.

Cautious optimism

How should management react to the picture that has just been painted? The present indications are good indeed and the future looks even brighter. The development of the human resource has been such that the workforce is well motivated, so that there is high individual performance and good productivity. The production per worker has increased by more than 50 per cent since the complex was first started up. Assuming that Phase 3 and the other expansions go ahead as planned, by the year 2000 the complex will not only be mining some 32 million tonnes per year of lignite but will have become a unique 'energy centre' at the heart of Southern India. The one thing the corporation should not do, and dare not do, is to rest upon its laurels.

Earlier, reference was made to the three Ms and the crucial importance of 'man' in that equation. Manpower is by far the most important resource that any company or country can have and a good manager will recognize that fact. Indeed, he will never forget it. It is true that India has manpower in abundance. The achievements of NLC demonstrate that man, given the necessary money and machines, can operate very successfully. Nevertheless, with the ambitious plans for expansion at Neyveli 'man' may still become a bottleneck. The corporation already faces a shortage of managerial talent, but it has not folded its arms. It is maintaining an advertising campaign for recruitment where it emphasizes three relevant motivating factors:

Education   Ecology   Environment

NLC has already built thirty-one schools, catering for more than 30,000 students. As part of a massive afforestation drive over four million trees have been planted. To develop the working environment parks, recreation centres, a stadium and swimming pools have been built. Several dispensaries and a modern hospital cater to the health of the employees and the supporting population. The population 'explosion', still a continuing threat in India, has been prevented by education in family planning, with the result that over 95 per cent of NLC employees follow the 'small family' norm.

Human resources development

It is very evident, therefore, that the NLC management has

recognized not only the short term, but also the long-term needs for success and are taking the appropriate steps. The desires and aspirations not only of its employees, but also their families and the community whose prosperity depends upon its continuing success, are being well covered.

The corporation's master plan to the end of the present century has targets not only for production and investment, but even more importantly, for the manpower and human resources required to sustain them. This is in line with the management's realization that *man* is its most important asset: far more important even than the lignite which it mines. It has been estimated that 40 per cent of the total staff are due to retire in the next three years. To prepare for their replacement in key areas in good time, a new concept, *mantor-protege*, has been introduced. The idea is to have an understudy in each of the key positions so that the present manager can guide and train his successor. This is a unique and most comprehensive programme in this area. Unique? Yes, we believe it to be unique, at least in terms of its comprehensive approach. We have found, as we have already detailed in Chapter 3, when dealing with 'delegation as a management tool', that professionally managed companies in the private sector, priding themselves on having an elaborate succession plan, have yet found themselves advertising for a chief executive. Of course, they use a post box address, but we are left wondering just how comprehensive their plans are. We believe that the failure is often due to the internal 'politics', which are allowed to dominate management thinking.[7]

Drawing conclusions

The story of the Neyveli Lignite Corporation is refreshing to review and an outstanding example to set before others, whether in the public sector or the private sector. The public sector, in particular, is continually criticized for its inertia: the 'dead hand' of bureaucracy is said to stifle all initiative. Not necessarily and not always, as the management and workers at NLC have plainly demonstrated. Given the appropriate authority and the will to achieve, even a public sector undertaking can achieve outstanding results. Indeed, NLC may be outstanding in India, but there are parallels in other parts of the world. There should, however, be many more.

The project had a most difficult start, despite the ready availability of the primary need and basis for success, high quality lignite. But thanks mainly to a determined management and a dedicated workforce, a remarkable turnaround was achieved. While the road was difficult and the task seemed at times impossible, the journey long and arduous, determination brought results. In retrospect, of course, the effort was well worth while and it was a great achievement. The success of NLC has had an impact far beyond its workforce, their families and the community in which they live and work. The steadily increasing and reliable generation of power at NLC has had a stimulating influence upon the entire economy not only of Tamil Nadu but the whole of Southern India. It has more than fulfilled Nehru's dream, as expressed when the plant was inaugurated in 1957 and has amply justified a nation's trust.

But let us not forget that sound management and effective leadership was at the root of it all. Management identified the cause of the problem and then exerted every effort not only to get it right, but to prepare for the future. The need to motivate the workforce was recognized, together with the need to maintain its quality by education. The success of preventive maintenance demonstrated once again the truth of that old adage: prevention is better than cure. It was recognized that growth was not only possible, but would make a major contribution to continuing success: in managerial circles this is called strategic planning and is a crucial element in success.[8]

Perpetuating bureaucracy

Having just seen, in the case of the turnaround at NLC, that what was really needed was a 'leader' who could cope with the 'dead hand' of bureaucracy and overcome its insidious influence, you will realize why we were so perturbed on reading a series of articles by Pradip N. Khandwalla on *Effective Turnaround Management*.[9] What disturbed us as we read these articles was the remedy that was being proposed. It was said, with truth, that 'very few managements have the skills of effectively turning round a sick unit'. Of course not. It is poor management that brought on the sickness: how can one expect that same poor management to cure itself? No, the *management* needs changing. But how? It was further said that 'a turnaround may be initiated by an individual or a small team at the top, but obviously, in sizeable organizations, it cannot be accomplished by just one or a few persons'. Why 'obviously'? It can and it has been done by one man - many times. That is, indeed, the continuing theme of this book, and we have just seen that it can be done with government-owned companies just as well as in the private sector. A successful turnaround is almost invariably the work of one man, not a team. True, that one man will build an effective team around himself, either by infusing new life into the existing management or by replacing it (both methods have worked), but it remains a one-man effort. A turnaround demands drastic change and it seems that in practice that change has to be autocratically imposed by one man who takes absolute command, at least for the time being.

This means that the remedy proposed by Khandwalla – an institutional system for preventing sickness – will never work. Company sickness can only be prevented from the *inside*, by good management, never from the outside. Those outside can maintain a close watch, and warn, but we doubt the effectiveness of even that attempt at prevention. Poor management will not listen, while good management will not need warning. So such a system would be completely redundant from the very beginning. The only way to reduce company sickness, in our view, is to improve the quality of management in general, by education. Education, not in management skills, but in the basic qualities of honesty, sincerity and sound morality. Managers who are prepared to do a good day's work for a day's pay and have a concern for the well-being of those under them will be excellent managers: a knowledge of what are called management techniques will take them very little further, since such techniques are largely just common sense.

An ideal model

Let us now make the point even more emphatically by taking one more example, again from India. We are going to look at the Damodar Valley Corporation (DVC), where a turnaround was again achieved by one man, P. C. Luther, and all within some two years. His three-point formula for success was somewhat different to that proposed by Drucker, with which we began this chapter, but was equally effective: discipline, accountability and dynamic welfare.

The Damodar Valley Corporation was set up in 1948, a year after India gained independence, as a joint venture between the central government and the state governments of Bihar and West Bengal. Its model was the Tennessee Valley Authority in the US. Its aim was flood control, controlled irrigation and power generation. By 1980 five major dams and some 2500 km of canals had been built, with power stations generating some 1400 MW. Power generation was largely from coal, since there are very large coalfields in Bihar and West Bengal. However, the coalfields, as they developed, relied entirely upon the power provided by DVC, and a vicious circle developed. Coal output fell, resulting in less power, which in its turn compelled an even lower coal output . . . then even less power. Of course the objective of DVC, apart from flood control and irrigation, was to generate power for all local industry, not only the coal fields, so a very serious situation developed.

While DVC grew rapidly in size, having some 18,000 employees by 1980, it was only generating some 40 per cent of its installed capacity. Although this installed capacity is a mere 3 per cent of the total installed capacity in India, this low output had a disastrous 'snowballing' effect. Since almost all the country's coal and steel production is within the Damodar Valley basin, failure to generate power *there* had an immediate and disastrous effect on India's economy. Indeed, it has been said that if DVC was to stop generating for only three weeks, the country's entire economy would come to a grinding halt! So crucial, then, is the role of DVC in India. And it was failing in its objectives.

What went wrong?

Nothing happens overnight in such a context as this. Deterioration set in over the years, with no one making any effort to halt what was going on. In 1980 a team of British experts were called in to 'diagnose' DVC's sickness. Their report makes interesting reading. They write of seventeen different unions, demarcation problems and gross overmanning, with each union trying to outdo its rivals by winning members and thus increasing its political power. There was conflict between the unions to such a degree that there was rioting and plant sabotage. The management, it seemed, did not dare to take action for fear of retaliation, while excessive overtime payments to the hourly paid staff so reduced the differential between them and the salaried staff that there was a great sense of unfair treatment and resentment throughout the management structure. It was said that one plant manager had been held captive in his office more than 300 times in one year.

Hearing this story, there seems to be no doubt what the root cause of the trouble was, and this was confirmed by the conclusions drawn by the British team. They felt that while the DVC labour unions had considerable potential and the employees in general were well paid, informal discussions made it very evident that there was a yearning among many employees for inspired leadership, starting at the top. Luther arrived in August 1980 to take over as chairman and chief executive and turned out to be the 'inspired leader', able to deal with a seemingly hopeless situation. His background seems to have been ideal.

Luther's diagnosis

It has been said with truth that half the solution to any problem is to appreciate and understand what the problem really is. This is just what Luther did. Describing the situation when he arrived, he said that there was a total lack of discipline and accountability. With nearly twenty unions and staff associations competing with one another in a very irresponsible fashion, an atmosphere of reckless militancy was created. The line managers had no authority or control and were in no way answerable to their superiors. Thus there was a total mismatch between responsibility and authority.

Speaking about the challenge that had faced him, Luther said some three years later that the best fuel for irresponsible militancy was a combination of two things:

1   Absence of grievance redressal machinery, and
2   An image of weakness in management

Having also established that DVC was overmanned, Luther refused to accept that in the Indian environment overmanning was inevitable, particularly in the public sector. He was quite candid about it, saying:

> It is often argued that the remedy for organizational obesity is ruled out by existing labour legislation, postures of unions and interference by politicians. My own experience does not support his contention. Whereas the treatment is undoubtedly inconvenient, arduous and even hazardous, it is certainly not impossible.

Luther indeed demonstrated that it *was* possible, as we shall see. He went on to administer the treatment and brought about a cure.

. . . and his prescription

Having diagnosed the problem – a diagnosis that coincided with that of the British team of experts – Luther went on to resolve the situation. He realized that there could be no 'magic cure' and that the turnaround was bound to take several years and a great deal of effort from everybody. So he went patiently to work, taking up first the challenge of indiscipline and militancy. At the DVC headquarters in Calcutta, staff came and went as they liked, there being no check whatever on their attendance. Physical checks were introduced, with the managers being encouraged to set an example. Within two months, a 98 per cent punctuality record had been attained. Next he sought to establish the manager's 'right to manage' at all the company's offices and plant installations. But for this concept to take root he had first to 'prepare the soil'. This he did by:

- Improving communication at all levels.
- Setting up an effective 'complaints' system.
- Refusing to yield to pressure tactics.
- Inculcating discipline and accountability, starting at the top.

The words 'starting at the top' were deliberate and full of significance for him, for they embodied his basic concept of proper management. He firmly believed that discipline and accountability flowed like water from the very top to the bottom. Water *cannot* climb up: if these principles were not seen at the very top then they would never be seen at the bottom. It should all begin then with Luther himself – and it did! He was injured and had to be hospitalized in the process.

This particular incident started on 1 October 1980, only three months after his arrival. He was expected in New Delhi on that day, so one of the DVC unions organized a demonstration within the headquarters building in Calcutta, designed to break the ban on demonstrations he had just imposed. But Luther was not in New Delhi. He turned up at the Calcutta offices and had to force his way through a huge mass of demonstrators. Some of them hit him on his neck and back. His response was decisive. The union organizing the demonstration was 'derecognized' and that decision stood despite efforts by the chief minister of West Bengal, Jyoti Basu to have it cancelled. Politics did not prevail and the lesson was learnt.

Next came his concept of 'dynamic welfare'. Through the benefits this brought he was able to secure the support and commitment of the large majority of the employees. He spent three-quarters of his time in the field, talking to the workers and even their families. He found that in some cases grievances going back for as long as four years had never been dealt with. So he streamlined the system and gave an undertaking that all grievances would be settled within 90 days, and the great majority of them almost immediately, at local level.

The result

In the first full year of Luther's stewardship (1981–2) DVC achieved results that had previously been considered to be completely unattainable. Energy generation increased to 6000 GWh, an increase of 34 per cent over the previous year, and net profit, which the previous year have been minimal, soared to Rs254 million. The

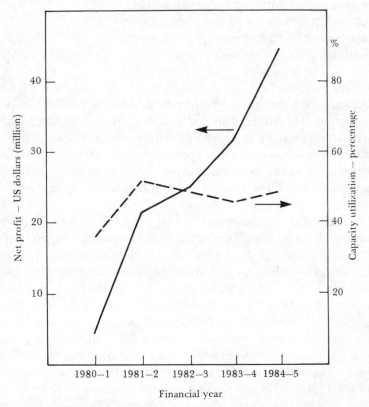

Figure 3   *A dramatic turnaround for the Damodar Valley Corporation. These graphs show very clearly indeed that once capacity utilization had been brought up to a proper level, profits soared.*
Source: The Centre for Monitoring the Indian Economy, Bombay.

improvement was no 'flash in the pan', but was sustained, as can be seen from Figure 3. Luther left to become chairman of the State Trading Corporation, a highly coveted post, in 1983, but as you can see from Figure 3, the results he had achieved were sustained. This demonstrates that the results were not due to the Luther 'personality' as such, but to the *changes* he had made, the transformation he had wrought, in the management of the company. Previously, administrative power and control had been concentrated at the headquarters offices at Calcutta, but Luther brought about substantial decentralization. Administrative control was shifted to divisional chiefs who were given the requisite financial authority. The function of the central office was then that of coordination and resource allocation. His care and sympathy for the employees, expressed in particular through the great improvements made in the handling of grievances, created a deep sense of 'belonging' among them.

Summary

We believe the lessons from our two examples found in India are clear. Management has both the duty and the right to manage, but that attitude must begin right at the top. If this right is abrogated, the company will always go downhill. A most important aspect of management is care and concern for the workforce and proper care 'pays off'. The workforce develops a sense of purpose and a feeling of 'belonging'. Luther, as chief executive, 'stuck his neck out' and got hurt – quite literally he 'got it in the neck'. But he persisted and was able to rally the workforce so that they were with him, seeing the beneficial effect for them of his policies. In fact, he developed what we have called a 'company culture', which may persist. A forceful character is needed to establish the situation, but once established it has its own momentum. Luther left, but the company continues to prosper, to the great benefit not only of the managers and workers, but above all the nation. A somewhat similar situation has developed at Neyveli, where the turnaround has not only been sustained but is being improved by Tandon's successor Narayanan. In both cases, India's economy has been at stake and the two 'doctors' not only diagnosed the sickness correctly, but administered the right 'prescription'.

References

1 Drucker, P. F., *The Changing World of the Executive*, Allied Publishers, 1982, p. 271.
2 Kharbanda, O. P. and Stallworthy, E. A., *Corporate Failure: Prediction, Panacea, Prevention*, McGraw-Hill, 1985, p. 224.
3 West, R., 'Pain and the power', *The Mail on Sunday*, 9 December 1984. (The article appeared under the banner headline: '2000 deaths – just the price of progress'.)
4 Thakore, D. and Gupta, G., 'Miracle at DVC', *Business World*, 12–25 October 1981, pp. 26-35; Gupta, S., 'A cloud on the horizon', *Business World*, 11–24 October 1982, pp. 16–19.
5 'Rs 1955 Crores for Neyveli expansion', *Economic Times*, 30 June, 14 July and 19 July 1986.
6 'NLC – a perennial source of thermal power', *Times of India*, 31 May 1985.
7 Kharbanda, O. P., 'Why the battle for succession?', *Times of India*, 31 January 1986.
8 Kharbanda, O. P. and Stallworthy, E. A., *Corporate Failure: Prediction, Panacea, Prevention*, McGraw-Hill, 1985. See Chapter 17, 'Corporate planning'.
9 Khandwalla, P. N., 'Effective turnaround management', series of 4 articles in *Economic Times*, 10 February–28 March 1986.

7 A monopoly disappears

We have already taken two case studies from India, both in the public sector, in Chapter 6. We thought it would now be interesting to take a case from the private sector. India may be the 'world's largest democracy', but that does not bring it any immunity from business failure, although because of government policy failure is the exception where perhaps it ought to be the rule. In a free economy it is broadly true that the survival of the fittest is the order of the day, although governments can and do come to the rescue from time to time. The unfit collapse and are liquidated or go bankrupt – but not necessarily in India. In India companies that fall sick rarely die, even when they might well be thought terminally ill, if we may pursue that particular analogy so far. In India companies are sustained in being for the sake of the employment they offer. We are not concerned here with the political aspect – the merits or demerits of the policy being implemented – but we cannot help noticing its results. Company sickness is a peculiarly Indian phenomenon: so much so that the word 'sickness' is now incorporated into the official jargon, with a formal definition. The various financial institutions, such as the Industrial Development Bank of India, the Industrial and Credit Corporation of India and the Industrial Finance Corporation, each have their own specific definition of 'sickness'.

Because of the magnitude of this particular problem in India, as shown in Table 6, there has been a deal of public concern and much public interest, reflected in the setting up of committees and the holding of numerous seminars, largely sponsored by various Chambers of Commerce throughout India. This interest has resulted in a steady flow of reports and books. A glance at the subjects dealt with, as detailed in Reference 1 at the end of this chapter, gives some idea of the prevalence of the concept of 'company sickness' in India.[1] Our objective in giving such an extensive list of references is to try and give our readers some idea of the 'flavour' of this particular subject. Of course, the literary output on this subject is not confined to India, it is worldwide, but the specific political climate in India seems to have developed 'corporate sickness' there to epidemic proportions. The disease seems to be infectious, since when we look at Metal Box (India) we see a sickly child with a very 'healthy' parent. But Metal Box (India) is not the only sickly child of this particular parent, who lives in the UK, since Metal Box (Nigeria) seems to have been in the same state. It was an Indian, Kuldip Puri, who was successful in accomplishing a 'turnaround' in the Nigerian company and he has now turned his attention to the Indian company, resulting in the public posing of a very pertinent question: 'Can Kuldip Puri turn Metal Box around?'[2] Let us see.

First a monopoly

When Metal Box first started up in India back in 1933 with a factory at

Table 6 *Public funds locked in sick units, India. This table probably represents but the tip of the iceberg, since advances by bank and institutions other than the Reserve Bank of India are not included, also advances to firms not officially declared 'sick' in accordance with the Reserve Bank of India's definition. Note the steady growth, from which there seems to be no respite*

As at the end December	Scheduled banks	Financial institutions	Total
1979	16.2	2.8	19.0
1980	18.1	3.3	21.4
1981	20.3	3.9	24.2
1982	25.8	6.0	31.8
1983	29.0	8.0	37.0
1984*	31.0	9.0	40.0

* Estimate.
All figures in Indian Rs billion.

Source: Centre for Monitoring the Indian Economy, Bombay.

Calcutta, it had a complete monopoly in India in its particular field and earned very high profits. The paid-up capital of Rs900,000 with which the company started grew to Rs5 million in the first ten years of operation and to Rs30 million in the next ten, largely through 'rights' issues. By 1974 the assets had grown to Rs70 million, but then the British holding was reduced to 60 per cent, as a consequence of a government-inspired process of 'Indianization'. By September 1983 the process had gone much further, the foreign holding being reduced to 40 per cent: control was now in Indian hands. Table 7 illustrates the progress of the company over the years leading up to that situation and it will be seen that the company was in a loss-making situation for some three years. Perhaps we should mention once again, so that the magnitude of these figures and those that follow can be appreciated by those not familiar with the Indian rupee, that ten Indian rupees are roughly equal to one US dollar. This is close enough to enable the order of magnitude of the figures given in Indian rupees to be assessed.

The company was very obviously in financial distress, but a discreet silence was maintained. The company only got into the headlines when it sold off its ballbearing factory for some Rs250 million. Then the articles in the press raised the question: Why this sale? Was it a 'distress' sale, designed to save a sinking ship? A much more pertinent question would have been: What on earth was Metal Box doing with a ballbearing factory? Let us see.

The product profile

The main product lines of Metal Box (India) matched that of its British parent: packaging products such as tin containers, pilfer-proof metal closures, crown corks, collapsible metal tubes (for toothpaste and similar products), followed by paper and plastic packaging. Later the company diversified in a closely related activity: the manufacture of packaging machinery and offset printing machines such as it itself used. This was an attempt at what is called in financial circles 'vertical integration'. Their ballbearing project, however, was a very different matter. It was in a completely unrelated field, although it was launched with much publicity. There is no doubt that this new development violated one of the key criteria for success. Peters and Waterman list eight such criteria in their book *In Search of Excellence*, and according to them the best companies 'stick to their knitting'.[3] Their review had shown them that the best companies 'never acquire a business they don't know how to run.' With this one exception, which constituted a mere 5 per cent of its turnover in 1982, when the company first began to make a loss, Metal Box was unique in India, offering the most comprehensive product range in containers and packaging available in that country.

Metal Box, with a virtual monopoly in packaging had a real head start over all its competitors. But yet the competition grew very rapidly and soon challenged that leading position. The market for packaging products was continually expanding, yet Metal Box was far too slow in adjusting to change and meeting the specific and novel packaging requirements of an expanding market. The overheads remained high and the sales staff were seen by the customer as high-handed and arrogant. No doubt Metal Box thought it had it 'all its own way', but it hadn't. Its monopoly was collapsing. Some of its lines, such as crown corks and metal containers, had only a small market, but it failed to convert what was a threat into an opportunity. Good management would have seized hold of the advantage it had in this field over all its competitors, by being able to produce at comparatively low cost (its plant was much older, and hence written off) and so undercut the competition and retain its monopoly. But nothing like this happened.

To what extent all this was a consequence of 'Indianization' is hard to say. The company entered in to this process rather late, the British managing director, Denis Alport, and most other expatriates not leaving the Indian company until 1969. This meant that by 1976, when the crisis developed, the Indian management had not had much time to learn 'how to do it'. In any event, it was the Indian management, under the then managing director P. K. Nanda, who introduced what we are sure was the 'last straw' that 'broke the camel's back', the ballbearing project. That project, which overran the initial estimates by some 25 per cent, finally costing Rs250 million, had prolonged teething troubles and the capacity utilization was dismal, as the following figures show most clearly:

	1980	1981	1982
Capacity utilization (per cent):	7	30	38

Above all, the quality of the product was such that it did not find acceptance in the Indian market, there being at the same time quite a liberal import policy. It seemed that this project was absolutely governed by Murphy's Law: everything that could go wrong *did* go wrong. The heavy interest burden and the operating losses brought in all a total cash loss of some Rs200 million. In retrospect the project, the brainchild of the then managing director P. K. Nanda, has to be seen as a disastrous nightmare. He kept the implementation of the project entirely to himself and one report suggests that the plant and machinery purchased on the recommendation of the parent company, who themselves were no experts in the manufacture of ballbearings, was defective.

Then the 'Peter Principle' took over. This is the title of a book by Dr Laurence J. Peter, wherein he said that he had discovered a rule in the business world of universal application.[4] In the author's own words:

> In a hierarchy individuals tend to rise to their levels of incompetence.

This was that people tend to be promoted till they reach a level beyond their competence. This, if true, is an obvious recipe for disaster. At all events, Nanda was promoted to the board of the parent company and Kuldip Puri took over. To be fair to them let us listen further to this industrial psychologist turned author:

> It was never my intention to decry the sins, mistakes, vanities and incompetence of my fellow human beings. I am at least as guilty as they. I have set forth my observations because I wanted to share the relief I find in laughter – that most satisfying coping mechanism whereby our personal misadventures and the general human conditions are seen to be absurd.

Having achieved a 'miracle' in Nigeria, it seems that Puri was now expected to give a repeat performance. He began with the obvious, and the ballbearing plant was finally sold to Tisco. Tisco drove a hard bargain, paying only Rs240 million, this figure including some Rs80 million of current assets.

Back from the brink

Metal Box (India), once a very healthy company, counted as a 'blue chip' on the Stock Exchange, found itself eventually on the brink of bankruptcy. The net worth of the company plunged from Rs220 million in September 1981 to Rs80 million by March 1985. Its share value, once a high of Rs28, was down to Rs10 in 1984. The debt/equity ratio, always a powerful indicator of company health, rose to an alarming 5·2/1·0 in 1985. The company was most certainly in need of a 'doctor' and it got one, in the form of Kuldip Puri. He was very pleased to come home and take up that particular role. He saw the 'sickness' as a bonus and its treatment a challenge. It took him a few months to come to grips with the problem, which apparently was much more serious than he had at first thought. His prescription, when produced, was short and sharp:

1   The ballbearing project was a 'dead weight'.
2   It was 'drowning' the profitable packaging business.
3   There was a need to restructure and reduce overheads.
4   The top priority was to establish liquidity.

The sale of the 'dead weight' was finally accomplished in June 1985, about a year after Kuldip Puri first took over. Over the same period the inventories had been drastically reduced and capital expenditure severely pruned. A major reorganization coupled with a spate of resignations reduced the number of managers by a third, to some 160, bringing with it a reduction in the cost of salaries of some 20 per cent. The head office in Calcutta took on a nice lean look, with a mere nineteen executives. The salaries of all executive officers in the company were 'frozen' and their 'perks' severely curtailed. Despite these hardships, the morale of the management rose, because it saw in Kuldip Puri a 'saviour'. At long last it could see the 'light at the end of the tunnel'. This is a quotation from a detailed report on the financial situation in the company,[5] but that particular choice of words reminds us that in this context appearances can sometimes deceive us. For instance, 'the light at the end of the tunnel could be a freight train'. However, in this particular case, the optimism seems to have been justified. Not only the spirits of the company management, but also the shares on the stock market revived, the share value having climbed back to Rs20 by August 1985, nearly twice the prevailing price when Kuldip Puri took over.

The slide down hill was not merely halted: it was reversed. The last two quarters of 1985 saw real earnings on production, and a net profit of some Rs10 million was earned in the year ending March 1986. This was a tremendous turnaround in view of the major losses over the past two years (Rs100 million and Rs60 million) as shown in Table 7. This was not quite the 'miracle' Kuldip Puri achieved in Nigeria, where he transformed a loss of Rs11 million in 1979 to a profit of Rs124 million by 1981. We keep the figures in rupees, rather than reverting to the Nigerian currency, to allow you to assess the magnitude of his achievement, first in Nigeria and then in India. But

Table 7 *Metal Box (India) goes down and up again. After three years operation at a loss, the company has at long last made a profit*

	1979–80	1980–1	1981–2	1982–3	1983–5
Sales and other income	1347^2	1113	1263	1435	1290^2
Net profit	57	23	10	(22)	(56)^2

Notes:
1   All figures are in million rupees.
2   Figures cover an 18-month period.
3   ( ) indicates a loss.
Source: Centre for Monitoring the Indian Economy, Bombay.

even if the transformation is not quite so dramatic, at least the Indian company has now been pulled 'back from the brink' and is beginning to 'recover its colour' – if we are to continue the analogy of a 'sick patient' now in its 'doctor's' hands.

Back on track

Having just used the analogy of a train in a tunnel, perhaps we dare continue the thought by saying that the company, almost derailed, is now back on the track and has a clear course to follow: a road mapped out by Kuldip Puri. It is reasonable to expect that the profit and loss account, for three long years in the red, but now back 'in the black', will stay that way. Despite its fluctuating fortunes, Metal Box (India) still has a very good reputation. When it advertised to fill some of the senior posts, such as accounts manager and general manager – finance, left open as a result of the spate of resignations we referred to earlier, there was a flood of applications. The company also managed to honour its interest payments despite its tight financial position, with the result that the bankers continued to have faith in the company and continued their support. To some extent, no doubt, the quality and the credentials of Kuldip Puri contributed to this situation. The mere presence at the helm of a personality with a history of success is often sufficient to restore confidence, long before his efforts yield their fruit. You will have noticed from the case histories we have studied and will study, that the bankers, in particular, often insist on the appointment of a 'doctor' with an established 'track record': they have confidence that he will accomplish a turnaround and save their money. Various financial 'devices' also made their contribution: the conversion of cumulative bonds worth Rs327 million in September 1985 brought the debt/equity ratio back to the much more reasonable and acceptable level of 3·7/1·0.

But of course, the turnaround is not yet complete. Indeed, it has only just started. Kuldip Puri's announced strategy is to bring the company back to the position it occupied *before* the notorious ballbearings project was initiated. How long will that take? No one knows, and even Kuldip Puri is not making any promises. But his target is clear enough. He not only wants to see the company fully restored to financial health: he wants it to regain its lost market share in its traditional product, the can. Can production at the moment constitutes some 70 per cent of the total annual output of Metal Box (India) but its market share, 50 per cent in 1982, has now dropped to 40 per cent. The company's fluctuating fortunes in this respect are set out in Table 8. These figures demonstrate that there is still ample room for growth. While the road may be long and arduous, the route is clear.

Table 8   *MBI's fluctuating market share. This table shows us that while Metal Box (India) improved their position significantly in 1986, they still have a long way to go if they are to regain their earlier position in the Indian market*

	1982 %	1983 %	1984 %	1985 %	1986 %
Cans	50	45	42	40	44
Crowns	35	29	32	36	42
Roll sealed closures	24	17	16	15	20
Collapsible tubes	32	20	19	18	21

Will the parent disown its child?

Metal Box (India) is one of six such companies associated with the parent company in London, the group as a whole having a turnover of some US$1800 million in 1984–5, with a profit of US$109 million. Metal Box is an undisputed market leader in the world of packaging, with a holding, now, of some 37 per cent in its Indian affiliate. During the bad days, there was a feeling in London that it would be as well to divest itself of the Indian operation, but to take that course at that time would have been very misguided. However, now that things are on the upturn and the Indian company has been restored to health, the parent company may well decide to sell off its remaining interest. There are plenty of contenders for the prize – India abounds with 'goenkas' – 'takeover' kings, as well as major companies who would be well pleased to further diversify, such as Birla, Thapar and Singhania. At the moment any such possibility is strongly denied, both in London and in Calcutta, but that is the normal reaction to all such rumours. There is no doubt that a very common 'follow-on' to a turnaround is a takeover, as several of our case histories demonstrate. Significantly enough, Richard Stanley, a director of the London company, on a farewell visit to Calcutta a few months prior to his retirement from the group, admitted:

> If a serious offer were indeed to be made, Metal Box plc would consider it on its merits. But I certainly haven't come over to Calcutta to sell our stake in our Indian affiliate.

So for the moment the ball seems to be the bidders' court.

Summary

We have now extended our case studies from the developing countries into the private sector. We see that the formula remains much the same. Get rid of the 'dead wood', motivate the management and the workforce, initiate change with courage and resolution. So far as the future of Metal Box (India) is concerned, it looks as though a 'serious offer' has been made and accepted although at the moment it is not for the divestiture of the Indian affiliate. The suitor seems to be MacNeill & Magor, who is to provide additional finance for the company's needs in respect of both fixed and working capital.[6] Three new directors have been placed on the board of Metal Box (India): B. M. Khaitan, the managing director of MacNeill & Magor, R. B. Magor and Deepak Khaitan. It is surmised that in due course the funds to be provided by MacNeill & Magor will be converted into equity, with a corresponding dilution of the parent company's holding. This arrangement may well prove satisfactory for all concerned, but one hopes that in the process the 'doctor' will be left in charge at least until his patient is fully recovered: there are very few of his stamp in India. No wonder they are in great demand and can almost name their salary.

References

1   Sarathi, V., *Company Failure in India*, New Heights Publishers, 1968; Simha, S. L. N., *Sickness of Industrial Units*, Institute for Financial Management and Research, 1977; Lal, S., *How to Protect Industrial Sickness: Symptoms and Rehabilitation*, Navrang, 1979; Gupta, L. C, *Financial Ratios as Forewarning Indicators of Corporate Sickness*, 1979; 'Problem Projects and their rehabilitation', *Industrial Credit and Investment Corporation of India*, 1977; National Council of Applied and Economic Research, *A Study of Industrial Sickness*, Punjab National Bank; Chakraworthy, S. K. and Sen P. K., *Industrial Sickness and Revival in India: Essays, Cases and Debates*, Indian Institute of Management, 1980; Kaveri, V. S., *How to Diagnose, Prevent and Cure Industrial Sickness*, Sultan Chand, 1983; Padaki, V. and Shanbhag, V., *Industrial Sickness: The Challenge in Indian Textiles*, Ahmedabad Textile Industry Research Association, 1984; Cherian, D., 'How to guarantee failure', *Business India*, 9–22 April 1984, p. 56; Bhagat, M., 'Physician, heal thyself', *Update*, 11–24 July 1984, pp. 44–51; Rungta, A. L., 'Cure for sick units', *Business India*, 10–23 September 1984, p. 156; Thacker, J. P., 'Sickness – disastrous impact on economy', *Economic Times*, 3 November 1985; Agarwal, R. C., 'Industrial sickness and its effect on bank's profitability', *Economic Times*, 19 March 1986.

2   Gupta, S., 'Can Kuldip Puri turn Metal Box around', *Business World*, August/September 1985, p. 44

3   Peters, T. J. and Waterman, R. H., *In Search of Excellence: Lessons from America's Best-Run Companies*, Harper & Row, 1982.

4   Peter, L. J., *Why Things Go Wrong or the Peter Principle Revisited*, George Allen & Unwin, 1985, p. 207.

5   Roy Subrata, 'Metal Box up for sale?', *Business India*, 12–25 September 1983, p. 62.

6   Roy, S., 'Metal Box – the MacNeill & Magor stake', *Business India*, 13–26 January 1986, p. 62.

8   Keeping Swiss watches ticking

Till now we have been looking at turnarounds accomplished with individual companies, rather than industries, although we have sometimes taken a look at an industry in order to assess and appreciate the climate in which that turnaround had been brought about. Each turnaround was initiated by a 'company doctor', as they are now commonly called in financial circles and we are seeking to learn the lessons in company management from the approach adopted by the man behind the turnaround. Now we are going to look at a turnaround, not in an individual company, but in a complete industry in one particular country – Switzerland. Since the scope is broader, we are not going to be able to identify the 'doctor' in quite the same way – it is more a surgical team who bring about the recovery – but nevertheless there are very valuable lessons in company management to be learned by a study of what has happened to the Swiss watch industry over the past decade.

A number of articles have been written about the transformation that has now taken place in the Swiss watch industry and the quality of what has happened is well presented by the titles of some of those articles:[1]

A last-minute comeback for Swiss watchmakers
A Doc for what ails Swiss watches
Can new management team keep Swiss watches ticking?
Brighter prospects for the Swiss watchmaking industry
Swiss watches: a timely recovery.

As you will see we are able to identify one or two members of that surgical team: names such as Dr Ernst Thomke and Dr Pierre Arnold come to the fore, but there must have been several others in the individual companies who played their part in the turnaround that has now been achieved. But what was the problem?

The story in brief

For centuries the craftsmanship to be found in the Swiss Alps in relation to clock and watchmaking has been renowned worldwide. Swiss watches were the epitome of precision and the Swiss watch industry dominated the world markets. The skills seem over the years to have spilled over, as it were, into their neighbour Germany, for Germany gained a somewhat similar reputation in relation to the manufacture of clocks, despite the fact that many tourists visiting Switzerland have taken home an old-fashioned cuckoo clock as a memento of their visit. But not only are the Swiss skilled craftsmen, they are a very conservative group of people, resistant to change. This has been amply demonstrated by the results of the numerous referendums that have been held in connection with a wide range of social and economic issues: almost invariably the result is to leave things as they are. It was this resistance to change that was, in the end, to bring the Swiss watch industry to its knees.

The titles we have quoted above demonstrate not only that the industry has been in trouble, but that it has made a comeback, but how did it get into trouble? Of course, the Swiss were not the only manufacturers of watches, but for a long time they were the only manufacturers of quality, high precision watches: the perfect time-keepers. But then the Japanese came on the scene, and started to dominate watch manufacture, just as they had begun to dominate so many other industries. They were able to produce a high quality watch at a low price, reflecting the latest technology. For instance, the Swiss had designed the self-winding watch, that never needed attention while it was worn for a few hours a day, but the mechanism was expensive. The Japanese came along with a cheaper battery-operated model that ran for a year or more on one battery and as a result they captured nearly 40 per cent of the world market. The Swiss had rested confident in their reputation, but reputation alone was not enough: price plays a significant role. The market had always recognized that precision timekeeping cost money and while a multitude bought cheap watches, accepting their lack of precision and reliability because that was all they could afford, there was a strong demand for the precision watch. But suddenly the cheap watch was also a precision watch, thanks to the new electronic quartz technology, so that the dominance of the Swiss disappeared almost overnight. The only solution was for the Swiss watch manufacturers to produce a cheap precision watch: but this demanded an industrial revolution in the industry, the transformation of production methods and the development of radical new designs, something that demanded the injection of very substantial sums in terms of capital for new plant and equipment.

Once again it was the bankers who came to the rescue. A group of five Swiss banks put up some US$500 million and the industry developed a technical solution. They copied the competition. A remarkable feature of Japanese industry is the way in which individual, competing companies in a specific industry will join together in research to bring about a new development, then each company takes that development and they start to compete for sales against one another on the open market. The Swiss did something like that: the industry banded together to design and produce a new, cheap, battery-operated plastic watch built on a robot-run assembly line. The number of separate parts was reduced from the current ninety to about fifty. They gave it a brand name: the *Swatch*. This new design, sleek and durable, found instant acceptance on the world market, backed as it was by the Swiss reputation for reliability. It sold for around US$25, whereas the cheapest 'standard' watch coming out of Switzerland had been costing at least US$50. With the cost of manufacture at around US$10, the Swiss had room to make a profit, and they did. They new watch came on the market in 1983 and sold a million in the first nine months. Rather neatly, to preserve as far as possible their traditional market, the *Swatch* was advertised as a stylish 'second watch', a fashion accessory rather than a device to tell the time. The implication was that everyone should still have a conventional Swiss watch, guaranteed to work under all conditions, even 200 metres down under the sea – as if the average person ever went in for deep sea diving! The *Swatch* was made available in a wide variety of dials, styles and colours: a watch to match every dress was the theme of the advertising. Before the introduction of this new product the Swiss share of the world market had dropped from some 70 per cent to less than 10 per cent by volume: a disastrous collapse. The position of Switzerland in the world 'league table' for watch production is given in Table 9. As this table demonstrates, the Swiss have not suffered as much value wise as they have in terms of

Table 9 *World watch production in 1985. This table lets us see that while Switzerland produces only 10 per cent of the world's watches in terms of number, in terms of value it takes nearly half the market*

	By volume %	By value %
Switzerland	10	45
Japan	35	35
Other Asian countries	50	14
Rest of the world	5	6

Source: Federation of the Swiss Watch Industry.

volume, since they still have nearly half the world market in terms of value. Indeed, they have succeeded in increasing the value of their sales worldwide once they had recovered their position, despite a substantial fall in the numbers sold, as is illustrated by Figure 4. The

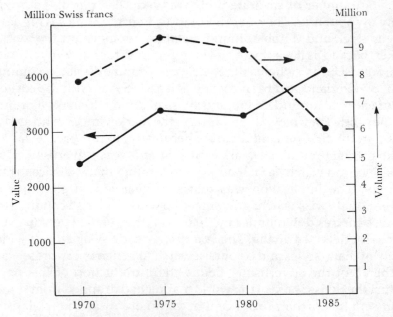

Figure 4   *Swiss watch sales. This graph demonstrates that in terms of value sales of Swiss watches have failed to keep pace with the growing demand for watches worldwide.* Source: *Federation of the Swiss Watch Industry.*

new product has initially provided a substantial boost to their market share, but it has accomplished much more than that. Its implementation has brought about a drastic change in attitudes, and provided a very necessary boost to morale in the industry in Switzerland. But how was this drastic change brought about in a society so insular and resistant to change?

The industry 'doctors'

If sick companies are to recover a 'doctor' is required, as we have already seen in the case studies we have taken so far. The doctor has to study the symptoms, make a diagnosis and then recommend the appropriate treatment. The treatment is almost inevitably drastic. When we come to look at the transformation that was brought about in the Swiss watch industry, we can identify two 'doctors' whose efforts complemented one another. We see the parallel in medicine, where a number of consultants are sometimes called in, and more particularly when it comes to surgery and a team of specialists, each with their own individual role to play, are brought together for the operation. There is also a proverb that is quite appropriate in this context: 'two heads are better than one'.

In the face of impending disaster, the two major companies in the watch industry in Switzerland, selling such well-known and honoured names as Omega, Longines and Tissot – the mere mention of the name immediately brings to mind an elegant watch – created a consortium in 1983 known as ASUAG-SSIH (Allgemeine Schweizer-izche Uhrenindustrie AG and Societe Suisse pour l'Industrie Horlogere). This consortium, which two years later led to a merger named SMH (Swiss Corporation for Microelectronics) had a managing committee of five members, but the most powerful of them was a physician – yes, literally as well as figuratively – Dr Ernst Thomke. At first sight, Dr Thomke could have been thought to have been a misfit in an industry dominated by engineers, but it was his selling acumen that made a major contribution to eventual success. He wanted to sell watches much as toothpaste is sold. With toothpaste you go into the supermarket and pick the brand that appeals to you off the shelf. All the brands are assumed to be of equivalent quality and your choice is largely motivated by brand advertising. He introduced a brand of watch, the *Swatch* and his prescription must have been the right one, because it worked. As a consequence Dr Thomke has been variously described as a 'genius' and as the 'saviour' of the Swiss watch industry, although he has critics, who have dubbed him a 'madman', the 'human bulldozer' and even 'Ayatollah Thomke', such is the resistance to change in some quarters.

There is no doubt that Dr Thomke was the father of the *Swatch*, a timepiece that has provided a precision industry with a break-through into the cheap quartz watch mass market. Not only did he introduce a revolutionary concept, the electronic watch, but at the same time he slashed costs by revolutionizing production methods. Above all, he taught the Swiss watch manufacturers to take notice of what was happening in the world about them, rather than just looking around their own industry and thinking what a lot of clever boys they were. Thanks to Dr Thomke and *Swatch* the worst may now be over. Dr Thomke came on to the scene in 1978 as the chief executive of an ASUAG subsidiary ETA, then the largest manu-facturer of watch components in Switzerland. His advent was resented, particularly by the engineers, but he brought results and that was what counted in an ailing industry. A charming personality and an accomplished musician, he has shown himself to be a tough boss and has been heard to say, though no doubt jokingly: 'I'm not a nice person'. At a 7.30 a.m. meeting one Monday morning, he was reported as yelling at a subordinate: 'Straighten out your department or you can pick up your last pay cheque tomorrow'. The department was reorganized and that particular individual kept his job! A very strong-willed personality, he had never done any jogging. Yet when a friend bet him a thousand dollars that he would not complete the New York Marathon (26·2 miles) in under four hours, he took him on, completed the course in a few seconds under four hours and won his bet. That, we feel, is a very interesting story in that it demonstrates his determination in the face of all odds.

But of course, strength of character is not all, nor is it enough of itself. There has to be a strong devotion to the subject in hand, in this case watches. We are told that so intense was Dr Thomke's interest in watches that he left school to work at ETA. But he also had a passion for learning, so went back to college at twenty, finally gaining his doctor's degree in his 'spare time'. However, he did not start practising, but opted for research at Beecham Pharmaceuticals, then moved over to marketing and became its sales manager. Instead of selling drugs as such, he organized free ski trips and concerts for doctors and their families: drug sales soared! When his first love, watches, got into trouble, he rejoined ASUAG and applied his gift of salesmanship to its problems.

The other 'doctor' was Dr Pierre Arnold. He came on to the scene somewhat later, when a diagnosis had been made and the 'treatment' was being applied. Retired, Pierre Arnold had been chief executive of the expanding and very successful retailing and distribution group Migros, a federation of independent co-operatives. He was also a director of Swissair and an ardent supporter of the application of electronics to watches. Although completely new to watches, he came to ASUAG with a reputation as a successful leader and 'strongman'. Described by one of his friends as a 'friendly bulldog', perhaps he was just what the Swiss watch industry needed at that time. Although he did not work full time, he seems to have provided a very necessary impetus. Laura Pilarski quotes him as saying:[1]

> What the watch industry is missing is someone to tell them what has to be done . . . already I feel welcomed . . . it's not a matter of doing a certain number of hours a day. My speciality, in a big organization like Migros, was to do the synthesis and synergy. I have many ideas in my head but I am not talking about them.

It is no wonder, in the face of this positive approach, and a proven record the ASUAG-SSIH board asked Arnold to head the combine. In doing so they passed over a number of very bright managers: managers who were eventually the unsung heroes of the most remarkable turnaround, for it was they who had to implement the drastic changes that were made.

So convinced was Arnold of the value of electronics, not only in watches, but in all industrial products, that he had made a mission of the concept. While at Migros he introduced courses on electronics at the adult education schools, displaying a missionary zeal in his continuing exhortation to 'go electronic'. For him it was not a 'fashion' but a stark necessity in the modern world. To drive home his message he actually wrote a book, *Living with Electronics*, a layman's guide in the world of transistors, microchips, computers and videos.[2] It lacks a section on electronics in watches, an omission that brought the industry in Switzerland close to disaster, but that particular disaster *could* have been avoided.

The electronic miracle

As long ago as the 1960s, the Swiss watch manufacturers were engaged in a US$2·5 million research programme to develop an all-electronic quartz watch. The technology was there, but unfortunately it remained in the laboratory and never reached the production line in Switzerland. But as has so often happened, the Japanese, building once again on the work of others, recognized the potential and the promise, took over the technology and put it into practice. Manufacturing quartz watches that were not only completely reliable but extremely accurate, the Japanese made deep inroads into the watch market, gaining a major share from the 'old timers', who slumbered on. Even in the face of this stiff competition the Swiss watch industry dithered, asserting that there was nothing to beat the precision mechanism they built: old traditions die hard!

The crisis deepened as time passed. The worldwide market share of the industry in Switzerland dropped from 70 per cent to less than 10 per cent by volume, two major groups ASUAG and SSIH were close to bankruptcy and the banks felt they had to come to the rescue. Outstanding loans were written off and in an effort to revive the industry, they compelled the amalgamation of ASUAG and SSIH, a group that now produces up to half the timepieces manufactured in Switzerland. The amalgamation and the dramatic revolution in manufacturing practice that followed, together with the inspired sales theme, began to show results in 1984. Exports rose by 13 per cent and the ASUAG-SSIH combine reached its breakeven point in sales volume, with a turnover of some US$650 million. As we have said already, the key to this revival in its fortunes was the *Swatch*, its father the flamboyant chief executive at ETA, one of ASUAG-SSIH's major production units. He certainly knew where he wanted to go, saying:[1]

> We have to start 'class' at an affordable price . . . .Consumers have become more price sensitive. The Japanese certainly have followed and stimulated the price-sensitivity of the market.

The figures now speak for themselves. An analysis has shown that the low-priced end of the watch market is by far the fastest-growing segment of the industry. Though margins are small there, the volume demand allows economy of scale and thus makes the low price sector financially attractive.

To give credit where credit is due, we should tell you that the basic production plan which resulted in this remarkable turnaround was drawn up by the consultants Hayek Engineering Ltd of Zurich. Of course the plan had to be implemented with enthusiasm and substantial team effort among the companies forming the group.

There has also been financial as well as production restructuring, so that the holding company now has three major manufacturing groups: movements and components, finished watches and industrial products. Initially it was operating completely independently and there was some cost duplication, particularly with administration, but a degree of centralization has eliminated this. However, it has already seen the danger of taking centralization too far. Its chief financial officer, Carl M. Meyer, says:

> We don't want to really centralise the group because we believe in independent profit centres, but a certain coordination was necessary.

Of course this industrial revolution has had its impact upon the workforce. It could hardly be otherwise. About two thirds of the watches manufactured by the group in 1984 were quartz models, and the workforce has been nearly halved, standing now at some 11,000. But you surely did not need us to tell you that by now.

The bankers take the lead

We have already mentioned that in this case – and as is so often the case – the bankers initiated the revival of the Swiss watch industry. They had to: their money was at risk. They saw that the only way to save the situation was by a substantial injection of money to fund the new capital investment that had to take place. As a result, they had a powerful voice in the restructuring of the industry that then took place. They provided new money of the order of US$500 million, used almost entirely for the development of new products and the modernization of production lines, the balance, perhaps some 10 per cent, going on a massive advertisement campaign.

The ASUAG-SSIH group is now almost wholly owned by the banks, but they are likely to 'privatize' it once the group is firmly on the road to recovery and making profits on a consistent basis. But there is no doubt that from now on, and even after they have divested themselves of this particular 'problem child', the banks will watch the watch industry – and not only the watch industry, much more closely than they have done in the past. Banks, we believe, have a duty of care, in as much as their loans play a significant role in the course that a company decides to take. Careless lending is very likely to lead to careless spending. One result of this is that most major banks now have specialist departments devoted to the care of ailing companies. Typical of these is a unit in the Corporate Financial

Division of the Midland Bank in the UK, where some fifty qualified specialists, including chartered accountants, conduct detailed assessments and make recommendations, following analysis of the situation in consultation with the directors of troubled companies who are their customers.[3] Here the banks did more than that, for they appointed a new board to run the company. Under a nine-person board there is a five-man management committee which includes Thomke and Meyer, who has a business degree from Harvard University in the US. This committee reports to the chairman, Arnold, and has a staff of sixty-five. One feels that Thomke would have been the logical choice for the top job and it was rumoured that he would quit if an outsider was brought in. An outsider *was* brought in and it is to his credit that he has worked amicably with Arnold for the good of the group, to the benefit both of the banks and their country.

Fashions and labels

The introduction of the *Swatch* in 1983, much against the wishes of the 'old timers', the watch craftsmen of Switzerland, seems to have stimulated the entire Swiss watch industry. How has this come about? It appears that the watch is no longer a 'once-in-a-lifetime' gift, nor is it the exclusive privilege of the rich. The wrist watch has become commonplace, even being worn by children from the age of five onwards and almost everyone has one or more. It seems that the wrist watch has become a fashion accessory, many of the ladies having a *Swatch* (or its equivalent) to match every dress. It appears from the statistics that in the OECD countries each and every one living there has 2·5 watches! Sales worldwide are still rising steadily, the figures for the US and Britain over the past ten years, as given below, speaking for themselves.

Watches purchased per 1000 persons

Year	United States	Britain
1975	240	274
1985	425	370

Of course, the bulk of these, probably some 90 per cent, are the low-priced electronic watches. In order to cash in on this growing trend, the fashion trade is now marketing watches under various 'house names', such as Tiffany, Garrard and even Christian Dior.

None of these companies manufacture watches, but they get them made with their label, and sometimes to their own design. Christian Dior, once having entered this particular market, increased its sales of wrist watches from 10,000 to 100,000 within four years. One wonders what is next in store for watches.

What of the future?

It is interesting to see the way in which a concept, once introduced, gains sway. Once having gone electronic, and having rationalized their industry by closing down those factories which were producing identical parts and competing for the same customers within the combine, they looked abroad, at Thomke's initiative, for markets not merely for their watches, but for watch parts. As a result they have won substantial orders from far-distant places such as Hong Kong and Japan and their parts business has become profitable in its own right, after three years of heavy losses.

The Japanese onslaught on the market was not only a price-cutting exercise. Watches were put on sale with truly novel features, such as the Seiko watch that came on the market in 1978 and was advertised with pride as the 'world's thinnest watch'. This was pushing quartz electronic technology to the limit. But Thomke, having had recourse to his medical dictionary, launched the project *Delirium Tremens* to counter this in 1979. Conventional watchmaking was a three-step process whereby the case and the movement were each fabricated separately and then assembled. ETA succeeded in reducing this to one single step by building the movement directly into the case. Within six months of launching the project the world's thinnest watch of all – the 2 mm thick *Concord Delirium* – came on the market. It was this major technological development that, used in the manufacture of the *Swatch*, contributed so much to cutting production costs.

The *Swatch* (Swiss watch) came in a tremendous variety of styles and we can imagine that the sales genius of Thomke was the main inspiration. Watches were on sale scented with banana, raspberry and mint: there was a 'very high precision' (VHP) model containing two quartz crystals instead of one. The first crystal clocks the time, while the second compensates for vibration and the effects of temperature upon the first crystal. However, this diversion to the 'cheap end' of the market has not caused the Swiss to relax in relation to their traditional product. They still retain their place as one of the world's finest jewellers, making luxury watches from precious metals, studded with gems and costing anything from US$1,000 to US$10,000. Value wise luxury watches still make up three quarters of their total sales volume, although in terms of quantity they now represent less than 20 per cent of total sales worldwide.

There seems to be an air of cautious optimism in relation to the future of the Swiss watch industry. A recent survey carried out by the Economic Research Department of the Union Bank of Switzerland, in close collaboration with the Federation of the Swiss Watch Industry, had some 170 companies respond to its questionnaire. Of them, some 63 per cent expected their business to increase, and only 3 per cent thought there was any possibility of decline. The future for workers in the industry, however, is by no means so rosy. Only 34 per cent of the companies expected to make any increase in their staff. Between 1970 and 1985 there has been a massive decline in manpower in the industry, from 90,000 to 32,000, but it appears that the worst is now over, since the latest figure represents a modest increase of 3 per cent over the previous year. It seems that the trade still has great confidence in maintaining their place in the 'top end' of the market, originally their whole market, as is displayed by the answers given to the prospects for the three basic segments of the trade, thus:

Reaction:	Positive	Negative	No opinion
	%	%	%
Expensive watches	80	6	14
Medium-priced watches	44	36	20
Cheap watches	58	25	17

Thus there is strong confidence that the expensive watch will continue to have a substantial market. The responses also show that the weak link in the chain is likely to be the medium-priced watch. We must wait to see to what extent this confidence is really justified. But the market is not the only problem Swiss watch manufacturers have to meet. There is also the problem of the continuing fall in the value of the US dollar, something over which they have no control at all. Then there is their relative failure to make sales in Japan. Although nearly two million Swiss watches were sold in Japan in 1985, and that might sound a very satisfactory achievement, it needs to be set in context. In fact it is only 2 per cent of the annual sales of watches in Japan, some 40 million. Since value wise nearly all the sales made were at the top end of the market, sales of Swiss watches took some 20 per cent of the Japanese market in terms of value, but the *Swatch* is hardly ever seen there. One interesting feature, perhaps demonstrating a market trend, is that one major Japanese watch manufacturer, *Casio* (who prefers to describe itself as a computer manufacturer) who concentrated on digital watches far more than did the Swiss, is now reverting to analog watches. It seems the customer prefers them, finding them more readily readable.

Summary

The Swiss watch has passed through a crisis of confidence and has survived, thanks largely to the initiative of the Swiss banks. The two 'doctors', each with a very different style, Dr Ernst Thomke and Dr Pierre Arnold, both played a crucial role in the revival of an industry. They both had an intense enthusiasm for watches, Dr Thomke from his youth, and Dr Arnold since his devotion to electronics. This resulted in their being an ideal combination. Thomke initiated the process of turnaround, while Arnold, coming in somewhat later, provided increased momentum to the turnaround by virtue of his technical knowledge and management skills. What is more, they both loved their country and were determined that the Swiss watch industry would not only survive but thrive.

References

1   Pilarski, L., 'A last-minute comeback for Swiss watchmakers', *Business Week*, 26 November, 1984, pp. 139–42; Pilarski, L., 'Can new management team keep Swiss watches ticking?' *International Marketing*, August 1985, pp. 23–4; Tully, S., 'A Doc for what ails Swiss watches', *Fortune*, no. 111, 4 February 1985, pp. 62–6; 'Brighter prospects for the Swiss watchmaking industry', *UBS Business Facts and Figures*, April 1986; 'Swiss watches: a timely recovery', *Economist*, no. 299, 17 May 1986, pp. 92–3.
2   Arnold, P., *Living with Electronics*, 1981. (Published in-house.)
3   Wheatley, D. J., 'Intensive care – life saving task for the profession', *Accountancy*, no. 94, August 1983, pp. 86–7.

Part Three

Even giants can bounce back

9 Transformation at General Motors

General Motors is not just a company – in the US it's an institution. Volumes have been written about this particular company and most of it in praise! If we go back to 1946 we find Peter Drucker, and he was by no means the first, writing a book with the title *Concept of the Corporation: A Study of General Motors*.[1] Then, some fifteen years ago now, came Alfred P. Sloan with his book *My Years with General Motors*.[2] General Motors is such an institution that you may well be surprised that it has a place in a book dealing with company turnarounds and company 'doctors'. We were, too! We had seen General Motors as a giant riding out the storm with equanimity, far too big ever to be flurried: quietly keeping up with current trends. We even included the story of its first 'plastic' sports car, the *Fiero*, in our book on successful projects.[3] General Motors is the largest corporation in the US, or perhaps the second, after Exxon. We do not really know: it depends to some extent upon how you measure size in such a context. Possibly it is also the largest corporation in the world. Its turnover is already more than US$90 billion and is expected to cross the US$100 billion barrier in 1986, more particularly since it has now gone on an acquisition spree. So why did General Motors ever have to have a 'doctor'?

Well, this may surprise you even more, but in 1980 General Motors made a loss. Figure 5 pictures both the sales and the profits at General Motors from 1977 onwards and it will be seen that while sales continued to rise steadily, profit took a serious dip in 1980. It is true that the loss was for one year only and the company made a quick recovery, but if one allows for the effect of escalation it will be realized that General Motors had been in the 'doldrums' for several

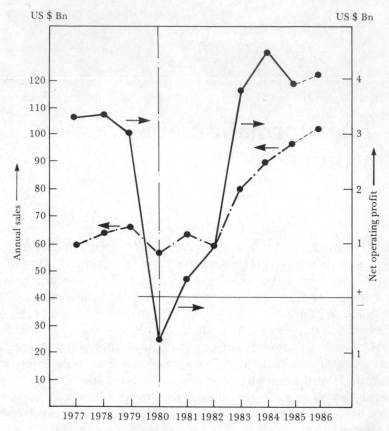

US $ Bn   US $ Bn

Figure 5   *Riding a cycle. This is a graphic demonstration of the way in which profits 'cycled' while sales, in terms of numbers, continued to rise.*
Source: Company accounts.

years. Now it has got back on course, but how did such a vast corporation ever get 'off course'?

Dropping into a 'pothole'

Leader writers can never resist an eye-catching title: nor can we! We saw the sudden sharp drop from profit to loss which we have just described above as a 'pothole' by a leader writer because General Motors is *the* car manufacturer and we thought it most expressive of what actually happened.[4] But how did General Motors ever run over that particular 'pothole'? The company is the industry leader, selling four out of every ten cars on the road in the US, and at the same time having 23 per cent of the world market, its closest runner up, Ford, having 20 per cent. Its total sales are greater than those of its major US rivals, Ford, Chrysler and AMC put together. General Motors is more than twice the size of Japan's biggest car makers, Toyota, and has nearly 800,000 employees. In fact it has by far the largest workforce of any single US company, being relatively labour intensive, particularly when compared with the other majors, who are all in oil. How could such a company ever get into trouble?

When Roger Smith took over as chairman of General Motors in 1980, that company (along with the other American car makers) was actually at a crucial stage in its history, although it perhaps did not quite realize it. With rising petrol prices, a consequence of the 'oil crisis' of 1973 and 1979, the fuel efficient cars produced by the Japanese were being favoured over the American 'fuel guzzlers'. In addition, the American car manufacturers had to cope with very high production costs. This was occasioned not only by the very high hourly rate paid to the American worker compared with other countries, such as Japan, but also by very poor productivity: a result of inefficient manufacturing practices. However, the company seemed obsessed by its turnover. All that mattered was the number of cars sold. So long as car sales continued to rise nothing else mattered. The company also seemed to have developed a tremendous inertia. As a result it ignored the trend and continued to operate as it had done in the 'good old days'. Then, suddenly, in 1980, the company came face to face with the realities of the situation. In one year a profit of US$3 billion disappeared, and there was a loss of US$760 million. That *was* a shock, even for a sleeping giant like General Motors.

Had anyone been looking, that 'nosedive' could have been predicted. General Motors at that time was the model of an uncompetitive and 'nearly comatose' American giant. Decisions trickled down the ladder from manager to manager: managers who were afraid to take risks. The company's answer to the strong Japanese challenge, which had been much strengthened by the oil crisis of 1973 and 1979 had been minimal. New front wheel drive models had been introduced, such as the Chevrolet *Cavalier* and the Oldsmobile *Ciera*, but these cars had failed to win back the converts to Toyotas and Datsuns. The cause of this weak response was clear enough: the highly bureaucratic and monolithic structure of the company. Its bureaucracy was such that it put the government bureaucrats in Washington to shame. It was more bureaucratic than the bureaucrats. Lee Iacocca no doubt read the situation correctly enough when he commented in his caustic way: 'Let the elephant sleep. Don't anyone wake the elephant'. Of course not. From his point of view, if the elephant stirred it could prove a dangerous competitor.

The 'doctor' from within

The general trend is for change to come from without, but this time it was initiated from within. The chairman of General Motors, Roger Smith, born in Columbus, Ohio and the son of a banker whose business, along with many others, failed in the depression took up the role of 'doctor'. The story of his rise to the top is straightforward and common enough. He was what some companies call a 'star' executive: a young man whose attributes marked him out as promising managerial material. His studies at the University of Michigan, interrupted by a two-year stint in the US Navy, finally brought him a business degree (MBA) in 1947. He then joined the accounts department at General Motors and never looked back. He went relatively rapidly straight to the top, becoming chairman in 1980, just in time to cope with the 'pothole'. He married a General Motors secretary, Barbara Ann, in 1954. Despite a happy family life he displayed a strong attachment to the company. It is perhaps significant that he started his business life with General Motors and had never seen anything else. In this he had what we shall see when we come to look at Japan more closely (Chapter 14) is the characteristically Japanese approach to employment. In the same spirit he is likely to stay on as chairman till company rules (a mandatory retirement age of sixty-five) compel him to retire in 1990. If he gets that far he will have served as chairman for just over ten years, the longest term since Alfred P. Sloan Jr, who served as chairman for twenty years. But if we are to judge from the impact of his first five years in office, he is likely to leave a far greater imprint on the company than ever Sloan did, for all his twenty years in the top office.

Strangely, Roger Smith did not at first appear to be the type of man who could 'doctor' an ailing company back to health. Many saw him as a man of 'grey mediocrity', tackling the problem in a traditional manner by cutting costs and the labour force. But he brought a novel and even oriental approach to the problem: he counselled *patience*. Writing in the house journal *GM Today* he advised:

Don't grab the first thing that comes along. Very rarely is that the right answer [referring to his move to cut jobs] . . . . I was probably one of the least popular chairmen ever when I began.

Roger Smith realized that General Motors had been 'sitting pretty', with a 60 per cent share of the American market for US-built cars and with its giant size it was a 'docile beast'.[5] In fact the company had grown so huge and was so completely decentralized (a policy adopted by Sloan way back in the 1930s) that it was impossible for it to react with speed to the changing situation in the market-place. No one could know what was happening throughout the organization as a whole. Each manufacturing entity was pursuing its own course. To quote David Cole, a director of automotive studies at the University of Michigan and son of a former General Motors president, it wasn't a matter of General Motors' 'left hand not knowing what its right hand was doing . . . its left *side* did not know what its right *side* was doing'.[6]

It probably says much for Roger Smith's quality of patience that in order to 'heal' the 'beast' (we now seem to have turned him into a veterinary surgeon, don't we) he had to turn into a reluctant revolutionary. To quote him once again, and the emphasis is ours: [7]

I'm not a guy that likes to change . . . but we *have* to change.

But having brought about the necessary changes, to which we shall come a little later, Roger Smith realized that the organizational framework within which he had to work was restricting the extent of change:[8]

The corporation has changed . . . [but] our economies of scale are different. Our manufacturing methods and designs are different. It might be that a better organization is needed.

So Roger Smith, despite his inherent conservatism, did not hesitate to consider changing the very structure of the company, describing what he had in mind as follows:[8]

It's a bottom-up look, not top-down – it's deciding how the engineers and others would design this corporation to be the most effective deliverer of our product.

To sceptics who doubted whether he would ever get anything out of the exercise, he responded by echoing their doubts, but at the same time demonstrated the quality of his approach to the problem by saying: 'I've been here thirty-three years (this was in 1983) and I don't remember a time like this when we said "start with a clean sheet of paper".' It would seem from this that the attitude of Roger Smith had become so liberal that he was prepared to change the very 'culture' of the monolith he had in his charge: but more of that later.

The 'doctor's' prescription

Roger Smith's problem (many would call it a nightmare) was to know where to start. He had to do 'first things first', but what came first? He was convinced that despite the multitude of things that were wrong, the company had an inherent strength which should be used. That it was strong was demonstrated by the fact that over sixty years, and having come through several periods of depression it had never made a loss – till now! Roger Smith made his own diagnosis, but he also called for comparative studies of costs as incurred by their Japanese affiliate, Isuzu Motors. General Motors had a minority interest in this company (34·2 per cent), acquired way back in 1971, but it was the troubles at General Motors ten years later that caused the company to start studying and so learning from its Japanese operations! That study revealed and so confirmed Roger Smith's impression that a car manufactured in Japan had a cost advantage of about US$2,500 when compared to a car manufactured in the US. Of course, that cost advantage was analysed in detail, that its lessons might be applied. So for once the management did not blame the usual scapegoat, the workers, deciding instead to look at its operations as a whole. So often the shopfloor worker gets all the blame for inefficient production, management failing to realize that if a worker cannot get the right materials at the right time in the right place, he can *never* operate efficiently. The world-famous management consultants, McKinsey & Co. were called in. They studied the organization of General Motors for two years and their recommendations formed the basis for a complete overhaul of the management structure.[9] In passing, we have here a very clear demonstration of the way in which consultants should be used. Roger Smith not only recognized that he would do well to call in the experts, but he also accepted their recommendations. So many get as far as asking for a report and paying for it, but from then on it is but another book on the chairman's bookshelf.

However, as we said, Roger Smith implemented the advice given him, thus making the most sweeping changes ever in his company's history. The workforce of 750,000 was effectively halved, being brought down to 367,000 by 1984. Since then (up to 1987) the workforce has been reduced by another third. In parallel with this drastic reduction in the workforce Roger Smith's prescription called for an upgrading of manufacturing technology, with the adoption of the Japanese techniques which had brought that saving of US$2,500 a car. To get at those techniques he sought and acquired partners, as detailed in Table 10. This list is not comprehensive, but it demonstrates very clearly Roger Smith's approach to the problem. He was an accountant through and through and he adopted the accountant's approach: he bought in his engineering skills.

The deals listed in Table 10, especially the last two, massive though they are, form an integral part of Roger Smith's 'blueprint' for General Motors beyond the year 2000. In his judgment the key to the future lies in electronics: hence the last two acquisitions. Table 10

Table 10 *General Motors buys experience. This table lists the companies in whom General Motors has an interest. It will be appreciated that each company contributes to the breadth of experience and knowledge available to the company*

Company	Year	GM stake %	GM investment US$ million	Product
Isuzu Motors	1971	34.2*	56	Pickup trucks, sub-compact cars
Suzuki Motors	1981	5.0*	38	Minicars
Fanuc	1982	50.0	5	Robots
Toyota Motor	1983	50.0	100	Sub-compact cars
Teknowledge	1984	13.0*	4	Artificial intelligence development
Philip Crosby Associates	1984	10.0*	4	Quality consulting
Daewoo Group	1984	50.0	100	Sub-compact cars
Electronic Data Systems (EDC)	1984	100.0*	2500	Data processing
Hughes Aircraft	1985	100.0*	5000	Electronics

Notes:
1 List does not purport to be complete listing of companies in which General Motors have an interest.
2 * indicates equity participation.

in effect lists some of Roger Smith's more dazzling moves since he took over the chairmanship of the company in 1981, moves more daring than any made by his most notable predecessor, A. P. Sloan Jr, when he was welding together a number of separate companies to form the giant GM back in the 1920s.[4] With reference to the acquisition of *Hughes Aircraft* the name of this company is misleading. It no longer manufactures aircraft, but is involved in a wide-range of related activities, such as the manufacture of microchips, lasers, communications satellites and air-to-air missiles – all highly dependent upon the application of electronics.

The approach adopted by Roger Smith demonstrates that he took hold of the Japanese threat and turned it into his opportunity. In effect, he 'joined them', a policy we shall see deployed to the full by other 'doctors' when we come to consider some 'classics from Japan' (Chapter 14). This approach startled Detroit, the home of automobile manufacture in the US, but the strategy was very sound. It was very apparent that the Japanese were ahead in the race, and joint ventures could benefit both partners. For instance, Toyota has a joint venture with General Motors, building small cars at a factory in California. The latest step in this direction is the plan to produce a completely new sub-compact car, *Saturn*, designed to revolutionize the American auto industry. The *Saturn* will be the first new label in General Motors since the introduction of the *Pontiac* in 1926 and it will make full use of the lessons being learnt from Japan. This US$5 billion project is unique. While drawing on decades of car manufacturing experience worldwide, the designers have started from scratch! To quote analyst Ann Knight of the Paine Webber Group:[13]

> One of Saturn's mandates is to pretend that nobody on earth has ever made a car and to essentially re-invent the wheel.

With some thirty-eight states in the US lobbying for its location, the plant is planned for Spring Hill, Tennessee. This was selected from several alternative locations in the US, each having its own attractive incentive package, offered by the local communities and authorities. The car will be computer designed, with a radically new engine and transmission. To ensure its success, the operation will start organizationally with a completely 'clean sheet'. An entirely new company, the *Saturn Corporation* has been set up as a wholly-owned subsidiary of General Motors, but with its own factory, its own engineering and design staff, its own labour contract, its own network of dealers and even its own president. Roger Smith is very clear about the purpose and intent of this radical approach, saying:[11]

We are not going to handicap him [the president] with a lot of preordained rules.

With this new freedom it is hoped that the new corporation can move swiftly to meet the Japanese challenge in respect of both price and quality. As Roger Smith says:

. . . we hope this car will be less labor intensive, less material intensive, less everything intensive than anything we have done before.

The project is now so far along the road that some idea can be gained as to its probable impact. The number of workers, thanks to considerable preassembly and automation, is expected to be a third of those employed in a conventional modern factory having the same output. In further imitation of the Japanese approach, it is expected that the unions will agree to be less restrictive. The complex software required for the highly computerized manufacturing and related sales operation is being designed by the recently acquired *Electronic Data Systems*. The intention, it is rumoured, is to cut out the paperwork so completely that there will not even be a mailboy!

Lest you get the impression that *Saturn* is the 'last word' in car concept and manufacture, let us tell you that Roger Smith has already dreamt up the next project, code named *Jupiter*. While the project has as yet no staff and no definition it already has a mandate.[12] That mandate is:

To develop an ultralight engine that will render obsolete one just completed for Saturn.

While it is still a 'dream' – project Saturn will take some five years to complete – it has a great deal of significance, since it is the dream of a conservative, cautious man. Roger Smith has continually advocated virtues such as patience and caution, yet he dreams! That means he has an objective, the very secret of success.

The 'doctor' employs a 'nurse'

Project Saturn is an in-house project, even though it is being implemented by a new and essentially independent company. Since it *is* in-house, it has acted as a catalyst in the changed and changing General Motors. The chairman, acquiring *Electronic Data Systems* in 1984 for US$1·5 billion, looked for that, too, to be a catalyst within the company. A child of the famous H. Ross Perot, now a most unorthodox director of General Motors and its most powerful and possibly largest single shareholder, *Electronic Data Systems* is seen by Roger Smith as the tool to integrate all General Motors' computer and telecommunications systems from basic design right through to its dealer network. For this he needs the support of Ross Perot, so let us look at him.

Ross Perot, born in Texarkana, East Texas in 1930, joined IBM in 1956 as a salesman. But he was such a super-salesman that in his fifth year with IBM he had completed his annual sales quota in only nineteen days. So, in accordance with company policy he took a lengthy vacation. He finally left IBM in 1962 to set up *Electronic Data Systems*, using but US$1,000 of his own money. His concept was simple enough. There were a great many companies enamoured of computers. They bought them, but then didn't know how to use them. So *Electronic Data Systems* set out to design, install and operate user systems. It was a purely service function: it did not propose to manufacture a thing. The company grew so fast that when it went public in 1968 Ross Perot found himself richer by some US$300 million. Today he is said to be the second richest man in the US and the governor of Texas finds it embarassing that this rich Texan does not sit at the top of the tree in General Motors. [13] That is the man, and Roger Smith had offered him a most challenging task.

Ross Perot found the prospect presented to him so fascinating that he allowed General Motors to acquire *Electronic Data Systems* for US$1 billion in cash and another US$500 million in GM shares. Perot's only condition, which Roger Smith, since it fully accorded with his own concept, willingly accepted, was that *Electronic Data Systems* be operated completely independently. Perot's objective, however, was different to that of Roger Smith. A merger would have downgraded EDS to the GM level. Remaining independent, 7,000 GM processing personnel augmented the EDS staff of some 13,500 and were upgraded, since some of the EDS excellence was bound to rub off on them. Perot has the knack of so motivating his employees that they are willing to work at salaries below the computer industry average, which is inordinately high on account of the scarcity of trained, experienced personnel. Perot agrees that the EDS approach could well benefit General Motors, being quoted as saying:[7]

> If you cut a finger at EDS, you'd go down to the doctor's office, get it sewed up and go home . . . cut your finger at GM, you go in the hospital on Thursday, lie around there until Tuesday afternoon, get a

suntan and leave with a hearing aid and orthopaedic shoes. It's almost that bad.

The task of integration now assigned to EDS is expected to take some four years, but the ultimate savings are expected to be enormous. In addition EDS is working on four 'hush-hush' projects, one code named GM400 and another, a giant US$8 billion project, code named GM10. Project GM10 is considered to be so revolutionary and so promising that a senior EDS executive is quoted as commenting:[9]

> If I were a state governor I would go after GM10 and forget about Saturn.

He is referring, of course, to the competition between the states to get the Saturn factory set up in their particular area of the country.

However, caution is advised, since robots have been reported to have misfired and scanners misread. Nevertheless, General Motors seems to be making a success of automation. Its first major application of MAP (manufacturing automation protocol), known within the company as project GMT400, has been a success. Three of General Motor's five commercial vehicles in the US are now being manufactured using this system and expenditure has already exceeded US$2·5 billion. Indeed, a total of US$40 billion is likely to be spent on automation by 1990.[14]

But to return to project GM10, this is said to be the largest new model programme ever undertaken anywhere in the car industry, calling for seven new plants, each with an annual capacity of some 1·5 million vehicles. Roger Smith is looking for something similar and as spectacular from his acquisition of Hughes Aircraft. His hopes are based on the idea that car development will come fastest via electronics. Despite all the electronic gadgetry, Roger Smith is convinced that the driver will still have to drive the car. However, as he says, 'it will be more fun, easier, safer and certainly more economical to drive'.[4] Hovering over all will be Hughes-manufactured satellites, linking together General Motors' global computer network! Incredible, isn't it, what size can do for you.

What a marriage!

Roger Smith and Ross Perot provide an interesting study in contrasts, yet on all basic issues they are very clear and at one. It would have been fascinating indeed to have watched the legendary founder of the Hughes empire integrated into the picture, but of course he is dead. Within a year of joining up with General Motors, Perot had correctly diagnosed the problems confronting the corporation. He grasped in a year what it had taken Roger Smith ten years to appreciate. Not only is he very perceptive and quick to appreciate a point, but he most refreshingly calls 'a spade a spade'. Sensing General Motors' poor image, he also saw the possibilities:[9]

> The interesting question is that people [meaning the GM workers] are better than the car. GM has had a system in place that stifles initiative and creativity. We need to unleash that because we have the resources to win against anybody.

The GM processing staff, on transfer to EDS, were unhappy. No doubt they missed the 'mollycoddling' to which they had become accustomed, as illustrated by Perot's reference to a 'cut finger' which we quoted earlier. Some of them told Perot that they felt more secure at GM, but Perot was blunt:[13]

> Get up in the morning and look in the mirror. You're your own job security. This is a business, not a social service.

He ought to know what he is talking about: a super-salesman with entrepreneurship in his blood. His diagnosis with respect to the constant complaints coming from GM employees on a wide range of issues was most perceptive:

> GM employees come from an industry that complains about the playing field not being level: in my view the playing field is never level.

Again he is speaking from experience. The playing field he found himself on was rougher than most.

The relative sizes of GM and EDS could give rise to the impression that EDS would adopt GM practices, but that was never the intention. In fact Roger Smith's objective was the very reverse: he was hoping that some of the EDS qualities would rub off on GM, and that was also the way Perot saw it. The GM executives in finance and marketing adopted an air of superiority in relation to EDS. They were going to look the company over and check up on its operations, but Perot knew just how to handle them. His comments were caustic:

> Some well-meaning guy from General Motors will show up and want us to do something, and if it's a good idea we'll do it. . . . If a guy comes down and just wants us to fill out forms, then we don't do it. . . . They're all good people, but their little view of the world is of

cluttering away in some little corner and their first impulse is to make us look like them. . . . We give them a hot meal, pat them on the back and say, 'No, we're not going to do this', and that's it.

Roger Smith welcomes Perot's presence and impact on the General Motors board and elsewhere. For one thing, it appears, he livens up board meetings and makes them interesting. He is a forceful proponent of the concept to 'push, push, push, harder, harder, harder' and what's more, although it is hardly within his remit, as Roger Smith says, 'he always comments on car quality and styling and everything else . . . [but] I wouldn't put him on the assembly line and hand him a welder's torch'. We wonder whether, when Perot heard that statement, he reminded Roger Smith that the 'welder's torch' should by then have been a relict of the past.

Summary

The story of the 'awakening giant' is a fascinating one, and Roger Smith now sees his 'pothole' as a blessing in disguise. It jolted them all awake, whereas the company could well have drifted along for several more years until it was finally drowned with its own inertia. The crisis so shook the organization that there was a real determination to do something before it was too late.

Judging from the results that have been achieved so far, General Motors has not only recovered from the shock but is now going on from strength to strength. And the most surprising thing of all is that the patient, cautious chairman no longer wants to take one step at a time, but is striving to make one great leap forward into the twenty-first century. Roger Smith, now that he has Perot behind him, seems to feel that the future itself can be designed and controlled – by computers, of course! He even seems to think that they can make their own 'luck', so large is General Motors becoming! Perot seems to share his enthusiasm – perhaps he inspired it – since he has said of the current developments:

It's like putting up the Eiffel Tower, the Golden Gate Bridge and launching the first satellite, all in one.

Will they succeed? Only time will tell, but the immediate prospects are promising.

References

1   Drucker, P., *Concept of a Corporation: A Study of General Motors*, John Day, 1972, p. 352.
2   Sloan, A. P. Jr, *My Years with General Motors*, Doubleday, 1972.
3   Kharbanda, O. P. and Stallworthy, E. A., *Successful Projects: All with a Moral for Management*, Gower, 1986.
4   Greenwald, J., 'Lulu is home now', *Time*, 17 June 1985, pp. 40–3.
5   Nicholson, T. *et al.*, 'Survival of the fittest', *Newsweek*, 25 June 1984, pp. 44–5.
6   O'Reilly, B., 'Is Perot good for General Motors?'. *Fortune*, no. 110, 6 August 1984, pp. 84–5.
7   Gelman, E. *et al.*, 'Wheels of the future', *Newsweek* 17 June 1985, pp. 40–6.
8   Burck, C. G., 'Will success spoil General Motors?'. *Fortune*, no. 108, August 1983, pp. 94.
9   'Survival of the fattest', *Economist*, no. 297, 12 October 1985, p. 45.
10   Seamonds, J. A. and Work, C. P., 'General Motors' $5 billion bet on a car to conquer imports', *US News & World Report*, no. 99, 5 August 1985, pp. 23–4.
11   DeMott, J., 'Saturn makes its debut at General Motors', *Time*, 21 January 1985, p. 34.
12   'GM moves into a new era', *Business Week*, 16 July 1984, p. 48.
13   Kleinfield, N. R., 'A new hobby and another target: GM – profile of H. Ross Perot', *International Herald Tribune*, 10–11 May 1986, p. 11.

10 Back from the brink

We take the title of this chapter from the book of that name by Sir Michael Edwardes.[1] This title, although used in the literature dealing with company turnarounds long before this particular book was published, has since became very popular as an apt description of the situation during the period of company turnaround. Sir Michael is a notable 'company doctor'. Chief executive of British Leyland for five years, he went on to write a book about his experiences there. He described those five years as an 'apocalyptic experience', incorporating that phrase in the subtitle to his book. From our old friend, the *Concise Oxford Dictionary* we gather that his experience at British Leyland was a succession of 'grand and violent' events. But British Leyland is by no means the only company, or even the only car company, to have been brought back from the brink by a series of grand and violent events.

If we turn from the UK to the USA we have the case of Chrysler, whose recovery can be attributed to another 'company doctor', Lee Iacocca. The son of Italian immigrants, he rose spectacularly to become president of the Ford Motor Company, only to be knocked down by his boss, Henry Ford II, who said 'I never liked him'. This was said after a thirty-year working association (1946–78), during which time Iacocca had risen in the company from student engineer to chief executive, only then to be dismissed from office. This could well have shattered a lesser man, but Iacocca not only determined to redress the situation, but as chief executive at Chrysler he transformed a dying company into a booming success. On leaving Ford he was immediately snapped up by Chrysler, who were then on the verge of bankruptcy. The legendary fight that developed between the two companies is vividly portrayed in his autobiography.[2] It is surprising that Iacocca stayed as long as he did at Ford, seeing that he and his boss were so alike. They were both ambitious, aggressive, opinionated and occasionally mule-headed. However, as president of Chrysler he put together an elaborate and realistic rescue plan that succeeded. Let us see the way in which this particular 'giant' was rescued from oblivion. Chrysler was indeed a 'giant' on the American scene, once ranking as the fourth largest industrial corporation in the US.

Crisis came to the company late in 1980. At a press conference early in December of that year Lee Iacocca revealed that there had been a disastrous slump in sales, that there was no cash in hand and that it would be necessary to seek another loan or guarantee from the government in Washington. He had already successfully negotiated a loan of US$1·5 billion, of which some US$800 million had already been taken up. From then on the bad news multiplied from day to day.[3] Failure seemed imminent. Payment to suppliers was postponed and production was cut. Chrysler was most certainly 'at the brink'.

The bail out

We have just mentioned that the US government came to the rescue of Chrysler with guarantees and loans totalling US$1·5 billion. The total losses incurred by the company between 1978 and 1982 were some US$3·5 billion. The government took the decision in principle to save the company because the stakes were so high. Governments cannot stand aloof and watch dispassionately when companies of the size of Chrysler are at risk. Unemployment is always a major concern, and the collapse of one company often leads to the failure of others, and 'public confidence' is destroyed. We shall see this even more clearly when we come to consider a second government bail out, with the banking company Continental Illinois. The drama in relation to Chrysler lasted some six months and this, together with the larger implications of this particular bail out, have been vividly described in a full-length book by Reich and Donahue.[4]

Had Chrysler been allowed to collapse, the implications would have been severe. The company, said to be worth US$3·5 billion, had debts totalling some US$6·7 billion. If allowed to 'die' there would have been a possible US$15 billion loss in taxes, welfare payments to be made, together with a wide range of other social costs. Misery would have spread far and wide. Not only would there have been the direct loss of some 150,000 jobs, but companies scattered right across America would have suffered, with many being brought to the brink. Inacocca was able to convince the authorities in Washington of the seriousness of the situation, but that was only the beginning of a mammoth task. The US$1·5 billion guarantee from the government was made conditional upon other concerned parties contributing their share. This involved many groups making substantial sacrifices. The labour union involved would have to accept a reduction in wages; lenders, such as local government offices and banks would have to wait for their money. Iacocca, a super-salesman, succeeded in his mission, but of course it all took time. Indeed, it took some six months, and negotiations were only completed just in time: just a few days before Chrysler would have had to declare itself bankrupt. With expenditure running at US$50 million a day, there was only US$1 million in cash left. How much closer *could* you get to disaster? Iacocca had met the crisis, and the company not only survived, but went on to health.

Nevertheless, the merits of this particular bail out have been challenged time and again. Was it justified? Was it the best course of action? The question has been the subject of debate by economists, sociologists and other professionals, with opinions being sharply divided. The trouble began back in 1974, when the recession in the US brought a steep drop in sales, major cuts in capital expenditure and the loss of key staff. The public did not like the cars on offer through Chrysler and the basic question was: how do you change the view of the marketplace? It was no use pumping money into the company if the cars would not sell. The sales problem was put very forcefully by the auto analyst Mary Ann Keller, who wrote:

> You can be philosophically in favour of bailing out Chrysler, but when it comes to spending your own money, it is a different matter. Chrysler could sell cars only if they were cheaper or substantially better than the competition. This is a consumer product after all. How would it change your life if Chrysler were not there?

According to several economists, the bail out was a blunder and what is more, their opinion remained unchanged three years later, even though by then the benefits had become very obvious. Typical of such criticism is that of the Nobel Laureate economist Milton Friedman:[5]

> Obviously it's a good thing for Chrysler and the country . . . but one

bad by-product is that it will lead people to believe bail outs are a good thing. A free enterprise system is one of profit and loss. If you guarantee against losses by bailing out losing companies, you remove the major monitoring device of a free market.

The book to which we have referred to above, *New deals: The Chrysler Revival and the American System* received some very attractive but mixed reviews in the international press. Even the headlines to these reviews have a story to tell. Reviewer Hampton asks 'Was the Chrysler bail out worth it?',[6] while Richard Lambert stirs the mud up with his caption: 'The Chrysler rescue – When bullying won the day'.[7] This latter reviewer considered the bail out to be an un-qualified success, as indeed it was, but went on to pose some questions of basic significance. He asks what was the *real* impact of government intervention and who *really* benefitted when Chrysler avoided bankruptcy. While the rescue most certainly worked, it seems there are moral issues involved. What obligations do we really have toward one another? To what extent should we share the risks, the costs and the rewards of economic change?

The truth is that no one knows the answer, chiefly because no one has the least idea what would have happened to the American economy had Chrysler actually collapsed. Of course, the experts had ideas about it, but estimates of the cost of failure could never be more than an 'order of magnitude' figure. There is obviously a choice, the choice between the price of government intervention and the social cost of failure, but since no one knows what that cost would have been, there can be no certain answer. However, it was most certainly a business drama: it has even been described as a love story between the Americans and their autos (as they call their cars over there). It is a love story with a happy ending, the villain being foreign imports, the underdog Chrysler and the hero Iacocca, rejected by his former employer, but now beloved.[8] Let us now take a closer look at the revival of Chrysler and how its hero, Iacocca, went about it.

Revived, but how?

Iacocca got the money, but then what? That is only the starting point. The very next question is: what are you going to do with it? Before going on to see what Iacocca actually did, it would be as well to get some understanding of the situation at Chrysler when he joined the company. Fortunately we can get that picture straight from the 'horse's mouth', since Iacocca has written an autobiography and there describes the Chrysler revival.[2] He tells us that within a few days of joining Chrysler he discovered that it was not functioning like a company at all. He compared Chrysler in 1978 to Italy in the 1860s – and he should know, since he was of Italian descent and well versed in that country's history. He described the situation in Chrysler as a cluster of little 'duchies': a bunch of 'mini-empires'. No one had the least concern or interest in what the others in the company were doing and how it affected their company. He even found that his own office was being used as a passage for other executives to fetch their coffee. There was no organization chart and thirty-five vice-presidents, each with his own particular domain.

The reputation of Chrysler had been sinking slowly but steadily for years, with its executives better known as golfers than as designers and makers of good cars. No wonder that the cars stalled, their brakes failed and some three and a half million had to be recalled over the years for free repairs. Then came the recession, with the car industry suffering more than most because of the unrestricted imports of cheaper cars from abroad. The Chrysler car had in fact by this time become a subject for popular jokes on the TV. As the story goes, someone would call Chrysler and ask: 'How's business?' or their managers would be pictured making a conference call to 'Dial-a-Prayer'! What did Iacocca do? He put first things first. He swept out the old management and axed the bad business practices, bringing in people he knew from Ford to be top managers. But that was only the beginning. He now had to convince the public that Chrysler was indeed alive and kicking, though perhaps not too well at the moment. So he took personal charge of advertising. Instead of selling cars, he sold trust. To quote from the advertising:[9]

I don't want you to buy a car on faith . . . I want you to compare. If you can find a better car, buy it.

The sales campaign was pursued without restraint, and resulted in Ford running a parallel campaign, so that both Chrysler and Ford were claiming that their cars were the best!

There is no doubt that Iacocca had the knack of getting the most out of people. He brought them to accomplish more than they ever thought they were able to accomplish and were capable of. No wonder he was well liked and was voted, year after year, in the Gallup polls, the most respectable businessman. But no man stands alone. For his efforts to be effective he had to have the right men in the right numbers at the right places and at the right time. This brought him to his next step, radical surgery to cut costs. The workforce was reduced to less than half (from 157,000 to 75,000), and at the same time the unions were persuaded to accept voluntary wage cuts. This brought the annual wage bill down from US$2·1 billion to US$1·5 billion. To be sure of getting results, Iacocca set targets for everyone and he was tough, insisting that the targets be met. To make sure that he was well understood, he used very plain English (or should we say American these days):

> I told you what I wanted done. It hasn't been done. Now do it, and I don't want any crap.

There was certainly no mincing of words here. Iacocca was also able to instil complete confidence in his plans among his associates and collaborators. A Japanese colleague, Tomio Kubo, chairman of the Mitsubishi Motors Corporation, said of him:[5]

> In the person of Mr Iacocca we have developed a sense of security about the corporation and its future . . . Iacocca shows signs of oriental wisdom.

Yes, with his 'oriental wisdom' he borrowed heavily and learnt much from Japan. He copied both their management and their manufacturing techniques. The number of parts employed in manufacture were reduced from 70,000 to 40,000 and the parts plants were built right next door to the assembly plants. In an effort at standardization, Iacocca took one car as the basic model, a building block for each of four differently sized models. This saved the billions of dollars normally required for the development of a series of separate models. To cut costs still further, Iacocca established joint ventures with various foreign manufacturers. This not only brought the economy of scale, but he benefitted from the lower production costs prevailing abroad and their superior design expertise. Iacocca did not accomplish all this alone, and that brings us to what we feel is a crucial aspect of his management style. He set up management teams to accomplish his objectives. His own team was a small group who could think strategically with him and they helped to change the corporate structure and culture towards ever more 'teamwork'. This resulted in individuals achieving the most outstanding results.[10]

The result – success!

All this effort brought results and the figures speak for themselves.

Costs were brought under control and productivity went up and up. In 1980 the company was manufacturing only 10.2 cars per employee per year, but by 1984 the figure had been doubled to 19.9.[11] Some twenty of the sixty plants had been closed or consolidated with others and over 1000 dealers had also gone. There were many new faces at the top – fifteen out of twenty-eight. Many of the newcomers had been his trusted managers at Ford. With the drastic cost cutting all round, the breakeven point was cut to less than half of what it was before, and a dramatic turnaround was achieved, as illustrated in Figure 6.[12] The turnaround was effectively completed during 1983 and the following year sales topped US$19 billion, while profits were US$2·4 billion. This was more than the company had earned during the whole of the previous fifty-eight years it had been in existence! As a consequence of this dramatic turnaround the price of the stock has risen five-fold between 1979 and 1983, from US$3·50 to over US$18. Yet the company is not resting on its laurels. Speaking to his workforce at the new Sterling Heights Plant in Michigan at the end of 1984, Iacocca had his audience roaring with approval when he declared: 'We have one and only one ambition: to be the best.'[11]

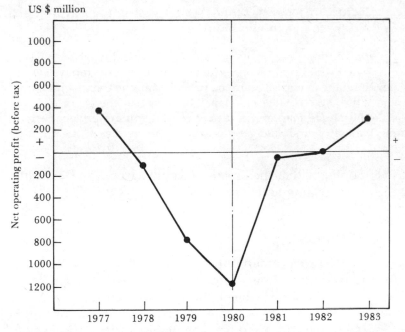

Figure 6 *Coming out of the red at Chrysler. This plot of operating profit/loss over the years shows the dramatic turnaround achieved by Iacocca.*
Source: Company accounts.

Whether he will ever really achieve that ambition is another matter, although that is the attitude – single-minded and determined – that is essential for success. To our mind he actually went down the wrong road. The government bail out was not the only option open at the time, but the alternative would have been a much more difficult road to follow, at least initially. Chrysler could have merged with a strong European firm (Mercedes was reportedly interested) and then the company would have risen to third in the world market.[13] But this route was not taken, and the only effective market for Chrysler is now the US. It will never now have the global market the other major car manufacturers have secured. But Iacocca hasn't given up. The technical press is now mooting the possibility that he may turn to building mini-vans in Romania, or that he may negotiate a deal with *Fiat* whereby they sell one another's cars.

Visiting Japan in April 1985, while the press there hailed him as the next presidential candidate, at the same time they deplored his flamboyant style and constant criticism of his competitors. Yet half a million copies of his autobiography have been sold in Japan. One wonders why. Perhaps it is the desire to 'know the enemy'. The visit was arranged to announce a major joint venture with Mitsubishi for the manufacture of 100,000 compact cars a year in the US. In Japan, Iacocca lived up to his known bluntness, saying:

> I have great admiration for the Japanese people and what they have accomplished. But I don't believe that the Japan we see today would exist without the generosity and the patience and the friendship of the people of the United States. . . . Japan has to realize the importance of its stake in the US market . . . it may be that you are protecting the wrong market; you should be protecting your market in the United States.

It is very unlikely that the Japanese would agree with him, but at least they were willing to listen.

Continental Illinois

Having looked at government intervention in the context of manufacturing, let us now see how it fared in the case of a bank. The rescue of Continental Illinois has been the largest such operation ever undertaken. While that rescue was carried out in accordance with the rules, it was felt that the official regulatory organization should have brought the rules to bear much earlier. Government intervention came only just in time and had it been much further delayed not only would Continental Illinois have collapsed but a number of other banks as well. There were a number of rather diverse reasons for failure, but the Latin American debts crisis played a significant role. In addition the bank had followed a super-aggressive lending policy, which led to a number of large loans to companies who later failed. One problem that banks have is that once trouble is seen on the horizon, it multiplies a thousand-fold. This happens because at the first signs of trouble, there is a 'run' on the bank, with many depositors seeking to withdraw their funds all at the same time. The management of the bank was also said to be suspect, one top officer being a heavy drinker, while another was said to be a regular user of cocaine.

Back in 1980 Continental Illinois was the seventh largest bank in the US, but it has now (1986) slipped down to eleventh place. It was a major lender in Latin America and North America to oil-based industries at a time when oil prices were soaring, but early in 1984 oil prices slumped. As a consequence Continental's bad debts mounted rapidly, finally reaching some US$4·5 billion. The magnitude of this debt was such that no private bank was large enough to bail Continental out and as a result the government *had* to step in. This it did through its Federal Deposit Insurance Corporation (FDIC). The arrangement finally made was that FDIC would take over the existing debt to the tune of US$3·5 billion, leaving US$1 billion to be written off by Continental, in effect a loss that would have to be funded by Continental Illinois shareholders.

How did this collapse come about? Here was a bank at the top of the ladder, priding itself upon its ability and having the confident slogan: 'We'll find a way'. Unfortunately the way it finally found was not the right way and it led the bank down and down. Now it has to find a very different way! During the four years from 1977 to 1981, a period of very rapid growth, the bank's assets doubled to some US$47 billion. This was due to a very rapid response to loan requests – almost 'grabbing' the business, the loans being granted being at the same time much bigger than were being offered by its competitors. In the end the loans exceeded the legal limits by virtue of the loans also being made through subsidiary companies. Further, the bank concluded a number of very unconventional deals, with bargain interest rates.[14]

Now Continental Illinois is wiser, having learnt a lesson and as a result things are very different. The bank is conducting itself far less aggressively and much more conservatively. Its top managers are no longer getting fat bonuses. The chairman, Roger E. Anderson, received US$892,000 in 1981 and was said to be the highest paid banker at that time. This was adduced as evidence that the bank was highly successful! Now the theme is 'work'. A recent (1986) advertisement had a whole page just filled with the word 'work' (some 300 times in all), while the copy at the bottom set out the bank's 1986 objectives. The advertisement declared that the real secret to making a bank work is in making *bankers* work. 'If you want the people working hard for us working hard for you', ran the advertisement, 'stop by and see a Continental banker. He's the one with his sleeves rolled up'. Their current slogan is: 'We work hard. We have to.' They are seeking to regain their position in the market place, since another advertisement, having listed the top twelve banks in 1980 and then in 1986, ascribes the drop in Continental's ranking to 'a well-publicized crisis' and then goes on to say: 'We have been given a second chance. A chance to work our way back by working hard for you.'

Enter the 'doctor'

The details of the road to recovery are interesting because once again the 'doctor' takes over, this time from within the company. More often than not, of course, the 'doctor' comes from without. This then means that he has no preconceived ideas and can start afresh to diagnose and prescribe. On the other hand an 'insider' can well have a head start, but he will need to have an open mind. David Taylor, who took over as chairman and chief executive from Anderson in April 1984, had to produce a 'miracle cure'. He first looked for rescue by his brethren, but a US$4·5 billion credit line arranged with 16 US banks proved insufficient. So he turned to the FDIC, who devised a US$7·5 billion package as an interim measure while the bank looked for a possible merger or some other alternative long-term solution.[15] It is unfortunate that the dire need for the government to sustain confidence in the banking system led to such willing and ready support, since it really conveyed the wrong message. Continental's management had been patently careless, even reckless, *yet* it was bailed out. A bad precedent!

A bank has only two assets, its money and its people. It has to rely upon its employees to create faith and confidence in the market-place, a most difficult task once doubt as to its ability has been sown.

So chairman David Taylor's first priority was to set up a team to go in at all levels to sort out the good managers from the bad. This is inevitably a long, hard process, inevitably unpleasant and likely to incur much bitter feeling. But it had to be done.[16] Further, bank policy had to change. Instead of pursuing the big commercial borrowers, it's loan officers had to encourage the medium-sized companies to come to them, since such customers will pay higher interest rates than the larger borrowers. Above all, the bank has to abandon its international activities, which after all were at the root of its problems. It is unfortunate that due to its continuing heavy involvement with the various regulatory bodies – a consequence of the crisis – its operations are likely to be slowed down, making it less responsive than it should be to its customers.

For the shareholders it remains a sorry story. Their investment has been practically wiped out. Before the run on the bank in May 1984 the shareholder's equity was more than US$1·7 billion. A year later it was a mere US$40 million.[17] Too bad for them, but for the bank itself? Well, 'all is well that ends well'!

Summary

In looking at Chrysler and its turnaround our attention has been captured, above all, by the man – Iacocca. His character dominates the scene. While he adopted many Japanese management techniques, yet he was also a very vocal critic of Japanese trade and business practices. But he arrived on the scene at Chrysler just at the right time. Knowing the industry well, he diagnosed the company's problems correctly. His prescription worked, judging by the results that were achieved, which we have reviewed above. A remarkable turnaround, a team effort, but a team led by a most competent leader.

When we come to Continental Illinois, we see a turnaround accomplished by a faceless organization. The new chairman, David Taylor, really had little to do with it, although his will be the job of keeping Continental Illinois on the right road now that the crisis is over. The man is still very important, but he came after the event. If he had come *before* the event, perhaps that event would never have happened at all. Who knows? But we see that a bank – and banks are usually the most conservative of institutions – can learn, and learn fast! In some countries, and particularly in the UK, bank failures are virtually unknown, so perhaps it is of interest to put the failure of

Continental Illinois into context by reminding ourselves that a bank failure is not all that uncommon in the US. The number of failures with federally insured banks in that country has gone as follows over the past few years:

	1980	1981	1982	1983	1984	1985
Failures	10	10	42	48	79	120

Truly a remarkable number we feel, even in such a vast country as the US, but it demonstrates how exceptional Continental Illinois was, since it was not allowed to fail and turn the 79 for 1984 into 80.

References

1   Edwardes, M., *Back from the Brink: An Apocalyptic Experience*, Collins, 1983.

2   Iacocca, L., with Novak, W., *Iacocca: An Autobiography*, Bantam Books, 1984.

3   Ross, I., 'Chrysler on the brink', *Fortune*, no. 103, 9 February, 1981, pp. 38–42.

4   Reich, R. B. and Donahue, J.D., *New Deals – The Chrysler Revival and the American System*, Times Books, 1985, p. 359.

5   Taylor, A. T., 'Iacocca's tightrope act', *Times*, 21 March 1983, pp. 40–8.

6   Hampton, W. J., 'Was the Chrysler bail out worth it', *Business Week*, 20 May 1985, pp. 10–11.

7   Lambert, R., 'The Chrysler rescue – When bullying won the day', *Financial Times*, 5 July 1985.

8   Douglas, M., 'Lessons from the big bailout', *Business & Society Review*, no. 55, Fall 1985, pp. 87–8.

9   Anderson, K., 'A spunky tycoon turned superstar', *Time*, 1 April 1985, pp. 12–19.

10 Adair, J., 'The special talents that set a leader apart', *International Management*, April 1985, p. 41.

11 Flax, S., 'Can Chrysler keep rolling along?', *Fortune*, no. 111, 7 January 1985, pp. 44–9.

12 'Corporate strategies – Can Chrysler keep its comeback rolling?', *Business Week*, 14 February 1983, pp. 58–62.

13 Drucker, P. F., *Innovation and Entrepreneurship*, Heinemann, 1985, p. 258.

14   Ehrbar, A. F., 'Continental Illinois', *Fortune*, no. 107, 7 February 1983, pp. 51–6.

15   Ehrbar, A. F., 'Continental's blow to safer banking', *Fortune*, 11 June 1984, pp. 67–8.

16   Ehrbar, A. F., 'Continental Illinois: salvaged but not really saved', *Business Week*, 6 August 1984, p. 20.

17   Greenhouse, S., 'Continental Illinois warns investors', *New York Times*, 10 May 1985.

11   The Italian touch

The Italian company Olivetti is known worldwide, yet when we look at its annual accounts towards the end of the 1970s we see a company in crying need of a 'doctor'. It was grossly undercapitalized, had a debt burden of more than US$1 billion and was losing US$6 million a month. Its shareholders had every cause for complaint: they had not received a dividend for four years. One observer tells us – and his choice of words is most interesting – that the company had received some 'emergency first aid'.[1] Although the main business of the company was ultra-modern office equipment, its managerial thinking was ancient, it had no strategic plan and its research and development effort and investment was miserly. If we are to continue our human analogy, the company was old, doddery and near to death. In financial terms it was heading for bankruptcy. A private company, the family management was weak and ineffective, seemed unaware of the technological revolution that was transforming its field of endeavour, and would not have been able to cope had it realized that it was falling behind in the race.

Olivetti had some thirty plants in ten countries and the sales graph maintained a steady upward trend, but so did losses and hence the debts. The basic reason for the continuing loss was the huge debt that had to be serviced. The family refused to go public, one step that could have done a great deal to resolve its financial difficulties. The analogy with old age is very appropriate, in that as one grows old one sees familiar faces disappearing and wonders how long it will be before one goes the same way. There had been a number of privately-owned companies in Italy with problems very similar to those of Olivetti and they had all gone the road of government 'bail out' or takeover. This was the last thing that the chairman of the company, Bruno Visentini, wanted to happen and early in 1978 he sought the advice of Carlo De Benedetti. He consulted a 'doctor', who within seven years transformed the company, making it Europe's largest office automation and data processing group. This has been achieved through both expansion and acquisition. Who looked for who is perhaps an open question, but the result has been spectacular, with an eighty-year old firm the subject of a major turnaround. The company's debts, which had been more than ten times the equity base, are now a mere 10 per cent of the equity and what accountants call the 'bottom line', once a red figure – US$72 million – is now black, and reads US$264 million![2]

Enter the 'doctor'

It seems that this was the opportunity and the challenge that De Benedetti had been waiting for, because he came to the task with great enthusiasm, taking control of the operations of the company with immediate effect. From the very first day he was instituting change in an effort to restore the confidence of the management and of the workers *in* the management.[3] Together with the chairman he worked out a rescue package, the object of which was to increase the paid-up capital of the company from US$69 million to US$115 million. De Benedetti himself put in US$17 million of this new capital, thus becoming the largest single shareholder, with a 20 per cent stake in the company. Though De Benedetti's investment was nominal in relation to that huge debt – US$1 billion – it was regarded as an act of faith. The company still remained a private company.

What was De Benedetti's assessment of the situation when he first sat in that chief executive's chair? In other words, what was his diagnosis? He tells us:[4]

[Olivetti was] . . . an organization that was like a coiled spring and only needed one to push it to get it to jump into life.

In other words, 'there was life in the old dog yet' and De Benedetti became the 'doctor' who revived the patient, but it required tremendous effort on his part. It seems that he acted quite dramatically, starting a typical day at six o'clock in the morning with a meeting with his top managerial team. This was a radical departure from previous managerial practice, even in that hot climate, and it seems that the objective was to impress upon management that change was in the air and so inspire confidence. It showed that a leader had arrived who meant business and was wasting no time. It appears that he had the personality that would bring results in such a context, for a long-time friend is quoted as saying of him:[3]

> Carlo has tremendous charisma and develops loyalty. You work well with him if you can stand the enormous demands he makes on you.

Another friend, a banker, adds:

> If you can stand the grind, perfect: if not, you might as well leave.

De Benedetti himself makes no mention of the pressure under which he began to put the management or the transformation in management style that he was bringing about. He implies that the management was fine, for he says:

> They just needed someone to be a leader . . . the company had within itself everything needed to make the turnaround.

He perhaps implied, with true Italian modesty, that he himself fulfilled that need.

The prescription

It seems that De Benedetti appraised the situation with which he was confronted very quickly indeed, for within days of his appearance on the scene he had stopped the production of products that were losing money, such as mechanical typewriters. This meant that the jobs had to go as well and at first the unions opposed such moves. However, De Benedetti told them that it was a question of 'do or die'. Interesting, isn't it, the way in which the human analogy continues to surface. De Benedetti produced facts and figures to convince the unions that it was in both their and their worker's long-term interests to face up to and accept the realities of the situation. Just to take one example, it took nine hours to build a mechanical calculator, but only thirty minutes to put together the latest electronic calculator. The revolution that De Benedetti was bringing about affected not only the workers on the shop floor but also the management. The staffing of the company was reviewed at all levels and executives who were surplus or who failed to perform effectively had to go. There was not only surplus staff as a consequence of the closing down of production, but the managerial organization itself was grossly over-staffed. The numbers of personnel, 61,000 in 1978, had fallen to 47,000 by 1984 and is still declining. Managerial staff was cut so ruthlessly that Elserino Paul, now vice-president for company strategy and one of the youngest first line managers when De Benedetti first appeared on the scene, became overnight one of the oldest. The dismissal and retirement programme created such a void that nearly a hundred competent senior managers were engaged to fill the gaps that had been created in the organization.

So what had De Benedetti done? He had injected new capital into the company to reduce the debt burden and had pruned the workforce so as to increase the overall efficiency of the company's operations. If you think back to all that we have said about turnaround strategy, you will already have decided what else he changed. His goal was very clear. He was determined to make Olivetti a world leader in the 'automated office of the future' and nothing less would do. To quote him once again:

> In *our* business, there is no future in becoming a second, third or fourth-rank company. Either you win or you die.

The emphasis is ours. His use of the word 'our' demonstrates how completely he has identified himself with his new activity. So De Benedetti upgraded the technology and increased prices to more realistic levels. The company also stopped chasing market share at the risk of profits. His long-term ambition is to surpass Fiat as Italy's

Table 11 *Turnaround at Olivetti. The dramatic change brought about between 1978 and 1985 is very apparent. Note the seven-fold increase in expenditure on research and development, to which we attribute much*

	1978	1984	1985
Sales (US$ billion)	0.9	2.6	3.9
Net profit (US$ billion)	(72.0)	201.0	264.0
Net profit (as a percentage of sales)	–	7.8	8.2
R&D (US$ million)	24.0	166.0	190.0
R&D as a percentage of sales	2.6	6.4	4.9

Notes:
( ) indicates debit figure.
R&D – research and development.

Source: Company accounts.

most influential company and his ultimate ambition is grander still. He hopes to be able to demonstrate that capitalism represents the best hope for the future and that Italian workers can equal any other workers in the world in terms of reliability and productivity. Meanwhile, the results that he has achieved so far are to be seen in Table 11. Truly a remarkable turnaround.

The man

How did Carlo De Benedetti get where he is today? We expect you have been wondering where that US$17 million came from that he invested in Olivetti when he took over. Well, De Benedetti was an electrical engineer by training, graduating with high honours from Turin Polytechnic in 1958. His father, also an engineer, had started a family business in Turin in the 1920s that was small but successful, producing flexible metal piping. The plant was bombed out during the Second World War and after the war his father had to start all over again. Carlo De Benedetti joined the family business when he graduated and under his management it prospered. The number of employees grew from eighty to some 500 and the company finally held 80 per cent of the total market in the specific products it manufactured. This failed to satisfy De Benedetti and he sought to expand. He started out on the road to expansion by buying up small, unprofitable companies producing car parts: there were plenty of them in Turin, the centre of the Italian car manufacturing industry. His energy and enthusiasm transformed the companies he acquired and they became profitable. It was this particular experience that prepared him for the role of 'doctor' at Olivetti much later. Earlier he was called in to diagnose Fiat's problems, but this did not work out. It was an ideal preparation, because he had learnt that drastic measures are acceptable if they bring results. In his takeover operations he had been quite ruthless in discarding the ineffective and the inefficient and in so doing had learnt, to use his own words:[3]

> . . . how people want to be motivated. They are frustrated when they are working in a company losing money. If you can switch from the red to the black, you're happy as the owner, but the employees and managers are even happier.

In the process of making people happy, De Benedetti had by 1976, through acquisition, divestment and expansion built up the family business so that it had become one of Italy's largest producers of car components. The group had an annual turnover of US$46 million. This was the result of two things: the right strategy and hard work. De Benedetti worked sixteen hours a day seven days a week. His reputation in the revival of ailing (or failing) companies brought him an invitation from an old friend, Gianni Agnelli, the chairman of Fiat, to become managing director of that great multinational. He now had a reputation as a 'company doctor'.

The offer from Fiat was tempting enough to cause De Benedetti to trade a controlling interest in the family business (60 per cent) against a 6 per cent block of Fiat common shares, making him the second largest stockholder after the Agnelli family. But notice the inherent caution. He still retains a 40 per cent interest in the thriving family business, but at the same time it is no longer his direct concern. However De Benedetti did not last long at Fiat. He only stayed for three months, leaving for reasons that have never been revealed by either party. It seems that he and Agnelli parted as friends and to this day their relationship is known to be one of cordiality and mutual respect. In the process of parting, De Benedetti emerged the richer by US$20 million and could easily have retired. But he did not. People like him probably never can retire: they are perpetually driven on by some inner force. At the time he was just coming up to forty and it seems that empire-building was in his blood. Within a few months he had acquired a controlling interest in Campagnie Industriali Riunite (CIR), one of Italy's oldest tanning companies. He then went on to acquire smaller firms, bringing them under the CIR umbrella and by 1978 the business had an annual turnover of US$84 million and had diversified to include cigarette-making machines, DIY tools and railway signalling equipment. Notice that the product is a matter of indifference to De Benedetti. He began his industrial career in a company making flexible hoses. He moved to car parts, then to cars, then to tanning, then to the very diverse products we have just listed.

It was at this point that Olivetti came into his life, and he into Olivetti's. He was just forty-two years old: a man in the prime of life. His approach to Olivetti was simple and bold. He staked the bulk of his fortune, buying US$17·3 million of Olivetti stock, in order to gain complete control. It seems that complete control is always his one essential condition, something that he insists upon before he will undertake a turnaround. Since Olivetti was a family-owned company, the family may well have been reluctant to hand over control, but it had no option. For Olivetti it was 'do or die'! This acceptance of the inevitable is something that we see time and again in our case studies and it always brings results. It is the refusal to accept the inevitable that brings disaster. In all probability the family was quietly grateful that De Benedetti was prepared to stake both his money and his reputation on what had all the appearance of a lost cause. But for De Benedetti there was no looking back.

Having taken a look at the man himself, you will now realize why, at fifty, he has been held out as an awe-inspiring example of entrepreneural management in Western Europe. In a poll held among some 8000 Italian executives in 1984, De Benedetti was far ahead of all the others, being elected *Il manager dell 'anno* (the manager of the year) for the second time in five years. In the same year the Zurich's journal *Weltwoche* selected De Benedetti as *Der beste Geschäftsfüer* in Italy. Again in the same year the magazine *Fortune* included him among their 'eleven best managers' in Western Europe and he was the only Italian in the list. So the accolades come, in Italian, German and English. It seems the press cannot speak too highly of one of the most imaginative and dazzling managers that the Italian business world has ever seen. Fluent in five languages, Italian, French, German, Schweizer-deutsch (the dialect of northern Switzerland) and, of course, English, he can most certainly communicate: yet another essential qualification for the good manager.

The turnaround strategy

We have already given some brief indication of the three-pronged strategy adopted by De Benedetti: the injection of new capital, the closing down of unprofitable lines and the ruthless cutting of costs. So far, so good. But how does one stop the company, in the process of time, falling once again into the lethargic state in which it was when he came to it? It seems that the De Benedetti solution is to drive ever onwards and ever upwards. He wants Olivetti to be the premier company in its field, but this ambition can have its pitfalls. The company is very much a 'one man business', in that its development and continuing progress depends very much on the drive of De Benedetti himself. He is the chief executive and, as always, it is the chief executive who finally makes or breaks a company. A tree usually rots from the top, since it is the top that provides the example and sets the pace. We have seen a company in trouble because its managing director had a pet project (ballbearings) that was completely different from the mainstream business of the company (Chapter 7). Metal Box (India) has been by no means the only company to suffer for such a reason. De Benedetti's 'pet project' seems to be acquisition, for which he seems to have a tremendous appetite, but he has by no means lost interest in the family business, even although he now has only a minority interest. That company has been acquiring companies as diverse from its original activities as was railway signalling from tanning, since the latest acquisitions have been in the food and allied trades. This spread of interest in its chief executive could threaten Olivetti's progress and has indeed caused the experts to ask whether microchips and pasta really mix.[4] However, De Benedetti seems confident enough.

De Benedetti's long-term strategy also bears his own unmistakable imprint, but it seems that while he may confidently expect, in the normal course of things, to be at the helm for many years to come, he has at the same time helped to develop the next line of command. You will remember that when assessing the elements of good management in Chapter 3 we saw that one of the most difficult aspects was the setting up of an heir apparent. It seems that De Benedetti has two. His two closest lieutenants are Piol and Levi, who are consulted regularly by him, although he does not hesitate to use outside advisers when he feels that to be necessary. In this way the strategic plan is created by him and then passed on for detailed implementation. Piol and Levi work very well together as a team, although these two 'pillars' in the Olivetti empire seem to have a very special relationship both between themselves and with De Benedetti. While he is the undisputed leader, in command, yet Piol has all the power and the day-to-day responsibility. Then just where does Levi fit in? Their relationship is perhaps best illustrated by the joke that has gone the rounds within the company, demonstrating that they share power and responsibility in what may well be a unique fashion. It is said that both Piol and Levi go bear-hunting. Piol goes out to find and kill the bear, in order that Levi may skin it. But then one day Piol arrives back at camp followed by a big bear, still alive, and says to Levi: 'Now then, Vittorio, you skin it while I go out and get another one.' Such is their ability to work together that they rarely have to go to De Benedetti for mediation between them. Indeed, it is alleged that when they do go it is only to give De Benedetti the feeling he is needed![5]

The marriage with AT & T

While De Benedetti has most certainly accomplished a turnaround at Olivetti, he does not seem to see it that way. Seeing that his rescue came while not only Italy but all Western Europe was in the throes of depression, one would have thought that the future could only be better, but De Benedetti sees trouble ahead. While the office automation market throughout the industrial world is expected to double by 1990, there will be strong competition for a place in that expanding market, with powerful contenders from the US, Japan and Western Europe. It is De Benedetti's ambition not only to be 'number 1' in Europe but also to be a world leader. It seems that the European market is far too fragmented to support Olivetti, so De Benedetti has been looking for support both eastwards towards Japan, and westwards towards the US, while still keeping his foothold firmly in Europe. His courtship with the American-based company AT & T convinced De Benedetti that the two groups really needed each other. Two years of arduous negotiations led to a linkup between the two companies in December 1983, whereby the giant AT & T, its 1984 revenue US$33·2 billion, took a 20 per cent shareholding in Olivetti for US$260 million. The company also holds an option to increase their holding to 40 per cent after four years. De Benedetti termed this a 'brilliant alliance' and AT & T expressed its high regard for De Benedetti in that it obtained a commitment from him that he would stay on as chief executive at Olivetti for at least ten years. James Olsen, vice-chairman of AT & T, who personally conducted the negotiations with De Benedetti, described him as 'visionary' and 'tough but fair'. Of their prospective partnership he is quoted as saying that it 'made good sense to us. It was a natural. We wanted an active presence in Europe and we were starting from scratch.'[3] De Benedetti went a step further, saying:

> I believe in marriage. We complement each other well. Technologically, Olivetti leads in data processing, AT & T has telecommunications. We are strong in applied technology, while AT & T is a leader in basic research.

With this alliance, De Benedetti feels confident enough to 'take on IBM'. The 'marriage' does indeed seem to be a 'marriage of equals', since despite the size of AT & T when compared with Olivetti, ultimate power at Olivetti does not rest with them: it stays with De Benedetti! In fact, as already stated, AT & T may well have made this a pre-condition for their collaboration.

While looking west, De Benedetti did not neglect to look east. Olivetti had a long-standing association with Toshiba of Japan, going back to 1961, but De Benedetti has encouraged a still closer partnership. The reasons are different than they were with AT & T, since if you want to sell in Japan you need, it seems, to manufacture there: a 'made in Japan' label is a must. So Toshiba has bought a 20 per cent stake in Olivetti's Japanese company, with exchange of products and joint ventures as possible future objectives.[6] Thanks to the AT & T connection, and a more recent distribution link-up with Xerox, Olivetti's personal computer sales have now reached third place worldwide, next only to IBM and Apple, and account for a third of their total sales worldwide.[7]

Looking beyond the balance sheet

There is no doubt that Olivetti has kept well up with the 'state of the art' in its particular field of endeavour. One visitor to one of the company's modern plants, set in the foothills of the Italian Alps, tells us that the workers are few, but that there are a large number of Olivetti-designed robots, operated by Olivetti-built computers.[8] Right at the beginning we mentioned Olivetti's miserably low expenditure on research and development, but since De Benedetti took over this has increased seven-fold. It will be some time before this effort bears fruit, since it takes some two years to develop a new product and there is always a danger that within another two years, such is the rate of development in electronics at the moment, that product may well have become obsolete. So one needs to sustain a constant effort just to stay in the same place. Olivetti had developed some high technology products when De Benedetti arrived, but there was no strategy that would enable the company to capitalize on this resource. Yet it is innovation that keeps a company ahead.

More recently (1985) De Benedetti has set up a share participation programme for the Olivetti employees. Some 12,000 employees opted to join the scheme within a short time of its introduction. This is a sound move, in that it increases motivation and encourages loyalty. The worker begins to feel that he is really working for himself as well as the company and tends to identify more closely with the company: a key aspect of what we have called elsewhere the 'Japanese miracle'. Now where will De Benedetti go? Perhaps it is all summed up for us in the title of yet another article in the *Economist*: 'Carlo De Benedetti – yesterday Italy, today Europe, tomorrow the world'.[9]

Summary

We have witnessed, in the transformation at Olivetti, the application of a few quite basic principles of turnaround strategy. But as always, it takes someone of a certain calibre to put it all into effect. De Benedetti is an outstanding example of a turnaround manager, and it seems he cannot stop exercising his turnaround skills, even though he is committed to Olivetti for the next ten years. One hopes that he realizes that despite that commitment he will not be there for ever and takes steps to ensure that there is an experienced, qualified team for a smooth takeover and to keep things going once he is no longer there. We gather that he still works an eighteen-hour day and has little time for social activities. His family live in Geneva and on a typical day he has flown from Turin to Paris, then flown onward to New York on Concorde to hold several business meetings there, returning the same evening to Turin. But not, notice, to his family. Is this too much? Not according to De Benedetti: he tells us that he enjoys it! Nevertheless, we would not recommend it as a sound management style. We still hold to the opinion we expressed in Chapter 3, that it is a poor manager that never takes a day off. Work must be tempered with play in order that both may be properly enjoyed.

References

1   Davidson, S., 'A mix of microchips and pasta', *Time*, 13 May 1985, pp. 38–9.
2   'Transforming the bottom line', *Economist*, no. 299, 26 April 1986, p. 69.
3   Painton, F., 'A dazzling comeback', *Time*, 18 February 1985, pp. 42–8.
4   Taggiasco, R. *et al.*, 'At Olivetti, success just fuels ambition', *Business Week*, 27 May 1985, pp. 44–50.
5   Turner, G., 'Inside Europe's giant companies – Olivetti goes bear hunting', *Long Range Planning*, no. 19, 13–20 April 1986.
6   Tagliabue, J., 'At Olivetti, success just fuels ambition', *Business Week*, 27 May 1985, p. 44.
7   Peterson, T., 'How Olivetti cloned its way to the top', *Business Week*, 16 June 1986, p. 78.

8 Friedman, A., 'Olivetti profits jump 41·5%', *Financial Times*, 23 April 1986.
9 'Carlo De Benedetti – Yesterday Italy, today Europe, tomorrow the world', *Economist*, no. 298, 28 February 1986, pp. 58–9.

12   When politics dominate

When we considered the turnaround at Chrysler in Chapter 10 we saw an ailing car manufacturing company rescued by government guarantees and loans, but politics played a very secondary role. But when we come to look at British Leyland we see a company where politics dominated. British Leyland was formed in 1968 by the merger of a number of manufacturing companies in the automotive industry, following a story of successive takeovers and mergers going back in all some twenty years. The automotive industry in the UK came under great pressure following that country's entry into the Common Market. Imports of European cars grew rapidly over the first few years, reaching more than 60 per cent of total sales. British Leyland was a wholly government-owned company that was making continuing losses, following a collapse in sales in 1974. Over the next ten years some £3 billion of taxpayer's money was being pumped into the company, but by 1986 the company had still to make a profit.

The 'doctor' is called in

In 1978 the Government decided to take decisive action and appoint Sir Michael Edwardes as chief executive. He started at the bottom of the ladder with the Chloride Group as a trainee manager in 1951 and was later given the job of reorganizing its Central African operations. So successful was he that on his return to the UK in 1972 he became its chief executive, moving to chairman some two years later. In six years he transformed Chloride, whose pretax profits rose as a consequence from $3·5 million to £26 million.[1] In 1975 he received the

Guardian 'Young Businessman of the Year' award. Three years later he had been persuaded to move to British Leyland to take on a job that many said was impossible. He proved them wrong in a five-year slog which, he says, taught him more than all his years with Chloride. 'My biggest contribution to BL', he said, 'was in the first three years. The fourth year was a year of consolidation. In the fifth I had begun to phase myself out'. Out he went, to be found shortly afterwards at ICL, another ailing company, but this time a company in the 'high-tech' field. We shall be looking at ICL and its progress later in this chapter, but let us first see what the 'doctor' did – and did not do – at BL.

The headlines in the economic and technical press tell it all. Let us quote a few in chronological order:

Back from the brink
How the pro tackled BL's Augean stables
Profits, Maestro, please
What is good for BL is good for Britain
Strong recovery in vehicle output at BL
Why GM has its eye on Leyland
Still holding the baby
A model that didn't work
BL's rejected suitors

These captions make it clear that the problems associated with BL have not as yet been finally resolved. The road to recovery has been rocky indeed.

While Sir Michael may well have brought British Leyland 'back from the brink' the company is still in great difficulty. What he *did* do was to continue to get government backing for the company, despite the pressure for privatization, which he felt would be disastrous. He planned and produced the Mini-Metro, a success for both British Leyland and for Britain. He laid the basis for cooperation between British Leyland and Honda of Japan, an association that is going from strength to strength. Throughout it was a struggle for survival, made much more difficult than it need have been by the continual political manoeuvring that took place.

There is no doubt that the root problem at British Leyland was poor management. As Sir Michael himself declared:[2]

Management simply lost control of the situation. Models were not, or could not be updated. Quality and production fell to unacceptable levels, and disputes reached four or five times the sort of level that a 'continuous production' industry can stand . . . Britain and the world blamed the unions and turned their back on British Leyland products. But the real blame lay with management, for they failed in their duty to manage.

It is interesting to note that the Government itself recognized and accepted the concept that managers should manage. He quotes Mrs Margaret Thatcher, the Prime Minister of the day, and heading a government whose policy was to privatize:

> I never want to take on another BL. We shouldn't be in it at all, but now we're in it we have to choose the time and we have to back Michael Edwardes' judgment. He's the manager, I'm not the manager. . . .

This attitude was maintained throughout. Despite being so closely involved and so desperately committed, Mrs Thatcher never showed the slightest inclination to interfere at British Leyland, not even in issues relating to employee relations, which were of prime importance to the government. This is of course as it should be. You should not have a dog and then bark yourself.

The diagnosis and the 'medicine'

Strong and hard decisions were needed if change was to be brought about in British Leyland. Sir Michael adopted a firm management line, displayed a resolve to meet the problems head on. He went direct to the employees, bypassing the unions, on all key issues. Till then the management had been weak and vacillating, blaming the unions for all its troubles. The situation in this respect is very similar to that encountered by P. C. Luther, the Indian 'doctor' whose story we tell in Chapter 8. His response to the situation he found at DVC was very similar to that of Sir Michael, and the comparison is interesting. While Sir Michael did not hesitate to give shock treatment when required, it is significant that he was able to transform management attitudes without replacing the managers. While, as Sir Michael himself made clear, the management was much at fault, the union attitude was also most disruptive and destructive, and his manner of dealing with them caused him to become known as 'the man who took on the unions'. But while he was busy reforming the management structure, he was also intro-ducing the latest production technology. Assembly lines were streamlined and more than fifty robots installed. In order to introduce a new model on the market in the shortest possible time he drew in Honda of Japan, adopting its new and fuel-efficient model, which came on the market as the Triumph *Acclaim*.

Sir Michael instituted his reforms from the top downwards. He reduced the size of the board so as to improve communications and reach consensus more quickly and he introduced decentralization to improve management efficiency and establish clear areas of responsibility. However, the comments on his activities in the technical press were not uniform in their praise. While he provided a 'survival package', the question was asked: 'Was it worth it?' Truly, the company has been brought back from the brink, but has it really turned its back on disaster? With an output of around half a million cars a year, British Leyland is extremely vulnerable in the market place. Its major competitors in the UK market, Nissan, Renault, Ford and Volkswagen, all have much bigger outputs, and thus benefit as British Leyland cannot from the economies of scale. The company must export or die, since its home market is nowhere near large enough to sustain it in economic production. The latest blow has been the sale of its highly profitable subsidiary, Jaguar Cars, a consequence of the Conservative Government's policy of privatization.

Is there a solution?

Sir Michael's major achievement, in our judgment, during his period at British Leyland was to make a sound diagnosis of the problem and to convince the Government that it should continue to fund the company till it was able to break even. But it has hardly reached that point as yet and it is now (1986) four years since he left. In 1984 there was a net loss of £60 million and an accumulated deficit of more than £500 million. There was a strong recovery in production through 1985, particularly with its commercial vehicles, which ran at a level some 30 per cent above the 1984 output and was nearly double that of all its competitors put together.[3] But the competition is fierce and the market limited.

There are many who consider privatization to be the only answer, and point to the successful turnaround at Jaguar achieved by Sir John Egan, who was actually appointed chief executive of that company by Sir Michael. General Motors, facing a declining share of the UK truck market, has shown a keen interest in taking over the truck and Land Rover divisions of British Leyland, but politics intervened yet again. There was much public clamour against the sale of British assets to an American company, once the negotiations became public. The affair reached a climax in March 1986 and in an effort to swing public opinion their way, General Motors took a series of full-page advertisements in the leading UK dailies, designed to demonstrate its commitment to Britain and its 'Britishness'. There was a banner headline, 'GM – a commitment to Britain for over 60 years', followed by details of their achievements. To quote:

> In good times and bad, in peace and in war, we have gone on investing in Britain. Producing in Britain. Exporting for Britain. Providing thousands of jobs. In our 60 years we have produced 5 million Vauxhalls. At Bedford we have produced 3.5 million commercial vehicles.

The closing headline ran: 'General Motors. The name behind a great British family'. But it was all to no avail. General Motors had promised to invest several hundred million pounds over five years, but politics held sway and their negotiators finally went home empty-handed. A month earlier the negotiations with Ford for a takeover of Austin Rover had also lapsed for the same reason.[4] Yet in some such arrangement must lie salvation for British Leyland. Lack of capital and a declining market compound the company's problems and consolidation seems the only effective answer. The volatility of the market is also a constant threat when manufacturing from such a small base. Public knowledge of the negotiations with Ford led to a drop in Austin Rover's market share in the UK from 18 per cent to 15 per cent. There is no doubt that uncertainty can kill in the motor industry, just as it will do any business.

Sir Michael left while there was still much to do, but in all probability he was not the man to complete the job. His task was to put British Leyland on the road to recovery, which he did, as illustrated in Figure 7. In our judgment a turnaround demands certain specific management skills, together with a certain toughness of mind and action, which are not necessarily appropriate once the turnaround has been accomplished. So it is better that the 'doctor' moves on to another patient, leaving the earlier one in the 'convalescent' stage. This he did, joining ICL. However, before he had time to implement reforms that were causing consternation among ICL's staider managers, Standard Telephone & Cable's Sir Kenneth Cornfield put in a successful bid for that company. Takeover instead of trauma? Let us see.

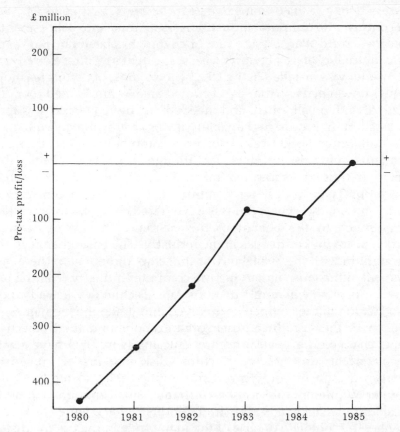

Figure 7   *Better, but still not good enough. This graph demonstrates quite clearly that while the losses at British Leyland have been brought back to zero, the company still has a long way to go.*
Source: Company reports.

From cars to computers

The car industry has grown up over a hundred years. The beginning of this century saw the introduction of mass production, with a degree of standardization. Over the years manufacture has spread till it is now worldwide. One doubts whether society will ever reach a point where everyone will want or use his own independent means of transport, but the long-term prospects for the industry remain bright, since there is continuing adaptation to a constantly changing operating environment. It seems that it takes some five years to introduce a new design to the market, and once on the market it can

expect to have a life of some five years before it disappears.[5] By way
of contrast, the computer industry has only come into being since the
Second World War, but the rate of change has been far more rapid
and dramatic. It is about 30 years ago that the first commercial
computer was installed in the UK, by Joe Lyons, of 'Lyons teashops'
fame. It weighed 400 tonnes, occupied an air-conditioned room the
size of a football pitch and needed its own electricity supply
substation. In processing capability it was approximately equivalent
to the kind of pocket calculator now commonly owned by maths
students going up to university, though much less reliable. Reliability in those days meant a 'mean time between failures' of about
two hours. Now a desk-top computer is to be seen in almost every
office and many homes. But this era of rapid change, while working
very much to the benefit of the customer, has brought many
problems to the companies in the industry. The basic change in size
brought in with the availability of the 'chip' did not stop there, as a
perusal of the journals serving the computer industry over the past
five years or so will amply demonstrate. Technology has advanced
too fast for all the companies involved and while the big names are
still there their products, their organizations and their objectives
have changed drastically and dramatically. Now they have a 256K
memory chip instead of 1K chips, disk systems of immensely
increased capacity and power, fibre optic cables to replace bulky
copper/aluminium cables and mainframes small enough to fit under
a table. Indeed some experts in the industry have gone so far as to
predict the complete demise of the mainframe in the not too distant
future as a prelude to the 'artificial intelligence'.

One company that had to face up to the problems created by this
climate of technological advance was ICL in the UK. This company
was formed in 1968 by the merger of ICT with English Electric
Computers, in itself the culmination of a series of mergers beginning
in 1959 with the combination of the Hollerith and Powers-Samas
punched card companies. This took place with the firm encouragement of the British Government, the intention being to create a major
UK company able to hold its own in this rapidly expanding field of
endeavour.[6]

The company adopted a very risky financial strategy based on
high revenue growth in the late 1970s and it failed to win through. It
looked for ever-increasing sales to cover its swiftly rising costs,
fuelled by rapid inflation in the UK. Predominantly manufacturers of
mainframe computers, that market failed to grow, so that costs per

machine soared. At the same time, margins were being squeezed by stiff competition. In an effort to reduce costs, the company closed its Dukinfield plant in October 1979, put a ban on recruitment and sought to reduce overheads. But the position continued to deteriorate, resulting in the closure of a second plant at Winsford in Cheshire. In 1979 ICL had 18 per cent of the home market, while its arch rival, IBM, held 24 per cent. The buying policy of the government of the day gave no preference to UK manufacturers, with the result that IBM was able to secure a number of major government orders, including a £10 million contract for computer facilities for the Vehicle Licensing Centre established at Swansea, South Wales. If ICL was not able to secure critical orders in its home market, what chance had it overseas? Yet ICL proceeded to venture into that market. The company borrowed heavily, reaching a debt/equity ratio of 1·3 in 1981, in an effort to expand its product line. However, the timing was all wrong, because recession set in. As a result, pre-tax profits plummeted. The Government, having taken away with one hand, by placing orders with IBM, now gave £320 million with the other, rescuing ICL with a loan.

Crisis and swift recovery

There was a historic board meeting on Sunday, 10 May 1981, lasting to the early hours of the following day (seven and a half hours in all), which resulted in the chairman and managing director resigning, to be replaced by Sir Christopher Laidlaw, formerly deputy chairman of British Petroleum, who took over as chairman, and Robb Wilmot, who came from the British subsidiary of Texas Instruments and took over as managing director. Sir Christopher looked after the financial side, while Robb Wilmot handled the immediate practicalities. Their first task was to stem the mounting losses, restore confidence and ensure the company's independent survival. The workforce was reduced by about a third (to some 22,000), cutting down both manufacturing and overhead costs. Mainframe computers constitute some 60 per cent of ICL's total business, but it also sought to establish itself ever more firmly in the desk-top computer market. Its very innovative product, a telephone-cum-terminal called the *One Per Desk*, was viewed as one of the industry's most revolutionary products of 1984.

The company was also courageous enough to abandon its policy of developing all its products itself and began to use technology shared with or bought from firms prepared to collaborate in the technical field. An outstanding example was the deal concluded with the Japanese company Fujitsu in relation to mainframe technology. This resulted, in April 1985, in the announcement of a new series 39 mainframe family. ICL has also entered the shop market in a big way. For instance, it has won a £10 million order to install its equipment in fifty of Marks and Spencer's biggest stores, including 3,000 of its 9518 point of sale (POS) terminals, together with tailor-made software.[7] All in all, ICL is on the 'up and up'.

The recovery, as we said, was led by Dr Wilmot, later supported by Peter Bonfield. The results of the efforts of these two 'doctors', working in tandem, was quite dramatic, as is illustrated by Figure 8. They were two contrasting personalities that complemented one another and so formed a very effective team. In three action-packed years ICL has moved back from striving merely to survive first into profit and then on into renewed growth. Despite this quite remarkable recovery displayed by these figures, the company still has a long way to go. How far is best demonstrated by making a comparison with its biggest competitor and standard setter, IBM. Compared with IBM, productivity has practically doubled, as is demonstrated in Figure 9. Yet, while having reached £43,000 per employee per year in 1984, it was then still only half the output achieved by IBM in that same year (US$120,000 per employee per year). This doubling in productivity at ICL between 1979 and 1984 must be attributed in the main to the drastic reduction that has been made in the workforce.

However, there has also been an accompanying drive to transform the managerial approach. This has been described in detail in three articles by Christopher Lorenz that first appeared in the *Financial Times*, under the general heading of 'Corporate Renewal'.[8] We are told that a crash programme of individual and company-wide education in management and marketing skills has revolutionized its operations. The old ICL was technology led, had a poor grasp of marketing and lacked clear strategies. The new ICL is now (1986) in much better shape. Not only has there been cost reduction, but also an improvement in productivity, tighter budgeting and planning, the provision of individual performance incentives, decentralized responsibility and intensive employee communications. All this has been achieved during the five years following that dramatic board meeting in 1981. But then a turnaround became a takeover. Where is that going to take ICL?

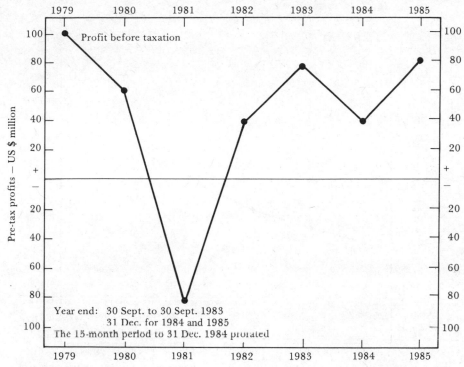

Figure 8 *The profits turnaround at ICL. This graph brings us a most graphic picture of the change wrought in profits in the three years following their plunge into the abyss in 1981, until their takeover by STC.*
Source: Company accounts.

Now a takeover

It seems that a common follow-up to a turnaround is a takeover and that is just what happened here. A bid from Standard Telephones and Cables (STC) came out of the blue and succeeded. STC was seeking to expand its international operations and broaden its product and service range to cover the converging fields of computers and telecommunications. It saw ICL as a logical extension to its activities. This tie-up made strategic sense: a marriage between communications and computer companies is a natural one since in a way they are 'made for each other'. It was not a takeover designed to 'rescue' ICL, but a part of STC company strategy.

The initial reaction of the ICL board to the takeover proposal, made on the 26 July 1984, was to reject the bid as totally inadequate. The board at that time was led by Sir Michael Edwardes, who had

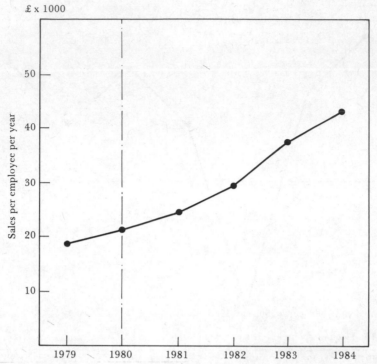

£ x 1000

Figure 9   *Output per employee at ICL. While the improvement in output per employee per year has been remarkable, it is still way below the achievement of IBM.*
Source: Company accounts.

come in as company 'doctor' and he conducted the negotiations with STC. There were some weeks of hard bargaining, as a result of which the terms were much improved and finally recommended to the shareholders for acceptance. STC at first held some 80 per cent of the shares, but it has since acquired the rest of the shares and ICL is now a wholly-owned subsidiary.

Following the takeover, and the appointment of Peter Bonfield as chairman and managing director, he found an excellent foil in Robb Wilmot. According to a *Financial Times* correspondent:[9]

> Talk to Robb Wilmot and you get 'a tour of the gardens of high technology'. Talk to Peter Bonfield and you get 'a thorough inspection of the kitchen'.

Together they formed a very effective team. Peter Bonfield was no stranger to ICL. He grew up there, his father having worked for the company for many years, but he was advised to get some international experience. So he went to Texas Instruments. One of the first tasks of Peter Bonfield, as he saw it, was to increase exports, since a global market was necessary in order to recover the very high product development costs, but this has not been very successful. Overall over half of the sales are still in the home market. An export breakthrough into the American market has still to come. One handicap in this respect is the lack of IBM compatibility. The company however hopes that the moves toward a common data-communication standard may ultimately solve some of its compatibility problems.[10]

It is interesting to note that since the takeover STC has been handling ICL very much at 'arms length'. It seems advisedly so, since STC itself has been in trouble. The same issue of *STC News* that carries a report of a further ICL success – a £3 million order from the DIY subsidiary of WH Smith for all sixty of its DIY stores for their HANDI electronic point of sale (EPOS) system, making a total of a 1000 systems sold to date – also reports on the front page a loss by STC for 1985 of £54 million.[11] At the same time ICL broke through the £1 billion turnover barrier, increased profits and was said to be strongly placed to exploit a growing market.

Summary

The history of both British Leyland and ICL makes it very clear that government funding can never be a solution. It may help to keep the 'patient' alive, but no more. The real solution always lies with proper management, who can cut costs and develop a sound company strategy. This calls for the right man at the right time. Whether Sir Michael Edwardes was the right man for British Leyland remains an open question. He certainly pulled the company back from the brink, but the continuing government involvement and the political bias that generated, seems to have prevented what might have been the better course, the sale of the various facilities to companies in the industry who could combine their resources with their own and so create a viable entity. This was the objective of the proposed takeover by General Motors of the vehicle divisions, but the Government backed away from that solution in the face of public criticism. A similar situation developed in relation to Westland, the only UK helicopter company, which was eventually taken over by a US company in the face of much opposition. But there the management was *not* government dependent, and pursued the course it thought best for the employees and the shareholders, irrespective of government policy. Business and politics will always be a disastrous mixture! When politics take over sound business practice goes out of the window. That is the lesson that *must* be learnt.

References

1   Spooner, P., 'UK squanders its management talent', *Chief Executive*, 5 June 1983, p. 4.
2   Edwards, M., *Back from the brink: An Apocalyptic Experience*, Collins, 1983.
3   Gooding, K., 'Strong recovery in vehicle output at BL', *Financial Times*, 5 December 1985.
4   'BL – Still holding the baby', *Economist*, no. 298, 29 March 1986 p. 43.
5   'The future of the automobile', *MIT Press*, 1984, p. 321. (Massachusetts Institute of Technology International Automobile Program.)
6   Marwood, D. C. L., 'ICL – Crisis and swift recovery', *Long Range Planning*, no. 18, April 1985, pp. 10–21.
7   'Marks ring up the changes with ICL', *STC News*, no. 334, February 1986, p. 6
8   Lorenz, C., 'Metamorphosis of a European laggard'; 'A painful process of change'; and 'How saturation training has focused the mind to dramatic effect', *Financial Times*, 12, 14 and 16 May 1986.
9   'Cultural change at ICL', *Financial Times*, 9 December 1985, p. 10.
10 'Continuing perils', *Economist*, no. 294, 2 February, 1985, pp. 72–3.
11 'STC counts the cost', *STC News*, no. 335, March 1986, p. 1.

Part Four

The fight for survival

13 Dunlop's dilemma

The name 'Dunlop' is well-known worldwide. Dunlop has been associated, first with bicycles and then with cars and other vehicles and finally with aircraft as a pneumatic tyre manufacturer. We believe that the company has been a manufacturer of pneumatic tyres almost since its invention and the company had what we might call a 'popular' image because long before the car came into mass production a great many people in a great many countries were riding the humble 'bike' and using Dunlop tyres. Dunlop grew over the years, starting in the UK but later developing overseas, until it became the world's leading tyre manufacturer, but it has long since lost that lead. How did this come about?

Overcapacity in Europe

Dunlop's problems, and the problems of the other tyre manu-facturers, developed to an acute stage in the late 1970s, as a result of massive over-production, particularly in the European end of the tyre industry. This problem was largely one of the industry's own making and it came about as the result of a continuing effort to produce and sell the 'last word' in tyres. It all began in the 1930s when it was noticed that the tyres of front-wheel drive Citroen cars in France wore out very quickly. After the Second World War Michelin introduced the use of a steel wire girdle under the tread to solve this problem. The 'girdle' reinforced and strengthened the tyre, so prolonging its life very substantially. This was very attractive to the user and sales of Michelin tyres leapt ahead. The other manufacturers researched hard during the 1960s in an endeavour to match the Michelin 'wired' tyre and Pirelli came the closest by incorporating a special textile thread in the canvas.

Another major design development first introduced by Michelin was what was called the 'radial' tyre. This gave a much smoother ride and was specially attractive to the owners of sports cars. Although rather more expensive than the standard tyre, the increased cost was more than recovered in use, because the tyre had a much longer life. In Europe the switch over to radial tyres took place with heavy lorries more quickly than with cars, since the design gave a tyre with much greater strength, thus allowing heavier loads to be carried. While the other manufacturers followed up these developments and even managed to come up at times with a better product than that being offered by Michelin, that company still retained and improved upon its lead in the market. Part of the strength of Michelin lay in its manufacturing techniques: it was operating more efficiently than many of its competitors – including Dunlop. Michelin's market share continued to grow, but the other manufacturers still prospered, because the market as a whole was growing at the rate of some 6 per cent per year right throughout the 1960s and 1970s, with an ever-expanding car market. But finally the market 'peaked out' and began to go into a decline. One substantial reason for this, apart from the declining sales of cars, was the fact that the technological improvements, driven on by the severe competition, resulted in tyres ever most resistant to wear and thus having a much longer life. So they did not require replacing as often as they did. By the end of the 1970s the industry, particularly in Europe, was in real trouble as a result.

Michelin rides out the storm

But not Michelin. In 1980 Michelin had 35 per cent of the car tyre market and 45 per cent of the truck tyre market in Europe and its share was still growing. The reputation of Michelin tyres was very good and the company still prospered. It still had a Michelin as chief executive and he seemed to have a very good 'feel' for the market. As he saw it he had three basic options before him in the struggle to maintain sales. They were:

1   Form a group with other tyre manufacturers.
2   Seek government help.
3   Do nothing.

The objective to be achieved by grouping together with other European tyre manufacturers would be to meet the growing invasion of the European tyre market by American and Japanese companies. But Dunlop had already tied up with Pirelli, though that particular association was not prospering, so Michelin doubted whether he could form any other grouping that would be successful. So he then considered the second alternative. He could have enlisted the support of both the EEC and individual governments in Western Europe, with a view to reducing the over-capacity there, but Michelin *personally* was not at all in favour of government intervention of any kind. He therefore followed the third course, and did nothing.

By doing nothing he was allowing the normal market forces to operate. With falling demand and over-capacity supply would exceed demand and prices would fall. That would settle the issue, resulting in the 'survival of the fittest'. Michelin was in a strong position and could well survive, riding out the storm. In any event, the competition wasn't doing all that well. Most of the American tyre companies selling in Europe, except Goodyear, were faring badly. Goodrich had by then (1980) abandoned the European market, while Uniroyal was just selling what it could. Firestone, another major US company, had closed two factories and 180 retail outlets in the UK and had also withdrawn from Switzerland. Goodyear, though not a company noted for its inventiveness, did have a strong base at home and its subsidiaries elsewhere in the world were doing well, so they decided to maintain a strong position in Europe.

So far as the European manufacturers themselves were concerned, Continental, a West German manufacturer, was still providing tyres for the cars manufactured by Volkswagen, staying in business despite not having made a profit on its tyre-making activities for fifteen years. It seems that it was felt that West Germany should have its own tyre manufacturing company at almost any price! Pirelli, the Italian-based manufacturer, was also in trouble, but we will come to them later. Has the Michelin strategy worked? At first sight it would appear so, with some competitors closing down and others cutting production severely, but the Michelin Group lost US$920 million during the years 1982–3, and as yet no major rival brand has actually disappeared from the market.

The rise and fall of Dunlop

Let us now see how Dunlop were faring while all this was going on.

Through the 1970s Dunlop had a dramatic rise in revenue, climbing from some £600 million in 1970 to £1·6 billion in 1979. Pretax profits matched this growth in revenue to begin with, rising from some £25 million in 1970 to £75 million in 1978, but then profits collapsed, as illustrated in Figure 10. They dropped to £10 million, in 1980, and the following year there was a loss of £10 million. Earnings per share followed a similar course. Reaching a peak of 18 pence a share in 1977, they fell to 3 pence a share by 1979, then came three years in succession with drastic losses (see Figure 10). What on earth had happened?

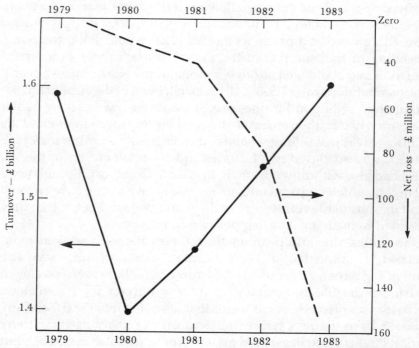

Figure 10   *Going the wrong way at Dunlop. This graph shows us that while a dramatic turnaround had been achieved in sales, it was not matched by rising profits: they worsened steadily.*
Source: Company accounts.

Dunlop had joined up with Pirelli of Italy in 1971 and it was this union, together with Dunlop's Malaysian connection, that brought the sudden, dramatic fall in profits. Pirelli was losing money steadily on tyre manufacture, as were so many other companies in the same business and it did not have a range of alternative, related products, as did Dunlop, to provide an alternative source of revenue. Beset with labour problems and declining productivity, Pirelli was in effect bankrupt, but it was not allowed to collapse. The Italian Government, as part of their socio-economic policy, was prepared to 'bail out' companies like Pirelli, provided it invested in factories in Southern Italy, a very depressed area. Pirelli was also leaning heavily on its partner, Dunlop. There was some sharing of markets, sharing of development costs and product diversification between the two companies, but the parent company, Dunlop, had a responsibility towards its shareholders and could not fund Pirelli indefinitely. The over-capacity in the industry as a whole made the situation potentially extremely serious, since there seemed no way out.

Wheeling and dealing

If we now turn to Malaysia, Dunlop had been manufacturing tyres there since 1963, pioneering in the area, having begun there with the acquisition and development of the rubber tree plantations. The name Dunlop was therefore well-known in Malaysia and the company's shares were much coveted. In July 1978 it became known that some four million Dunlop shares had been transferred to nominees in the Far East, and buying from the Far East continued all through 1979 and the first half of 1980. Institutional holders in the UK, such as insurance companies, were the main sellers. Then it transpired that a local group headed by Ghaffar Baba, a golf-playing Malaysian politician was behind this buying and his objective, as finally disclosed in the local press, was to acquire Dunlop as a whole, both the manufacturing interests and, more particularly, the plantations in Malaysia. To accomplish this Ghaffar Baba began to exert both public pressure through the media, and political pressure. Most of Dunlop's plantations were in Malacca, one of the Malaysian states, and the home state of both Mr Baba and his associate Mr C. A. Eng in a company they had set up for the purpose called *Goodyield Holdings*. Their intentions, as leaked to the press, were neither specific nor clear, and it seemed, not above board. In an attempt to find out what was going on, a British Government department with responsibility for overseas trade, the Department of Trade, scrutinized the entire affair in the Far East, issuing a report in February 1981 wherein it said:

We have shown how the holdings of the Goodyield group and connected shareholdings were treated as a 'pool', and it is possible that the 'pool' in the wider sense reached 5 per cent before the group declared its interest.

In order to comply with English law, a holding of 5 per cent in a public company had to be publicly declared, while if the holding exceeded 30 per cent the concerned individual or group was required to bid for the entire company. The group led by Mr Baba had no choice but to admit that it had acquired a holding of some 5 per cent in Dunlop. From then the Goodyield Holdings interest in Dunlop continued to grow, with each purchase of shares bringing an outcry against the Dunlop management by the other shareholders. Finally, Mr Baba declared his desire to purchase the Dunlop plantations in Malaysia, and the sale was finally concluded in March 1982. Meanwhile the Goodyield interest continued to grow, finally reaching 30 per cent. At this point Mr Baba joined the Dunlop board. Both he and Mr Eng attended one board meeting, but thereafter they left their representation in the hands of alternates. The Malaysian development continued to receive much publicity. It may well have been exciting news in Malaysia, but it brought no benefits to Dunlop, whose shares were much depressed. Dunlop was clearly under threat: Mr Baba might well, in the end, buy up the balance of the shares 'for a song'.

To appreciate the extent of the threat, it must be remembered that whereas in France and Italy companies will be rescued in the national interest, that did not normally happen in the UK and the Government was most unlikely to intervene. Companies in trouble fail or survive in response to the law of 'the survival of the fittest'. So what could Dunlop do?

The Dunlop response

In an attempt to counter the 'offshore' threat the Dunlop board developed a three-pronged strategy. It had to be executed very quickly, because profitability had collapsed and time was running out. The company had an inherent weakness following its union with Pirelli, and in addition its major customer, British Leyland, was steadily losing its share of the car market. All this when the UK was going through a period of severe depression. The three-pronged approach to the crisis developed by the Dunlop board was:

1 Seek Government aid.
2 Restructure the company.
3 Offload Pirelli.

At the time of crisis a Labour Government was in power, and it was hoped that it might be receptive to a plea for help. In response to a formal request the Department of Industry carried out an in-depth study and concluded that the company needed a cash injection of some £50 million to see it through. The then Labour Government suggested that this should be raised partly through a rights issue and partly as equity provided by the National Enterprise Board. But for the National Enterprise Board to take up an interest was seen as 'back door' nationalization: something the Dunlop board was not prepared to accept. Then came a change in government and all that the incoming Conservatives were prepared to offer Dunlop was a loan of £6 million, made conditional upon it embarking upon new investment. But this Dunlop could never contemplate: retrenchment, not investment and job creation, was for them the order of the day in its industry.

The policy of restructuring was also initiated, but it was not prosecuted in depth or with vigour. It was decided to concentrate on high-volume products, such as radial car and truck tyres and motor cycle tyres. As a consequence, Dunlop became the first major company in the tyre industry to close down a factory. It shut down its major tyre manufacturing facility at Speke, near Liverpool, and this closure was followed by several others. As a result the workforce fell sharply, from 43,000 in 1975 to some 22,000 in 1983. Finally, the Pirelli connection was closed out in 1981. Dunlop received £20·4 million in compensation, but this was nothing when compared with the investment the company had made in Pirelli over ten sterile years. But still, something is always better than nothing and this drain on profits came to an end.

Enter the Japanese

Dunlop had diversified quite widely over the years, both in terms of products and countries. Some of these activities were quite profitable, although often shared with other minority interests. But by 1982 it had become very clear that the profitable parts of the business could no longer sustain the European tyre manufacturing business, which was losing steadily. The European tyre business had to go: but

how? Who would buy a losing business? On the other hand, to close
the factories down would be a most expensive process, because of
the tremendous redundancy payments that would have to be met.
So Dunlop turned to Japan. Dunlop, with a large shareholding in the
Sumitomo Rubber Company, had better links in Japan than any
other non-Japanese tyre company, so it opened negotiations with
Sumitomo. The Japanese tyre industry was seeking to broaden its
base in line with that of its own car industry. While the industry
commanded a strong share of the world export market, it had not
been particularly successful in setting up manufacturing operations
overseas. In addition, Sumitomo was not particularly happy with
the large stake in its company held by Dunlop. It would have liked to
have seen it reduced, thus improving its rating in the stock market.
So Sumitomo sought to combine this with the purchase of part or all
of Dunlop's tyre manufacturing operations. The most complicated
negotiations went on for months over the years 1982–3, with Dunlop
continually playing down the possibility of a deal so as not to upset
its Japanese partners. The negotiations were further complicated by
the Malaysian intervention which we described above, and the
position for Dunlop was further worsened by the pressure on it from
its bankers to get a quick result. It is here that the Japanese virtue of
patience can bring rich dividends, as we shall see in more detail
when we come to consider entrepreneural activities in that country
in some detail in the following chapter.

Sumitomo did very well out of all this 'wheeling and dealing', but
where did it all get Dunlop? The company's status, as assessed by
Performance Analysis Services Ltd over these traumatic years is
presented in Table 12. We gave a brief outline of this company's
method of assessment in Chapter 3, but to remind you, the PAS
score is an assessment of the company's 'health' on a scale from 1 to
100. Once a company gets below 20 on this scale it is considered to be
at risk, so Dunlop was very much at risk from 1980 onwards, with the
final disaster looming ever nearer with each passing year. The Z-
score is a parallel assessment, but since the formulae, published by
Altman, are in the public domain, it is felt to be of interest and value
to quote it. Altman said that if the Z-score was less than 1·8, then
failure was certain.[2] That was for the US. For the UK, the number
might be a little lower, perhaps 1·5, but quite evidently, according to
Altman, there was no hope for Dunlop. The other significant
warning signal is the growth in debt/equity ratio.

Table 12 *Assessing the Dunlop accounts. This extract from the company profile for Dunlop, with profitability, working capital and financial risk assessment on a scale from 1 to 100, shows a movement from bad to worse. The alternative figures for the year ending 31 December 1983 show the impact on the company status had it been able to secure the support it was seeking. (With thanks to Performance Analysis Services Limited, for permission to publish.)*

Year end	Profit ability	Working capital	Financial risk	PAS score	Z score	Debt/ equity
31 Dec. 84	1	1	–	2	−5.0	
31 Dec. 83	2	1	1	4	−3.90	1.42:1
31 Dec. 82	2	2	3	11	−2.34	1.03:1
31 Dec. 81	3	1	2	10	−2.23	1.09:1
With £200 million equity and £100 million long-term loan:						
31 Dec. 83	4	4	5	37	1.81	

Remarks:
Risk rating 5.
Going concern qualification.

The banks call in the 'doctor' – at last

The banks, who looked at that debt/equity ratio with dismay, having advanced the money, finally called in Sir Michael Edwardes, fresh from his triumph at British Leyland, to repeat his 'magic'. While at British Leyland he had been described as the 'man who took on the unions', at Dunlop the first reaction of the workers was very different to what it had been at British Leyland. They wanted to talk and made no threats. Indeed, although Sir Michael, on arrival, made a clean sweep of the main board (with the exception of those Malayan directors we mentioned earlier), the Dunlop workforce did not tremble. Dunlop had a major factory in Coventry and the last time Sir Michael wielded power in Coventry two factories closed. Yet a union leader there does not see that clear out as an ugly portent, but rather as a hopeful sign, saying:[3]

> It was necessary to prune the company from the top and he did it. I don't think he will chop jobs here. We have so much work and we have a good set-up, with successful local management and no industrial relations problems. I think Edwardes is the man to invest in and capitalize on that set-up.

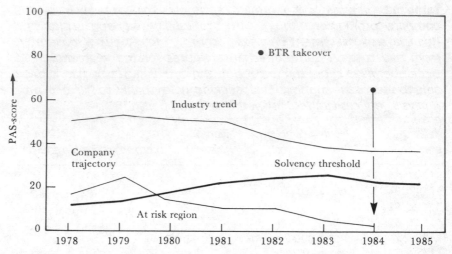

Figure 11   *Dunlop in context. This plot of the PAS-score for Dunlop, set against the industry trend, shows that the company had been very much at risk since 1980. (With thanks to Performance Analysis Services Limited, London, for permission to publish.)*

But Sir Michael had no opportunity to 'capitalize on that set-up': time was running out fast. The company was very much on the brink of disaster, as is most graphically indicated in Figure 11 and a takeover took over – once again!

From turnaround to takeover

The company BTR plc is one of Britain's largest, fastest-growing and broadest-based conglomerates and all of a sudden it offered to take over poor, weak, limping Dunlop. The proposal came as a surprise to the banks, and much credit must go to Sir Michael, who conducted the negotiations. He managed to get BTR to increase its initial offer for the company very substantially. BTR is active in construction, industrial, energy and electrical consumer goods, and Dunlop just disappeared into its maw. BTR has net assets in the order of £1 billion, while little Dunlop was valued on acquisition at £65 million and so now represents but some 5 per cent of BTR's total activities. Looking at the annual accounts of BTR for the year ending 28 December 1985 for signs of Dunlop, we see that BTR may have written its initial investment of £65 million in that company down to some £45 million, judging by a goodwill write-off of around £110

Table 13 *Progress at BTR (construction, industrial, energy and electrical consumer goods). This outline of the annual accounts for BTR for the year ending 28 December 1985, together with the PAS assessment as was given for Dunlop in Table 12, shows a very different picture. Here we have a very healthy company. (With thanks to Performance Analysis Services Limited, London, for permission to publish.)*

Annual accounts for year ending 28 December 85

	28.12.85	29.12.84	31.12.83
	£m	£m	£m
Turnover	3881	3487	1970
Interest	132	88	63
Profit before tax	362	284	171
Margin	9.3%	8.1%	8.7%
Net dividend (after scrip)	5.83p	4.33p	2.83p
EPS (after scrip)	16p	12.2p	8.5p
Ex'ord items	34	26	13
NTA	1099		
NA/share	62p (after scrip issue)		

Year end	Profit-ability	Working capital	Financial risk	Short-term liquidity	PAS score
28 December 1985 (after conversion and Cornhill cash)	8	4	5	7	64
28 December 1985 (as per accounts)	7	3	3	6	50
29 December 1984	7	2	4	4	46
31 December 1983	7	1	4	2	36

million noted in the directors' report and statement of accounting policy.

To give you some idea as to the immensity and complexity of BTR, we present as Table 13 highlights from the annual accounts of the company as at the 28 December 1985, together with the assessment of the company as made by Performance Analysis Services Limited. The historic trend of the PAS score for BTR, as given below, is most interesting.

	1980	1981	1982	1983	1984	1985
PAS score:	66	58	62	36	46	50(64)

The latest PAS score of 50 contrasts with a collapse to an estimated 22 on the acquisition of bankrupt Dunlop. The board's own view on Dunlop, as given in the report with the annual accounts, is that Dunlop is developing soundly and shows much promise. It describes the takeover as a 'smooth transfer'.

Where does BTR go next? Financial commentators generally seem preoccupied with speculation as to who is likely to be BTR's next target, with a major acquisition in 1986 viewed as inevitable. Sir Owen Green, the chief executive, and due to retire, but who will stay on as chairman to the end of 1986, has said in interviews any new acquisition was likely to be in US manufacturing, and that a 'policy of growth' was the key management motivator. It seems that BTR has a strong management team, with a remarkable ability for turning around the companies it takes over and also obtaining ever-increasing returns from mature companies that might have been thought to have attained a plateau in terms of growth. The company's financial realism is demonstrated by its sale of Cornhill Insurance, noted in Table 13. It seems that originally BTR had aspirations to run an insurance business, but apparently it had second thoughts once it had had practical experience, via Cornhill. It was a very intelligent disposal, associated as it was with an open acknowledgement of the fact that, contrary to original expectations, it was outside the realm of BTR's expertise to manage, and that if the funds were deployed elsewhere they could well earn twice as much as they were earning through Cornhill. We trust our readers are taking notice!

We like to look at the chief executive, rather than the company as an entity, to get to know how it is done, but in the case of BTR this is difficult. Sir Owen Green, the man who has built a £5,000 million business and ranks as one of Britain's most outstanding wealth creators, seems to get remarkably little publicity. For years he has bluntly refused all requests to be interviewed by journalists. But while Sir Owen keeps a low profile, he seeks an ever higher profile for his company, with the shares now being quoted on both the Frankfurt and Tokio stock exchanges. The purpose, of course, is to have greater flexibility in raising funds around the world.

Summary

Dunlop is a classic case of a lack of decisive action until it was almost too late. Whether Sir Michael Edwardes would have been able to turn the company around is a moot point, but in any event he never had the opportunity to demonstrate that particular skill. He did, however, demonstrate his skill at negotiation when BTR came along with its takeover bid. It must be remembered that he had very few bargaining counters on his side of the table, with Dunlop on the verge of bankruptcy.

This reluctance to take decisive action is a recurring phenomenon when we look at companies in trouble and we can only hope our readers pay attention, and learn the lesson. Once the warning signs are there, there can never be any merit in delaying tactics. Far better to 'grasp the bull by the horns', as the saying goes, and take positive, bold, decisive action.

References

1   'Dunlop's dilemma – flat tyres in Europe', *Economist*, no. 291, 2 June 1984, p. 75; 'Dunlop – chipped blue-chip patched up', pp. 64–6; 'Dunlop retreading', pp. 76–7.
2   Altman, E. I., *Corporate Financial Distress. A Complete Guide to Predictions, Avoiding and Dealing with Bankruptcy*, Wiley, 1983.
3   Walters, P., 'Workforce fate in lap of Little Moe', *Coventry Evening Telegraph*, 20 November, 1984, p. 6.

14   Classics from Japan

Japan has emerged from the ashes to reach the top of the industrial league of nations in about three decades, a remarkable achievement by any standard. The experts ascribe this miracle primarily to the Japanese style of management, which has been the subject of a host of books in recent years. Developed and developing countries alike have been exhorted to look to Japan and learn.[1] Having begun as a mere imitator, Japan is now seen as the great example for imitation. What a role reversal! Thanks to its productivity, which has steadily increased over the years, together with extremely harmonious management–worker relationships, Japan has come to dominate industry after industry. So impressive has been the progress of Japan in the industrial sphere that many industrialized nations, including the US, now study and seek to emulate the Japanese style of management. With respect to the US, this has its own irony, since most of the so-called Japanese concepts originated in the US, following the substantial activities of US nationals in Japan immediately after the Second World War. This contrast has been most tersely summed up by the co-founder of the Honda Motor Company in the words 'Japanese and American management is 95 per cent the same and different in all important respects'. What are these differences?

In Japan, men and women are the focus of all that is done. The individual is at the centre and family life merges into that of the corporation. Parents may be involved at the time of hiring and they are even rewarded for their offspring's achievements. All decisions are by consensus, so important is the individual and their views felt to be. No one is left out of anything. This assures commitment, so essential to proper performance, and brings with it a harmonious work team: an approach which seems to ensure success most of the time, although not always, as we shall see. Salary is normally related to seniority, while promotion is on merit. This can lead to what many in the Western world would consider to be an anomalous situation: the head of the group receiving a lower salary than some members of his team. Director and worker usually wear the same uniform and eat in the same canteen. Further, Japanese workers and managers are encouraged to continue learning throughout their working career. Specialists broaden their knowledge of allied fields and, with considerable job rotation, can step into a colleague's shoes at short notice. A Japanese worker may well spend some 500 days in training during a ten-year work span. This cross-fertilization encourages creativity and has led to a spate of suggestions for the improvement of productivity and quality. Individuals and groups are recognized and rewarded for such achievements and share such financial gains that may follow. It all sounds wonderful, yet Japan has its failed and bankrupt companies.

Impact of bankruptcy laws

In Figure 12 we compare the company bankruptcy rate between Germany and Japan. We have chosen to compare Japan with Germany since bankruptcy laws differ from country to country and the insolvency laws in Germany have certain peculiarities. The laws there are so strict that very few companies apply for *Vergleich* (bankrputcy). The Government is currently seeking to change the law and so make it easier for companies to go bankrupt, but the bankers there lobby powerfully against it, having lost a lot of money in such cases of bankruptcy as have occurred. A typical illustration of what happens is the case of AEG-Telefunken, a company that in the face of crisis applied for *Vergleich*. It was thereby able to shed some 60 per cent of its debt to the bankers and is now operating profitably.

In Japan the banks also play a powerful role in relation to firms that are likely to go bankrupt, but in a very different way. They play a protective role, stepping in at the first sign of trouble and propping up the company with further loans.[2] Despite this continuing support from the banks, corporate bankruptcy is on the increase in Japan, just as it is in the rest of the world. In 1983 19,000 firms collapsed, 2000 more than in the previous year.[3] In Chapter 4 we considered the activities of a notable company 'doctor', Umeo Oyamo, and we saw

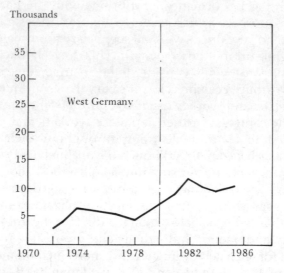

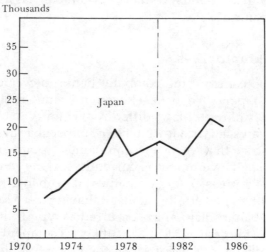

Figure 12   *Company bankruptcies. The number of officially recorded bankruptcies in West Germany and Japan are compared.*
Sources: Tokyo Shoko and the Federal Statistics Office.

that he found plenty to do. His story, while demonstrating his own personal ability, also highlights the significant role played by the banks in Japan. It is always the banks who call in the 'doctor', since they are always by far the largest creditors and potentially the greatest sufferers if the company should 'die'.

The Japanese financial system

It has to be remembered that the key features in the post-1945 financial system in Japan were largely imposed by the US occupying authorities and modelled on their own markets at that time. Two features predominated, regulated interest rates and strict compartmentalization between institutions, and the system was highly protected from external influences. The Japanese financial system has three layers, the regulatory authorities, public finance and private finance. The main consideration when the system was first developed was to engineer an economic recovery, the financial markets being a conduit for this rather than a growth sector in their own right. Funds were scarce and had to be allocated to the areas where they were most productive. While the system succeeded in channelling funds with great precision to core industries, there was a side effect. This structured and protected environment allowed the financial sector to grow without being subject to the pressures seen in other industrialized countries. The reward for the private sector was low inflation coupled with great confidence in the value of money and the integrity of the banking system. The system was designed to and was well able to provide plentiful funds for industry at low interest rates, although the consumer sector suffered, in that lending there was very restricted and expensive. But one major result was that the plentiful funds flowed into ill-managed companies as well as the successful ones for far too long. Hence a role for Umeo Oyamo. But there have been others.

The Japanese cultural system

Before considering what those who have gone to live in Japan to do business have achieved, we thought it would help in an appreciation of their effort to try and illustrate how *different* life is there, as compared to what they have been accustomed to. Not in the factory, which we have already touched upon, but in the street. It appears that in Japan great stress is laid on maintaining a smooth, even human relationship.[4] This anxiety not to upset things goes so far that there is permissiveness in lying. This is done either explicitly (*tatemae*, with apparent intention) or implicitly (*honne*, the actual intention). The Japanese rarely say 'no': they wouldn't wish to upset you. Instead they say 'yes, but . . . ', the emphasis being on the emotional aspect, rather than the logical.

It seems that the cultural shock occasioned to Westerners living in Japan can be such that it brings on mental disorders, or they take to excessive drinking, wife beating or, in extreme cases, are even driven to suicide.[5] Silence, often difficult to cope with, has a very different meaning in Japan, and their way of saying 'no', to which we have just referred, seems to create tremendous problems. Then there are straightforward cultural differences: the Japanese urinate in the streets, smile with no particular meaning, slurp when eating their soup and stare at foreigners. All this can be very disconcerting and even traumatic for sensitive souls. The foreigner, it seems, will always be treated as people with only a peripheral role to play in Japanese society and this isolation makes daily life very difficult.

The strange foreigner

We thought that in view of the special problems that developing a successful business in Japan must have, it would be particularly interesting to a worldwide readership to look at the way in which individual foreigners have, despite all, achieved success. The Japanese have the word 'gaijin' to describe a foreigner and it means more than foreigner: it means an outsider. And that is what foreigners *always* are in Japan: they can never be a part of Japan's clannish economic elite. Yet, despite this inbred attitude, despite Japan being a tough market, hedged about not only with cultural tripwires but bureaucratic red tape, some foreigners have been able to get in and make a success of the companies they run. The statistics tell the story. Direct investment in Japan from abroad has increased four-fold in the last ten years, and there has been a great increase in foreign executives holding managerial roles in Japanese companies. Today more than 3000 American companies have offices or factories in Japan and the number of foreign companies is growing at the rate of some 600 a year.[6] Gaijin companies (to use the Japanese description) have sometimes been able to outpace their local rivals and become undisputed industry leaders in their particular field. Many executives now arrive in Japan fluent in the Japanese language and holding management degrees.

Among the well-known names who now operate successful Japanese companies are IBM, Nestlé, Coca-Cola, Texas Instruments and Schick. These companies have created many job opportunities for the Japanese – IBM alone is said to employ more than 17,000, thus making a substantial contribution to the Japanese economy, while at the same time being a powerful stimulus to the Japanese computer industry. Then there are the hybrids – joint ventures between overseas companies and local companies. Typical of these are Caterpillar-Mitsubishi, Asahai-Dow, McDonalds Japan and Fuji-Xerox. It is however what we might call, though with no disrespect intended, the 'small fry' who are the most interesting from our particular point of view. It is the small company and the individualist who is going to have the greatest difficulty in overcoming and surmounting the isolationist tradition that is still so powerful in Japan. Let us look at a few of them. While we can discern no set formula for their success, since they seem very often to make up the rules as they proceed, they all display certain essential qualities: patience, perseverance and flexibility.

Billiard cues provide the cue

Richard Helmstetter first started making billiard cues in Chicago in 1966, on leaving school. He was making 'custom' cues, that is cues designed for specific users or styles of play. So successful was he that he was making cues for twenty-seven of the world's top thirty professionals. While he had a flourishing business, he nevertheless commented:

> The Japanese were knocking me off . . . I'd come out with a catalogue and six months later they would be making the same cues – cheaper.

His solution was to invade the enemy's territory. He went to Japan to set up a joint venture with local partners, but within the year he had lost his 'seed money', US$280,000. Not a typical Japanese joint venture, he now jokingly recalls. Undaunted, he started up his own pool-cue factory in Tokyo in 1969. He now has two factories employing in all some eighty people and has a virtual monopoly, while eighteen of his former rivals failed. The company, Adam Limited, exports to ninety countries. This global market is neatly divided into two halves: Helmstetter dominates the expensive top end, while the bottom end is dominated by the Taiwanese.

What sort of a man is Richard Helmstetter? He is said to be fluent in Japanese, to have very fast reflexes and the patience of Buddha. He has succeeded, it appears, by beating the Japanese at their own game. Convinced that detailed business negotiations were never going to be a success using translators, he managed for himself and learnt from his mistakes. One mistake was to pay equal wages to both men and women, which led to strikes and walkouts. He had gone against the prevailing culture and says of this incident:

> Workers like responsibility as long as it has definite limits. The hierarchy gives everyone a place. Everyone needs a title and a name card.

The end result was a compromise between his own style and Japanese culture. Sometimes he rolls up his sleeves and works alongside his employees turning up a cue on his own private lathe. He listens thoughtfully to what is said to him, adopting a paternal attitude. One consequence is that he has acted as the honoured 'go-between' at the weddings of nine of his employees. Notice the way in which the company and the family are being integrated. His advice to those seeking to pierce the Japanese market is simple and straightforward:[4]

> Japan is a closed market, but there are cracks. If people put the same energy into opening them as looking for tax loopholes, they'd do alright. . . . You shouldn't expect fair treatment. . . . The foreigner has half the chance a Japanese does to survive in the [same] business.

He believes – and his own experience is proof enough – that if the gaijin will combine the technical advantage which he has to exploit with the Japanese way of management he can be successful, even in Japan.

Traditions die hard

Tetra Pak is a Swedish maker of milk cartons who set up in Japan in 1957. The project had all the elements for success: it was a brand new product, it had unbeatable technology and a vast market – all milk was then sold in Japan in clumsy glass bottles. Tetra Pak began by linking with Kyodo Nyugyo, one of the big four in the dairy products industry in Japan, but within a year the project had collapsed. As it turns out, that was a very good thing. The reason for failure was that consumers would not buy milk they couldn't see. In addition, the retailers misinterpreted the advice concerning a longer shelf life and failed to refrigerate their stocks. Yasunori Katssuymama, now a Tetra Pak veteran, provides us with both the prognosis and the cure. He said:

> It was exactly what we'd been most afraid of . . . if you want to introduce a new concept you need a strong organization. The answer follows: you have to do it yourself.

That was what Richard Helmstetter found, and that is what Tetra Pak now found. So the company started again, with a wholly owned subsidiary. This was then something completely novel in Japan and would not normally have been allowed. It was here that the initial fiasco proved a blessing in disguise. No one believed the company could possibly succeed, for there was no precedent, except one flop. This led the Ministry of International Trade and Industry (MITI) to believe that there were no Japanese competitors that could get hurt. So they let the 'paper tiger' in. They completely overlooked the fact that it was a replacement product and were proved sadly wrong! Today Tetra Pak is a most successful company, the initial three-man office having grown into a company with annual sales of US$260 million, 840 workers making over five billion cartons a year. Milk in glass bottles is now a matter of history and Tetra Pak cartons are sold worldwide, packaging some 2000 products, marketed by some hundred companies selling products ranging from yoghurt to Spanish wine.

Behind all this stood Yasunori Katssuymama, who says that the secret of success is the creation of a long-term commitment to the customer. It took him eight years to get one particular customer on to his books, while the average is three years. Innovation just will not come overnight. There was no real expansion of business for the first ten years. He says:

> Getting a new concept accepted takes a long time and our Swedish headquarters showed immense patience. We also had to keep flexible to cope with rapid market changes.

For its success in Japan Yasunori Katssuymama gives his Swedish headquarters full credit. Its philosophy, as applied to its Japanese venture, was that it could be wrong for 20 per cent of the time, but it must prove right for the other 80 per cent.

The soft donut pierces a hard market

Here we are introduced to a very unusual aspect of Japanese culture, where faith is said to be at the heart of the success that has been achieved. Back in 1971 Mister Donut of America sold its franchise rights to Duskin of Japan for the sum of US$425,000, plus a 2·5 per cent yearly royalty. The Duskin Donut is now in the front rank of Japan's fast food industry, with 1985 sales of US$180 million, an increase of 18 per cent over the previous year. But the credit goes not

only to Duskin, but to the American company. All Duskin employees must study the precepts of *Ittoen*, a service-orientated
unorthodox religious sect. They have to say the Duskin prayer
together both morning and evening. The president of the company,
Shigeharu Komai, says:

> The idea is to put the heart ahead of business . . . the American
> Minister Donut succeeded to a degree, but they lacked the creativity to
> go further. If we didn't make our donuts the American way, there
> wouldn't have been any point to it.

This meant that it had to educate the consumer's taste: he had to
learn to like and want a completely novel product. Where did the
Duskin creativity come in? It was in discarding the notion that
foreign food products could not succeed in Japan. It altered the
product only slightly to make it completely acceptable. The approach
adopted was, with the full cooperation of Mister Donut, to set up a
full scale mock-up in Osaka for many weeks of market testing, some
of the employees themselves playing the customer. This detailed
work led to the discovery that the Japanese preferred a fluffy donut
(or should we spell it 'doughnut' at this point?). Having established
the customer preference, the first store was opened in a remote
Osaka suburb and sales turned out to be ten times that forecast. Now
there are nearly 500 outlets in Japan. We believe this to be a good
example of the truism that prevention is better than cure. There was
no immediate failure, as in the two previous cases we have looked at,
because the ground had been well prepared for success. They had
ensured market acceptance before they 'went to town'.

The software is not so soft

Our next invader in the Japanese market came from the US. One Bill
Totten was a salesman for Californian-based Software Development
Corporation (SDC) and he visited Japan in 1969 to assess the
prospects there for mainframe computer software. He reported that
there was a vast potential, but his company was not as impressed as
he was. As a consequence Totten quit and set up a software company
in Japan that has now grown to be the biggest in its field. That
company's programs, such as ASSIST (in Japanese, KK Ashisuto)
are sold and serviced in Japan and compete successfully even with
the products of the giants in the business, such as IBM and Fujitsu.
But it was no easy road and the story brings us some more lessons in
relation to competing against the Japanese.

After leaving SDC, Totten obtained the rights to market two computer software programs developed by SDC's competitors. A year later he had learnt a great deal about the Japanese culture and had become fluent in the language, but had not sold a thing. He then got together five partners and capital of US$5,000 and set up a Japanese joint stock holding company, called *Ashisuto*, but for months disaster loomed large. Totten took no salary and borrowed from his accountant to meet his payroll obligations – he must have been a very good salesman! But finally he managed to turn the corner. It took him nearly six years to build up the credibility of his company but from then on there was no looking back. The average growth rate since 1978 has been 66 per cent per year, sales for 1985 were US$25 million, with a forecast for 1976 of US$50 million. We are told that Totten has found it no handicap being a foreigner, but of course he has learnt both the language and the system. There is a mass of regulations and an enormous amount of form filling, but since everyone is in the same boat so far as that is concerned it is no handicap. So, as Totten himself says:[6]

> If you want to make an issue of that kind of thing, you can . . . or you can hire a cheap clerk, and she does it for you, and the problem goes away.

In this quiet and unassuming fashion Totten is effectively meeting the Japanese competition, using an imported software package that has been translated into Japanese and 'debugged' on a Japanese computer. The emphasis is on salesmanship and this seems to be at the root of his success. Hi salesmen are well trained and are required to make fifteen calls a week, while he himself meets his clients regularly, even perhaps to the point of overdoing it. To quote him once again:

> We have consistently oversupported our products. Buy our horse and we not only lead you to the water, we force you to drink.

We consider this to be a most remarkable success story, in that not only have all the normal hurdles been overcome, but that most abnormal hurdle, the application of overseas software to the Japanese language and their computers. Patience and persistence brought its rewards.

The Italians learn too, but not so fast

We have looked at the turnaround with Olivetti brought about by Dr

Carlo De Benedetti in some detail earlier (Chapter 11) and we saw its collaboration with Toshiba as a part of that company's worldwide strategy. Olivetti had been doing business in Japan for twenty-five years, but it was that alliance that brought the breakthrough. It completed a 'triad' which was the kernel of Olivetti's long-term strategy, bringing it a leading role in three great markets, the US, Europe and Japan. For us it illustrates yet another principle in company turnaround that should always be carefully assessed, summed up by Olivetti's president in Japan, Paolo Venturini in the words:

> Don't beat them, join them . . . you can be part of a 'triad' . . . or sooner or later you can be financially dead.

Sales for Olivetti in Japan increased four-fold over the ten years from 1972 to 1982, but now the going is getting tougher. This illustrates a very specific quality always found in the Japanese: they come back competitively in strength, taking over the product. We saw that earlier with billiard cues, and Olivetti found that the same thing happened with the electronic typewriter. They introduced the very first electronic typewriter on to the Japanese market in 1983, but within the year the Japanese had caught up. It seems that any new product launch, however novel, will only keep its lead for a few months. Hence the success of the strategy demonstrated by all the case studies we have taken so far in this look at Japan: join them and manufacture locally. Toshiba, a long-time supplier to Olivetti, is now manufacturing Olivetti products in Japan and at the same time has secured a greater presence in Europe. Yet this particular approach has succeeded in containing the Japanese competition. The Japanese have competed successfully for many years worldwide and this has been attributed to their specific management techniques: techniques which cannot be readily adopted in other countries. No, but there is no difficulty at all in using those techniques in Japan itself, and then 'joining them' by not only selling your product in Japan itself, but exporting from that base worldwide, with all the competitive advantage thereby gained. This is undoubtedly the secret of success in Japan – and not only Japan, for the principle can be applied elsewhere as well.

Rollers 'roll' into Japan

Let us take one more example to reinforce the principle we seem to have established by telling the 'Dynapac' story. Dynapac is a Swedish company manufacturing road-making equipment, such as road rollers. Its association with Japan goes back many years and it was first represented in Japan by the Swedish trading group *Gadilius*. However, the company did not feel that it was getting its share of the Japanese market, while at the same time Japanese companies in the same field, such as Sakai and Kawasaki, were expanding rapidly in their overseas markets and presenting a strong challenge. To meet that challenge Dynapac felt that it had to have a base of its own in Japan itself. As Per Hyman, who looks after its Japanese interests, puts it:[7]

> When you have an important Japanese competitor you have to compete in his home market.

How did Dynapac put this principle into practice? At first it looked for a local distributor but this approach was unsuccessful. Having already looked at a number of parallel cases, we could have told it why, couldn't we! Its next step was to consider licensing a local producer, or even setting up its own manufacturing company in Japan. This brought it into contact with Watanabe, a well-established family company specializing in road-making equipment that happened to be complementary to the range manufactured by Dynapac. The two companies set up a joint venture, with the intention of ultimately manufacturing Dynapac machines in the Watanabe factory, which was located at Kawaguchi, a northern suburb of Tokyo. So far, so good. But within a year Watanabe found itself in deep financial trouble, having made severe losses on a major contract in Iraq. So serious was the situation that Watanabe became involved in bankruptcy proceedings. The company had a very good name in Japan and a valuable asset in the form of a strong distribution network, so Dynapac decided to bid for the business. But sale to a foreign company met a great deal of opposition, the court-appointed administrator making every effort to sell the company to a local firm. But when no one was interested, the deal with Dynapac was clinched. This took in all some eighteen months, but Dynapac had already had some experience of working in Japan, knew how things went and had the patience to 'sit it out'. The end result, the establishment of *Dynapac Watanabe*.

Dynapac KK is born

The Swedes worked hard to develop their business in Japan and were very successful, so much so that they believed that the Dynapac name had been totally accepted locally, with the name Watanabe no longer providing the Japanese aura. So in July 1984 the word Watanabe was removed from the company name and Dynapac KK was born. Sales from the Japanese factory have grown from Yen3·2 billion (£10·8 million) in 1982 to more than Yen4 billion by 1984 and Dynapac's share of the domestic vibratory compactor market, its traditional product line, had grown significantly, all as illustrated in Figure 13. A major Watanabe product line was static rollers, and Dynapac has introduced a new series of machines which have more than doubled its share of the market, as illustrated in Figure 13. This increased market share has yet to make its impact on profits, but there is no doubt that that will come. Dynapac, despite

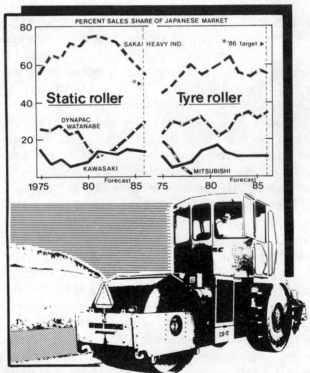

Figure 13   *The Dynapac drama. The Dynapac C5–12 deadweight roller illustrated above, which has recently been working on the M1 motorway in the UK, was made in the Swedish company's Watanabe company factory in Japan, now known as Dynapac KK. The graphs illustrate that Dynapac are increasing sales while the sales of their Japanese competitors are falling. (With thanks to the* Financial Times, *for permission to publish.)*

its name, is now a fully integrated *Japanese* company and therefore has ready access to the cheapest finance available anywhere in the developed world, provided by the Japanese banks, as described at the beginning of this chapter. To take full advantage of this facility, Dynapac has borrowed as much as it can, rather than injecting new equity of its own. This means that lack of immediate profit has no great significance, since the investment from Sweden is minimal. Per Hyman, president of the Japanese company, is most optimistic about the future, since the company is already covering all its operating costs. He expects a profit by 1987, five years after the formation of the company, all in accordance with its original corporate plan.

The plan has been maintained despite the problems created by the state of the factory it took over. The propaganda in relation to Japanese production is such that one expects every Japanese factory to be an 'immaculate modern plant, a model for the West'. But the Watanabe factory was a complex of six old buildings, dirty and nondescript and barely adequate. The factory no doubt 'grew like Topsy' and as is so often the case with family-owned companies, Watanabe never thought of, let alone got so far as to invest money in, improving the appearance of the buildings or modernizing the equipment. To quote Per Hyman once again:[7]

> We spent our first year reconditioning the machine tools and bringing the floors up to standard.

The Japanese windfall

We have already mentioned one benefit of being a Japanese company: the availability of cheap finance. There are many more. Dynapac KK was able to take advantage of the Japanese 'culture' by tying up with a Japanese trading company on deals involving construction equipment both at home and abroad. Not only did this bring it large overseas construction projects but it was able to shelter under the Japanese 'umbrella', with its project loans, credit and aid facilities. It seems that despite its 'foreign' (gaijin) label the company is at no disadvantage when it comes to financial arrangements. Indeed, the Swedish Group has ways and means to integrate their Japanese operation with its manufacturing facilities both at home in Sweden and also in the US. Wherever there is an advantage in terms of either price or quality products can be interchanged – it is the Japanese car makers who have become masters of this particular art, but others can copy. Of course, there are disadvantages as well, one in particular being a difficulty in getting suitable graduate staff from the Japanese universities. Per Hyman, who obviously has a most intimate knowledge of Japanese *mores*, says characteristically:

> When a person graduates from university, he goes first for the famous Japanese companies and then for the big foreign companies. Newcomers like us are further down the list. . . . Apart from new graduates and retirees, there is very little movement of personnel in Japan.

Well, one cannot pick and choose: it is all part of the 'package' but it seems to be a most attractive package indeed. Dynapac has charted a most unusual course, yet it is a course which we feel many other companies facing Japanese competition could well imitate. Unfortunately, such cases are not widely publicized and the possibilities are not really appreciated. One has to seek out such cases as we have given here from a great welter of paper but if and when such success stories become more widely known there could well be a torrent of such ventures, if only to meet the Japanese at their own doorstep, the policy they themselves have applied so successfully in so many countries. But knowing too their attitude to the 'gaijin' we would expect their government to quickly find ways of stemming the flood. But meanwhile many more are riding with the flood. Let us just share a few headlines with you, for they paint the picture very well: [8, 9, 10, 11]

US Drugmakers move in for a bigger piece of the action
The Street's street war with Japan
European car makers start honking at the Japanese
Cracking the Japanese market from the inside

The process is continuing and growing.

Summary

Japan is noted as being an overprotected market, although it takes full advantage of the unprotected free markets elsewhere in the world. Because of this, Western manufacturers have had great difficulty in penetrating the Japanese market. Apart from import restrictions, there is a rigid and expensive trading and distribution system which *has* to be used. All this is exclusively Japanese and there is no way in which foreign agencies can enter that field. However, as we show through examples from several different and disparate fields of endeavour, the peculiarities of the Japanese system can be used to advantage, once they are understood. For instance, since Japanese workers are hardly ever dismissed – how can you possibly turn someone out of the family – once a company is in financial trouble and cannot support its workforce, and the banks have reached their limit so far as loans are concerned, the next step is to go bankrupt. The bankruptcy procedure is very similar to that in the US, the bankruptcy court appointing an administrator whose prime task is to reconstruct the business. This may well involve the elimination of a number of jobs, so what the company cannot do the court will do – but only most reluctantly. As we have seen, Dynapac used this route to buy up Watanabe and so turn its Japanese operation into a genuine thriving Japanese company.

We believe our several case studies also make it very clear that speaking Japanese fluently and understanding the Japanese methods of working are crucial to success. You will remember that we saw the same thing when we reviewed the success of John Willis as a company 'doctor' in France. His chief contribution was a detailed knowledge of local practices and procedures. When we look at Japan we see a 'bamboo curtain' – but it can be crossed. We have shown you how.

References

1 Pascale, R. T. and Athos, A. G., *The Art of Japanese Management – Applications for American Executives*, Simon & Schuster, 1982.

2 Hoshino, Y., 'An analysis of corporate bankruptcies in Japan', *Management International Review*, no. 24, 2 November 1984, pp. 70–7.

3 Saito, T., 'Japan's Economy – Need for a Two-prong Policy', *Fuji Bank Bulletin*, July-August 1984, pp. 3–4.

4 Inuta, Mitsura, 'Permissiveness to lying – a feature of Japanese culture', *Japanese Management Newsletter*, 1 April 1985, pp. 1–2.

5 Whymant, R., 'Adapting to life in Japan has costs for Westerners', *International Herald Tribune*, 26 May 1986, p. 5.

6 Dahlby, T. and Lewis D., 'Gaijin Success Stories', *Newsweek*, 3 March 1986, pp. 38–41.

7 Rodger, I., 'Competing in Japan – Dynapac rolls to the rescue', *Financial Times*, 27 December 1985.

8 Bartlett, S., 'US drugmakers move in for a bigger piece of the action', *Business Week*, 22 April 1985, pp. 30–1.

9 Helm, L., 'The Street's street war with Japan', *Business Week*, 22 April 1985, p. 31.

10   Jones, D. E., 'European carmakers start honking at the Japanese', *Business Week*, 22 April 1985, p. 32.
11   Joseph, J., 'Cracking the Japanese market from the inside', *Business Week*, 27 May 1985, pp. 50–2.

15 Disparate examples from Europe

Businesses large and small, in countries large and small, can get into trouble and need a helping hand if they are to ride out their particular storm, and each case has its own special lessons. The wider we cast our net, the more we are likely to learn. Having seen what can happen in Japan, we thought we would come back to Europe to take up three more cases that carry significant lessons. Our examples come from three very different countries, although they are all three part of Western Europe: the UK, Finland and Switzerland. These three countries are indeed very, very different in size, in culture and in business tradition. We have already taken up some outstanding examples of the work of company 'doctors' in the UK, but they concerned major companies where the story of their difficulties reached the headlines in the national press, but now we want to look at the struggle for survival by a small, insignificant company, a 'small business'.

The role of the small business

These days the 'small business' is considered to be of supreme importance in the struggle to recover from the economic depression of the past few years, and this is particularly true of the UK. The Conservative Government led by Margaret Thatcher, now well into its second term, have always laid stress on the importance of the small business to the economy and have done their very best to stimulate and encourage the development of the small business. It is seen as making a great contribution to the solution of the very serious unemployment problem in the UK, since the vast majority of small businesses are run by what are commonly called the 'self-employed' and they are very obviously the people who work for themselves and keep what they earn (apart from taxation) who are going to be the most enthusiastic and hardworking. During the period from 1979, when they first came into power, to 1983 the Conservative Government passed over 760 measures designed to support the small firm. They enjoy generous loan guarantee schemes and since 1981 the individual, as well as the corporation, has been given tax relief on investment in a new or expanding business. Of course, not all such incentives are used for the purpose intended and one letter to the editor of the *Economist* in this context declared:[1]

> Junk all subsidies and tax incentives for small businesses. There is no shortage of money available if you know where to look and if you don't know (or can't find out) then you shouldn't be in business in the first place.

We believe that there is a lot of truth in that sentiment, especially when we call to mind what has been happening in India in relation to the small business. There, too, have been a variety of incentives, including low-interest loans, tax holidays, sales tax and excise tax exemption, all designed to encourage the development of the small business in that country. But there, too, the help given has not always been used as it should. As our letter writer suggests, the easy availability of finance attracts the incompetent and it is extremely difficult to weed such persons out. Neither in the UK nor in India is there any assessment of the capabilities and credentials of the budding entrepreneur. Although much good advice is on offer, no one is there to see that it is taken. In India there has also been gross misuse of the facilities set up to assist the small business by the bigger companies: misuse so serious as to warrant a full-length book on the subject.[2] The message of the book can be summed up by saying that those for whom the small-scale industry policy in India was never intended have exploited it up to the hilt. Due to vagueness in defining the ownership aspect large companies promoted SSI units and reaped the financial reward. Some forty major companies such as Tata and Birla, and even multinationals such as GEC and Hindustan Lever, set up small companiese to take undue advantage of the legislation. Thus the policy to encourage and support the small business in India has become largely a farce and probably is best abandoned. After all, if our letter writer from the UK is right, those who succeed would succeed in any case, while those who fall by the wayside should never have set out in the first place.

Those who start up a small business should always be full of hope and confidence: here we turn to Japan. We have had a lot to say about the Japanese style of management and the way in which Japanese financial policy has given great support to Japanese companies, enabling them to expand and conquer so many markets, but now we meet the suggestion that perhaps we have all been brainwashed, and the Japanese economic miracle has an entirely different cause. Teresa Gorman exhorts us to look rather at the small business in Japan.[3] She says that the financial experts would like us to believe that Japan's success has been brought about by giant corporations, whose actions have been moulded and controlled by the higher wisdom of MITI, Japan's powerful Ministry of International Trade and Industry. This is not so, in her view. She asserts that Japan's miracle ingredient is a mixture of low taxation and an apparently chaotic mass of tiny companies. Throughout the 1950s and 1960s Japan adopted a deliberate policy of reducing tax, with the result that new companies were set up at the rate of nearly a million a year, capital investment increasing thereby at the rate of some 30 per cent per year. Now, it seems, Japan has the biggest self-employed and small-business sector of all the OECD nations. Even the Hondas, the Sonys and the Nissans began in a small way, through the efforts of one creative, innovative entrepreneur. Akio Morita and Masara Ibuka built Sony up from nothing, while Soichira Honda was a garage mechanic who attached a tiny motor to his bicycle, thus inventing the scooter. The authorities at the time gave him no encouragement whatever. Instead they told him it wouldn't work: it would not be possible to take along enough petrol to make it a feasible proposition. But Soichira Honda persevered, and we all know where his company stands today. So, concludes Teresa Gorman, 'the enterprise culture is Japan's strength, not any mysterious wisdom of its civil servants'. But let us come back to the UK and turn from the general to the particular, by looking at the history and experiences of one particular small business.

How it all began

We are going to look at a small company, Hermotronics Ltd, that found it a constant struggle to get finance and to establish its credibility in the marketplace.[4] Big business pays 'lip service' to the concept that small businesses are very desirable and that they will support them, but when it comes to exercising their purchasing power, they only consider their own financial advantage: nothing else. This was a lesson that Frank Harper-Jones and his three colleagues, seeking to set up a new business in high-technology electronics, learnt the hard way.

This little team of budding entrepreneurs first tried, without success, to effect a 'management buyout' of the company that employed them, Sintered Glass Products, part of the Sale Tinley Group until it was split off and sold in 1983. The company produced glass beads for miniature electric lamps, but it was losing money. Failing to buy up this 'going concern' our team next set up their own company, Hermotronics Ltd, of which Frank Harper-Jones, then fifty-three years old, was managing director. The objective was the manufacture of protective circuit boxes (called 'micropackages' in the trade) for microelectronic circuits. These 'gold-plated tins' protect circuits used in arduous conditions, such as inside missiles or under water. While the total market for this particular product in the UK was small, some £25 million a year at that point, it was growing fast and there was only one company in the UK manufacturing it, Marconi Osram Valve, and that company was selling almost exclusively to its parent GEC, Britain's major electronic and electrical manufacturing group. The rest of the market was supplied by import from either the US or the other members of the EEC. In this context Hermotronics should have had a signal advantage over its foreign competitor, since in this particular industry the customer works very closely with the supplier in order to ensure that the product, which is in effect 'custom built', is designed, manufactured and tested in accordance with its own specific requirements. Dr Peter Barnwell, a director of the Murray Electronics Venture Fund and non-executive chairman of the company, certainly seemed to think that it had a future. His reason:

> One of the basic problems of the UK electronics industry is that it does not have the infrastructure to support it.

Here was a little bit of that 'infrastructure' in prospect.

Disaster looms large

Hermotronics set up a factory at Slough, Berkshire, borrowing £453,000 to serve as equity, and also creating loan stock of £175,000.

But it quickly began to run out of funds, having grossly under-estimated the time that it would take the Ministry of Defence and the telecommunications companies who would use its product to evaluate it and place orders. It seems that, apart from any evaluation as such, potential customers were just not willing to take the risk of purchasing from a new and unknown supplier. An understandable attitude, but if maintained how can a new product ever get into the market? The company, first formed in April 1984, had spent £628,000 by September 1985 and was forced to raise another £500,000. This was done in the form of a 'rights issue' through the Business Expansion Scheme (BES). This involved some complex legal arrangements, since there were several hundred investors in BES, whose interests had to be protected. So far Hermotronics were following the classic route: there are any number of small companies who underestimate the funds they will require to carry on until they are in commercial production and the money starts to flow in. Just to illustrate this point, for it is so important, an article in the journal *Across the Board* had as its title the question: 'Why do so many small businesses flop?'[5] While it went on to add 'and some succeed', the examples it quotes are salutary. The case of Joe Atkins (presumably fictitious) bears directly upon the situation with Hermotronics. Joe saved US$25,000 and borrowed US$50,000 to set up a small ready-to-wear shop for men. The entire amount was spent on the store and its stock, so that on opening day his bank balance was US$2·60. He had not provided for working capital, was squeezed for cash and went bankrupt within six months. The writers of the article ask: 'Should not the lender have reviewed Joe's unrealistic costings and given him some sound advice?' Very possibly, but it is not always as easy as that. Coming back to Hermotronics and its particular problems, Peter Hyatt, a partner in Reville Russell the accountants, who helped Hermotronics organize the rights issue, is quoted as saying:[4]

> Naturally, start-ups have no track record. That makes many people cautious about asking for what they really need, with the result that they are under-funded some two years later.

The second round of financing helped bring Hermotronics back from the brink and immediate disaster was averted. The company troubles, both financial and technical, are beginning to recede, the product is steadily gaining acceptance and the future is beginning to look quite bright as we write (July 1986).

The company strategy

We have pointed out before the need for a corporate strategy and have laid great stress on the fact that while the development of a corporation plan will be a team effort by the top executives of a company, nevertheless the chief executive should take the lead and provide the inspiration. So important, we feel, is this aspect of company management to company success, that we devoted a whole chapter (corporate planning) to the subject when we examined the prediction, panacea and prevention of corporate failure.[6] Hermotronic had a plan. They proposed to persuade the large electronics companies to buy the Hermotronic package instead of the US equivalent and then go on to the development of a cheaper 'sealed in glass' device. You will remember that that was where its experience lay: in the manufacture of miniature glass items. Hermotronics was in fact successful in winning six prototype orders for its new product, but it realized that it had to begin by offering something that was already accepted and familiar. As Martin Perrin, the finance director, explains:

> If you launch straight into the market with a new company offering a new product, that really would be stretching it. So we decided to sell something that we knew people would already want so as to build up credibility.

There was keen interest in the company's products from the very beginning, but it took time to convert that interest into actual orders. No one rejected the product, but they were slow to order. As we have already seen, this delay disrupted the company's cash flow forecasts and a thin order book also meant that production costs were not as competitive as they could be once production had been built up. So in the beginning sales merely trickled in. In the first twelve months sales actually totalled £9,720, while costs totalled £123,570. The founders were 'strapped for cash', having put up a total of £50,000 for a 25 per cent share, but the influx of the further funding of course resulted in a reduction of their share. The primary lesson, we believe, is that the small business *can* succeed: but it will always be an uphill struggle, with much depending upon the enthusiasm and initiative of those who first set the business up and their having enough liquid cash to get over that initial hump.

Change your partner and thrive

Let us now take a very different case, from Finland. Valmet of Finland built lifts (elevators to our American readers) under licence from the Swiss lift manufacturer Schindler, who is second only to Otis, the leaders in the industry. We are going to look at Valmet's activities in the lift building industry, but lifts actually played a very small part in Valmet's activities, representing a bare 1·5 per cent of its turnover. Valmet is a state-owned metals and engineering group, seen by the Government primarily as a job provider, in accordance with the socialistic concepts prevailing in Finland. When advertising, the company claims to be a 'leading developer of reliable technology' and it consists of six operating groups:

Paper machinery.
Shipbuilding.
Automation.
Transportation equipment (which we assume includes lifts).
Tractors.
Defence equipment.

Valmet grew and prospered, but it became clear that its very survival in the lift business depended upon it being able to export and sell lifts outside Finland. The home market was just not big enough to sustain the operation. Finland, in terms of land area, is one of the largest countries in Europe, but her population is one of the smallest, with less than 5 million inhabitants. The basis of the Finnish economy is wood processing and the metal industries and the country had achieved high technological standards both in these industries and many others. This means that it has technological knowhow to export, and Valmet sought to do just that. However, its lift licensor Schindler would not allow this. No doubt it saw Valmet as a threat to its own activities elsewhere in Europe and particularly Scandinavia. But Valmet did not leave it there. It turned to the US–based world leader Otis who, it seems, was very pleased to make friends with the Finns. Otis is the largest lift manufacturer in the world and had a strong worldwide presence, operating in some 130 countries, but *not* in Scandinavia.

Now the fun begins

Valmet's desire to cooperate with Otis was helped by a change in government policy in Finland in 1980, whereby the state-owned companies were free to run on normal commercial lines, as were companies in the private sector. That is, profit was to be the top priority. One consequence of this change in policy was that the state-owned companies in Finland began to enjoy a great deal of independence: an independence which Valmet exercised to the full in its negotiations with Otis and the other companies who sought to play a role. Valmet's chief executive, Matti Kankaanpää played a key role in those negotiations: he was the 'doctor' who wrought the change.

Negotiations were opened with Otis in secret, and secrecy was maintained until the agreement was signed. When what was happening became public knowledge (in January 1986) another major engineering group in Finland manufacturing lifts, Kone, sought to intervene. Kone asked for a chance to make an offer or to collaborate. But Otis had included in its preliminary agreement with Valmet a clause banning them from having liaison talks with any of its competitors, Matti Kankaanpää refusing to entertain Kone's offer or to have any discussions whatever with them about it. Kone did not take this 'blank wall' lying down. The directors contacted Valmet's shareholders directly, as has now become almost standard practice in 'takeover raids', first in the US and now in the UK. Kone also enlisted the support of the Finnish Ministry of Trade and Industry, who had responsibility for practically all the state-owned industries in Finland. With their support Kone promptly put in an offer to Valmet, but Matti Kankaapää played for time. He did this by formally asking the advice of the Commission for Foreign Investments. Meanwhile Kone pushed ever harder, making two further offers, each successively more attractive to the Valmet shareholders. Valmet had a government-appointment supervisory board, but this was a political body, and while it might have viewed Kone's offer very favourably, it was not in a position to make a decision. The board had to refer it to Matti Kankaanpää and his co-directors, who had already refused to talk to Kone.

There are now a lot of similiarities between the 'Valmet affair' and the 'Westland affair' in the UK. In both cases there was an attractive American offer, seeking to cooperate with a locally-based company. With Westland the 'other party' was a European consortium, while with Valmet it was a local Finnish company. But, as in the UK, the majority of the Finnish politicians favoured the local company, two ministers who preferred the American deal having to resign over the issue. As with Westland, it was the management who preferred collaboration with the 'other' (Otis) and for much the same reason – it saw Otis as offering better long-term prospects. The directors of Valmet, led by Matti Kankaanpää, were sure that they could not find a better partner than Otis, but the subject became a controversial political football. However, after weeks of threats, meetings and continuing indecision, Matti Kankaanpää had his way and the American offer was accepted. It would seem that he played a very similar and firm role to Sir John Cuckney at Westland Helicopters and also seemed to adopt a very similar style. There were no heroic gestures: just quiet diplomacy, associated however, with a solid determination to do that which he thought best for the company.

The outcome

The end of the matter was that Otis acquired a controlling interest (70 per cent) in Valmet's lift business for some US$20 million and the company is now actively seeking not only to expand Valmet's share of the home market, currently some 30 per cent, but also get a similar share of the market in Norway, Sweden and Denmark, countries where Otis has but 3 per cent of the lift market. Not only has Otis acquired a local lift manufacturer but a strong local service and maintenance network, a very essential asset.

Of course, Kone had not been idle. Having lost out with Valmet, Kone has sought to consolidate its position by acquiring a number of lift-manufacturing concerns – in Italy, Germany and Canada. It felt that if it was not careful its strong Scandinavian base could be quickly eroded, now that its local competitor had all the strength of a world leader behind it. Till Valmet came along, Otis had to serve the Nordic market from its factories in the UK, France or Italy, but now its lifts can be built in Finland. If Otis is successful in achieving its declared objective, 30 per cent of the total Scandinavian market, lift manufacture at Valmet could climb to 1400 units a year, five times what it was in pre-Otis days. But it will have to face determined opposition, since Kone has said that it will not be adverse to selling lifts at a loss if the situation demands it. Then what happens? Well, Otis has countered by saying that it will sell lifts 'at any price' to meet its declared sales target of 30 per cent of the total market.[7] All very nice for those building blocks of flats and office blocks there! But now let us go to the other end of Europe and an entirely different field of endeavour, drug and fine chemicals manufacture.

A financially successful marriage, but . . .

There were two Swiss companies, J. R. Geigy and Ciba, who had been operating completely independently for more than fifty years, their factories being within a couple of kilometres of each other on the same side of the Rhine at Basel. These two companies merged together in 1970 and the story of that merger is most fascinating. It merits a book and a book has indeed been written about it.[8] Mike Hyde, in his foreword to the book, says:

> . . . a variety of events and circumstances . . . conspired to push both Ciba and Geigy simultaneously, albeit unwittingly, towards fusion. Paul Erni [the author] speaks of this as the 'upshot of a unique confluence' of the two companies' respective streams of development during the years immediately preceding the merger.
>
> If a merger . . . is to succeed then some kind of order must be imposed from the start. Ciba-Geigy are to be congratulated for having put theirs into effect as soon as possible . . . this is the only marriage of two large companies in which the new company can be seen to be operating with financial success within such a short period . . . Ciba-Geigy have weathered the recession crisis much better than many of their competitors . . . an example of the whole proving greater than the sum of its parts.

We have a word for that: synergy. But there were troubles, to which we shall come later, and during all this the company seems to have been 'lulled' to sleep for two long years. It had a few nightmares too, but hopefully all that is now behind them.

The historical background

Geigy was founded way back in 1788 by a chemist, Johan Geigy, who began by making dyewoods for the local silk industry. In the 1930s the company began to make agricultural chemicals, including the notorious DDT, which was a discovery of one of its chemists. He received the Nobel Prize for his discovery, but now one wonders. The royalties from DDT financed Geigy's drug research and in the late 1960s it achieved a breakthrough with the development of a corn herbicide, triazine, which had the most desirable characteristic of killing weeds without killing the crop.

Now Ciba. That company also began with a Basel dyehouse in 1856, but in time it too developed a wide range of fine chemical products, such as insecticides, synthetic resin and toiletries. Ciba sold on the international market much more widely than Geigy, although it was less profitable. Perhaps its lower profits were due in part to the one-man rule of its ageing chairman, Robert Käppeli. Talks about a 'marriage' between the companies began in the late 1960s, culminating in a merger in 1970. But then the troubles began. The management boards and the executive committees of the two companies were lumped together, with the result that they became large and cumbersome and could seldom reach consensus. This had repercussions at all levels, with the staff remaining loyal to their own old company and its traditions.

Troubles never come singly

The company's patent on their Triazine herbicide, which had been its biggest money-spinner in the US, expired in the mid-1970s and a number of other companies started to offer the product at very competitive prices. A new and better herbicide, Dual, came along too late to stem the fall in sales. At the same time its dyestuffs started to lose money and then, in 1978, the company was faced with the biggest drug liability case ever. This arose in Japan and related to its product, *Entero-Viaform*, sold as a cure for diarrhoea. The drug was alleged to cause a disease of the spinal and optic nerves called subacute myelo-optic neuropathy (SMON). Some 11,000 Japanese fell victim to this disease, with many being paralysed or blinded. The Japanese Government banned the drug in 1970 and over 7400 victims sued the company, which, however, asserted that its drug could not have been the actual cause of the trouble. However, during a trial that lasted eight years it could not come up with any other cause and had finally to pay some US$200 million in settlement of the claims that had been lodged against it.

Following the ban in Japan, the company would have been wise to have withdrawn the product elsewhere, but it did not, despite demands for this from doctors and consumer groups. The company's response was to caution (on the label) against excessive dosage. However, the warning was not always heeded, since cases of SMON were reported in Australia, Britain and even the company's home country Switzerland. Nine more countries then banned the drug, with Swedish doctors boycotting it after forty-two cases had been reported in their country. Ciba-Geigy settled all these cases out of court but it did not finally phase out the drug until 1982.

Somebody, somewhere was very short-sighted, for the company's 'image' suffered severely. And not only its image, but its profits.

Change by consensus

Since the merger an ex-Geigy executive, Samuel Koechlin, had been chairman of the company, but he had to retire because of ill-health and Albert Bodmer took over. He was the first chemist ever to become a chief executive and he operated by seeking consensus. In this, of course, either consciously or unconsciously he was imitating the Japanese style of management, and it proved successful. The executive committee was first called upon to answer a series of questions:

Are we too much of a gentlemen's club?
Are we too slow at the top?
Are we too kind to each other?

   It decided (collectively) that the answer to all these questions was 'yes', so it then went on to do something about it, still in collective fashion. In late 1980 forty executives met at an old country house outside Basel for further heart searching and decided that they had too many employees, that they had been 'gypping' the share-holders, that they had to centralize their strategic planning and that they must increase profits to US$250 million by the end of 1983.[9] For the more curious of our readers, we would advise that a 'gyppy' is an Egyptian soldier, so that a 'gyppy tummy' is the diarrhoea that tends to afflict visitors to hot countries. It seems that these executives still had their late product for the cure of diarrhoea very much on their minds, to liken their treatment of their shareholders to that.

   So the purge began. To set an example to the company worldwide, 600 jobs were axed at Basel and there were cuts in manpower and inventories everywhere. It became the craze. Personnel that left were not replaced – new hiring was frozen – and three unprofitable products, with annual sales of some US$100 million, were sold off. Dyestuffs, now largely unprofitable, were cut back. Albert Bodmer, now firmly in the saddle, was simple and straight about it, saying: 'We saw that no new fibres would be developed this century, so no new dyestuffs would be needed.' But notice that he began with 'we': this was change by consensus. One should also note the simplicity of the statement: yet it was firm and bold. The photographic division at

Ilford in the UK was another loser: some US$250 million had been lost during those 'sleepy' years. So 2000 staff went at Ilford, and the division broke even. Pharmaceuticals seem to be a problem that may well persist, with a complete lack of new products to stimulate the market. Henri Schramak, a board member, comments:

> Because we had most merger troubles in pharmaceuticals, and people fought each other instead of working together ten years ago, we're now in the middle of a 'new product' gap, which we recognize will be with us for quite some time.

Consensus still prevails. This time it is not Albert Bodmer, but Henri Schramak who tells us what is going on. The development of a new pharmaceutical product takes a very long time. It can be five years at least before the laboratory discovery appears for trials, and then it has to be accepted by the appropriate authorities before it can be placed on the market, a process that in its turn can also take years. So Ciba-Geigy will have to live with its present portfolio, unless it can license from others. Nevertheless it has quite a commanding share of the market in pharmaceuticals, having a 5 per cent share of the beta-blocker market for hypertension (second only to ICI); a 15 per cent share of the world market in arthritic medicines (second only to Merck) and is the leader in the drugs for the control of depression and epilepsy.

What is more, Ciba-Geigy is exploring new fields: it is researching in biotechnology and thinking of developing into electronic equipment. The company currently has 150 scientists working on gene splicing and hoping to come up with new and cheaper drugs, and plant strains that are less dependent upon agricultural chemicals for rapid growth and protection from disease. The turnaround strategy has succeeded, as can be seen from the data in Table 14. Profits have doubled in the two years from 1980 to 1982, in stark contrast to companies in the same field. Dupont profits dropped by 44 per cent, Hoechst by 43 per cent and Bayer by 78 per cent over the same period. While Ciba-Geigy's earnings on sales are low when compared with other drug manufacturers, they are above average when compared with the generality of European chemical manufacturers.

In 1984 Ciba-Geigy broke its own personal 'billion barrier' by turning in after-tax income of SFr1·2 billion. On the basis of its 1984 results Ciba-Geigy, when compared with other chemicals manufacturers worldwide, registered the most improvement over the

Table 14   *The Ciba-Geigy results. This data lets us see the way in which earnings grew from year to year once decisive action was taken. Of special significance is the increasing return on sales*

Year	Sales	Earnings	Earnings as a percentage of sales
	US$ million	US$ million	%
1978	5541	223	4.0
1979	6209	205	3.3
1980	6693	171	2.6
1981	7618	292	3.8
1982	6887	310	4.5
1983	6762	356	5.3
1984	6721	457	6.8
1985	8854	715	8.1

Source: Chemical Insight.

previous year. Its sale of the Airwick Group brought it SFr500 million, which in all probability will be used to further its research into biotechnology. It appears that 1985 was another record year and 1986 may well prove the best yet, since due to its very strong financial position Ciba-Geigy was able to finance more than 80 per cent of its cash requirements from its internal resources. All in all, consensus is seen to work. While our objective has been to seek out the 'doctor', with a view to seeing how he achieves his dramatic results, here we see equally solid results being achieved by a committee, through consensus. Our earlier case studies in this chapter, from the UK and from Finland, brought us much the same lesson, in that no dominant figure emerged while the turnaround was accomplished. Yet in each case the turnaround *was* accomplished – most successfully.

Summary

The future is always uncertain and with Ciba-Geigy it is likely to be very uncertain, despite its successful turnaround. Much depends upon whether the present momentum can be maintained. If it falls asleep once again it will be lost. The merger, the drug that sent it to sleep, offers us a classic illustration of the old saying, that while mergers will always result in bigger companies, they do not necessarily result in a *better* company. Fortunately for Ciba-Geigy the very managers who dozed off, when awoken by a loss, much as that dormant giant General Motors was (Chapter 9) also resolved the crisis. The 'doctor' – in this case, 'doctors' – came from within.

References

1   Letter to the Editor in *Economist*, no. 288, 13 August 1983, p. 6.
2   Goyal, S. K., Chalapati Rao, K. S. and Kumer, N., *The Small Sector and Big Business*, Indian Institute of Public Administration, 1983.
3   Gorman, T., 'The Japan giant's small beginnings', *Today*, 17 July 1986, p. 16.
4   Dawkins, W., 'A struggle for credibility', *Financial Times*, 17 December 1985, p. 10.
5   Burr, P. L. and Heckmann, R. J., 'Why do so many businesses flop?', *Across the Board*, no. 16, 1979, pp. 46–8.
6   Kharbanda, O. P. and Stallworthy, E. A., *Corporate Failure: Prediction, Panacea and Prevention*, McGraw-Hill, 1985.
7   Virtanen, Ollo, 'Ups and downs of a Finnish takeover', *Financial Times*, 25 March 1986, p. 24.
8   Erni, P., *The Basel Marriage – History of the Ciba-Geigy Merger*, Neue Zürcher Zeitung, 1979.
9   Kinhead, G., 'Ciba-Geigy's big sleep is over', *Fortune*, no. 108, 11 July 1983, p. 92.

16 Getting back on track

Volkswagenwerk AG of Wolfsburg, West Germany, has a most remarkable history. Surprisingly enough, it is actually the youngest of the European car manufacturers, being brought to life in 1934. That first factory was designed to produce a 'people's car', the brainchild of Dr Ferdinand Porsche.[1] Production of this car was restarted after the Second World War and it became known in the popular jargon as the *Beetle*. In all some 21 million were sold worldwide before production ceased at Wolfsburg. The *Beetle* has now been replaced by the *Golf*. This is currently Volkswagen's best-selling car and the core of its business. Launched as the successor to the long-running *Beetle*, the company's fate hung on the reception accorded the new car in the market when it was launched in 1974. Results have more than lived up to expectations and it is probable that the *Golf* will be on the market as long as the *Beetle* although like the *Beetle* it will be subject to modification over the years. The first *Golf* sold more than 6 million before a new version came on the market in 1983. This model has already sold more than a million and was Europe's best-selling car for the next two years. In West Germany itself the *Golf* has been that country's best-selling model ever since it came on the market.[2]

This sounds very much like a success story and indeed it is, but Volkswagen has nevertheless been 'in the red' twice in its history: first in 1974 in the wake of the energy crisis and again some ten years later, over the years 1984–5. The manner in which disaster was averted is not only interesting in itself, but carries very significant lessons for management, particularly when operating in a volatile market. At each crisis there was a change of chairman and it is his actions that we wish to study. It should be noted that these losses were incurred despite the fact that sales were maintained, as illustrated in Figure 14. How did this come about?

The cloudy 1970s

The sharp rise in fuel costs that resulted from what has become

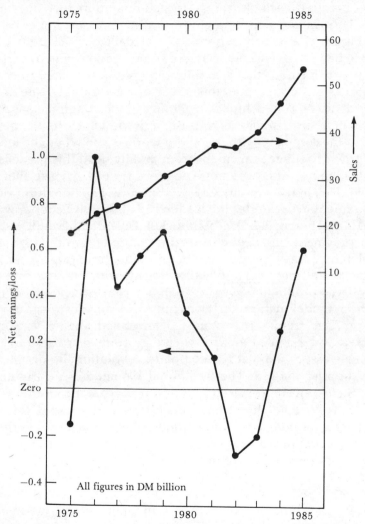

Figure 14 *From loss to profit. These two graphs illustrate that whilst sales maintained their momentum, profits have fluctuated dramatically.*
Source: Company accounts.

known as the 'oil crisis' brought problems to many industries and the car industry, as one might expect, felt its impact more severely than most. Volkswagen were not immune and suffered heavy losses over two years, as indicated in Figure 14. In 1974 Volkswagen suffered a loss of some US$300 million on worldwide sales of US$6·6 billion. Then Toni Schmücker took over as chairman – and 'doctor' – and achieved a most remarkable turnaround. Within two years profits bounced back, reaching US$400 million in 1976 on sales of nearly US$9 billion. The momentum was maintained, as can be seen from Figure 14 and Toni Schmücker was hailed as the 'hero' of the day. He had achieved a net swing of some US$600 million, a change in company fortunes that was fully reflected in the share prices.

There is no doubt that this reversal was entirely due to the stewardship of Toni Schmücker. He was indeed a miracle worker, but his greatness is best seen in the attitude which he adopted to those in the company with whom he worked and whom he led. He gave praise to the management team and its head, his predecessor Rudolf Leiding. This was not a matter of words, praise that was hollow. The praise was indeed well-deserved. The efforts of the management team, under the leadership of Rudolf Leiding, were a sound base upon which Toni Schmücker could build. Rudolf Leiding was a pragmatic engineer and during his brief tenure (1971–4) he completed a crash programme to replace the dying *Beetle*. The change was effected very speedily indeed, with the result that the Volkswagen production line was changed from a 'thirties model' to a 'seventies model' at a stroke. It was not only a drastic change in form, but a change from a rear-mounted air-cooled engine to a front-mounted water-cooled engine, a change from rear drive to front drive, all associated with a complete revolution in design and production techniques. The traditional VW models, nearly half of them *Beetles*, were replaced within five years by entirely new models. This could never have been achieved without the solid engineering foundation laid by Rudolf Leiding. The changes that he made were so drastic and so complete that one VW veteran in the company was moved to comment:

> The only thing left standing in the plants were the walls.

These new models were the foundation upon which Toni Schmücker could and did build, achieving ever-mounting sales and profits.

However, while Rudolf Leiding and his team, working round the clock, transformed the factory, he could not transform the men. The attitude of the union officials proved his undoing. Through the works councils and supervisory boards they exerted considerable influence and would not listen to his pleas for wage restraint. He actually wrote a personal letter to each employee at home on the subject, but this attempt to bypass the officials was much resented and he finally had to leave. He was replaced, as we have said, by Toni Schmücker, who had already demonstrated that he was a very effective troubleshooter and was a car industry veteran, having had over twenty-five years experience with Ford at its Cologne Works. Starting there as an apprentice, he rose to be head of purchasing, and finally director of sales and marketing before leaving to go to Rheinstahl in 1968.

Rheinstahl, when Toni Schmücker went there, was an ailing steel and machinery company, but he achieved a turnaround by persuading the unions to accept the closure of the loss-making operations and the consequent loss of jobs. Having achieved this turnaround, Toni Schmücker led Rheinstahl into a merger with August-Thyssen–Hütte, Germany's largest steelmaker, joining their board. It was at this point in his career that he was persuaded to come to the rescue of Volkswagen. He did not come easily, once he saw the situation with which he would have to cope: no liquidity and too many people working in the plant. But VW was an industry giant, employing some 200,000 people, and he saw it as a challenge which he agreed to take up. He arrived at Wolfsburg alone, without wife, secretary or dog![3]

The 'doctor' clears the clouds

Toni Schmücker saw as his first task the accomplishment of that which Rudolf Leiding had striven after but had failed to do: the drastic reduction of the workforce. He got his way, reducing the workforce by some 25,000 to bring it into line with output. He was involved in agonizing negotiations, but by offering substantial redundancy payments (which the company could hardly afford but would prove cheaper in the long run) he got his way. As had been demonstrated under the leadership of Rudolf Leiding, there were plenty of able people in management, who were drawn in by Toni Schmücker with words of exhortation such as 'You're my team and we are going to do this together'. He was able to inspire them as much by example as anything, since he devoted his entire time to his work. He stayed on the job alone throughout the week, only going home to his wife in Essen at weekends.

It is manifest that the major problem before him was that of man management. This problem was intensified by the fact that the way his predecessors had left things gave the impression that it was the Metalworkers Union and the Social Democrats who actually ran Volkswagen. But Toni Schmücker had developed the knack of getting along with the unions, despite the fact that it was said of him that while he listened to what they had to say, he nevertheless did what *he* wanted to do. In fact, such an attitude must always be seen in good management and effective managers. The manager is there to manage, so his *must* be the final decision. He must have been a really persuasive character, since not only did he get the unions to agree to substantial reductions in the workforce at Wolfsburg but also, eventually, to the setting up of a production facility in the US. He achieved his ends by establishing a cooperative relationship with the workers and their unions on the basis of a 'do or die' philosophy that has worked so often. You will remember Chrysler, whose story we told in Chapter 10, and British Leyland in Chapter 12.

This was well demonstrated by the fact that on one occasion a senior union official, Loderer, chaired a shareholders' meeting on one occasion in the absence of the chairman, Hans Birnbaum, who was taken ill. When questioned about this Toni Schmücker made his attitude very clear, saying:

> Herr Loderer is the deputy chairman and that's what a deputy is for. We have no reason to try and hide him. After all the workers are as much a part of this company as the stockholders.

We have had Toni Schmücker described to us. He is said to be cool and poised, always immaculately dressed and excellent in communicating his ideas to others. He prefers to talk 'face to face' rather than write memos. He does this because 'he wants to hear how you sound' – see the gestures, listen to the tone of voice. These are essential aspects of good communication. The one imparting the information should know how it is received – indeed, *whether* it is received. In writing about project management we devoted a whole chapter to this one aspect, so important did we feel it to be. That chapter was headed 'The project manager really must listen' – the manager must be both communicator and receiver.[4] To be a good receiver he must *listen* – listening, it seems, while vital, is terribly difficult for most people. But not for Toni Schmücker.

Getting results

Instead of striving for volume and market share, Toni Schmücker encouraged his team to go 'up market' as they say, for profits. The models available were increased in variety, and quality was maintained at an extremely high standard. Thus the selling price per unit went up, and by 1978, while the output was about the same as in 1971 (some 2·3 million per year), the sales grossed US$13·3 billion, nearly three times the value of sales in 1971, an increase far in excess of inflation. By 1979 its range extended from the low-priced *Polo*, through various *Golf* models to the *Audi* range, which was intruding upon what is known as *Mercedes* country. Diesel engines were introduced in 1976 and these have been a particular source of strength in the market for Volkswagen, continuing its reputation for reliability and ruggedness.

Despite the remarkable change that had been achieved, the profits were still not there. The return on sales was only just over 2 per cent, whereas General Motors was making more than 5 per cent. So Toni Schmücker introduced more rigorous systems for cost control, including strict budgeting procedures. The progress made over the years is illustrated graphically in Figure 15. We can imagine the pleasure that one can get from results of this sort. Indeed, Toni Schmücker was said to have so completely identified himself with VW, and was so happy in his work, that he could not envisage anything 'after VW'. Yet, despite his success, his reign came to an end, as such reigns always must. Yet the 'show' went on.

The second crisis at VW

We have always maintained that troubles never come overnight. There are always 'early warning signals', there to be looked for: signals which if ignored will inevitably lead to disaster. Just as VW (and Toni Schmücker) was 'riding high' it encountered two major problems, both of which were of its own making. As part of its diversification policy Volkswagen bought Triumph-Adler in 1978. This West German company, a major manufacturer of office equipment, was a continuing burden from the time it was acquired. It has incurred losses year after year.

The second problem was in connection with the US plant at Westmoreland in Pennsylvania. This factory was opened in 1978 as

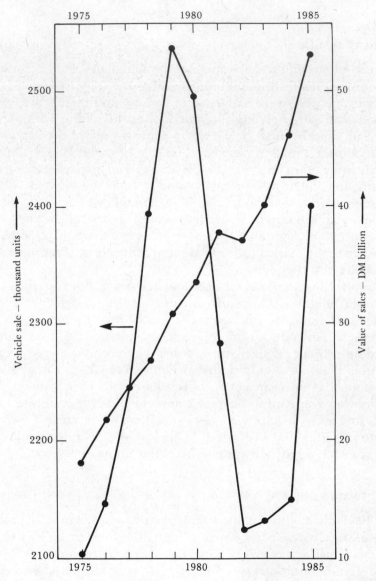

Figure 15 *Sales in DM and vehicles. These graphs demonstrate the continuing growth of the company worldwide. Notice the way in which the value of sales has been maintained, despite quite wide fluctuations in the volume of sales.*
Source: Company accounts.

part of Toni Schmücker's strategy, but was beset with very serious quality problems. For instance, in 1983 some million cars (the *Rabbit*, the name first given to the *Golf* in the US) had to be recalled. [3] The loss of its reputation for reliability caused sales to collapse in the US and it had yet to get back to its pre-1983 level. Strangely, this recall of the *Rabbit* coincided with a growing preference among Americans for European cars made in Europe, probably because they had more confidence in the quality of an overseas product. The end result of these adverse circumstances was another collapse in profits, in 1982, as illustrated in Figure 14, demanding a radical review of the situation and a change in strategy. Since there was a major problem in the US market it seemed appropriate to recall Carl Hahn, who had an intimate knowledge of the American market, having headed the US company from 1959 to 1964. He left Volkswagen in 1972 to head a West German tyre company, but he responded to the call and returned to the fold. On his return, investigating the situation in the US, he was appalled at the poor quality of the cars being produced there. It *looked* like a VW, but that was about all that could be said for it. To quote Carl Hahn:[2]

> I can't describe how it felt to drive a car that looked like a *VW* on the outside but didn't feel like a *VW* on the inside. In its driving behaviour it wasn't a *VW* any more.

We have assessed the 'miracle' of one 'doctor', succeeding where his predecesors had failed. He achieved a turnaround, but it seems it could not be sustained – or perhaps he lost his 'magic touch' in the course of time. He was chief executive for six years from 1975 to 1981. We have a theory that the best man to bring about a turnaround is not necessarily the best man to run the company once turnaround has been achieved. It seems to us that the qualities called for to bring about a turnaround, such as a degree of ruthlessness, are not necessarily the dominant qualities called for in continuing operation. However that may be, the situation was resolved by the fact that Toni Schmücker had a heart attack on 11 June 1981 and while he recovered he did not feel able to take up his duties once more. In view of the specific problem facing the company at that time, with the US company, Hahn was very evidently a natural choice.

One 'doctor' replaces another

It is interesting to note that Carl Hahn, like Toni Schmücker, came with a reputation as a 'doctor'. Having joined Continental Tyre of Hanover, he brought a great change there, described as transforming it 'from a purely German concern to a European force in the industry.[5] Having arrived at Volkswagen, he certainly conformed to pattern. Within nine months of his joining the company once again, Hahn had brought a great change in the product in the US. He cleared out all the gimmicks, such as simulated wood veneer trim on the dashboard, colour-coordinated interiors, plush carpeting and an excess of chrome trim. He went 'back to basics', as it were, seeking to elevate good engineering and quality production above all else. He even got rid of the name *Rabbit*, replacing it with the name *Golf*, which meanwhile had gained worldwide acceptance. There was by then a 'Golf' cult, just as previously there had been a 'Beetle' cult. Hahn took over as chairman of the Volkswagen Group in 1982 and by 1984 sales of the *Golf* had grown to 177,000 units a year, from the previous level of 156,000 units, and sales continue to grow. Confidence has been restored in the product in the American market, thanks to Hahn's 'doctoring' and Americans have come to love VW engineering. The profitability of the US operation has been further improved by substantial imports of German-built models, chiefly serving the higher end of the market. For instance, while the Audi *Quattro* series accounts for only 20 per cent of US sales, it contributes to about a third of the profits, since an *Audi* brings in nearly 50 per cent more profit per car than does the *Golf*. The interlacing network of sales of cars and the provision of parts is illustrated in Figure 16 and it will be seen that apart from Wolfsburg and Westmoreland, the other major factory is located in Brazil, in line with the current pattern of globalization in car manufacture.

While the problems in the US market were the most significant, they were not the only sources of loss in the group. There were also losses in Latin America. In 1979 Volkswagen had more than 50 per cent of the market there, but as a consequence of hyper-inflation and the clamping on of severe credit controls, the car market collapsed almost overnight. As a result Volkswagen lost some US$12 million in Brazil in 1983, and a further US$93 million in Mexico. Sales in Brazil were halved.

At the same time there were problems at home. There was a metalworkers' strike in South Germany, which could not have come at a worse time. Volkswagen is largely self-sufficient, but it does purchase certain items from outside suppliers. As a result of the strike the production lines at Wolfsburg came to a halt for some six weeks in 1984, due to a lack of but six parts. This cost Volkswagen some 160,000 cars and cut back its profits very severely. Nevertheless, under the guidance of Carl Hahn the company has ridden

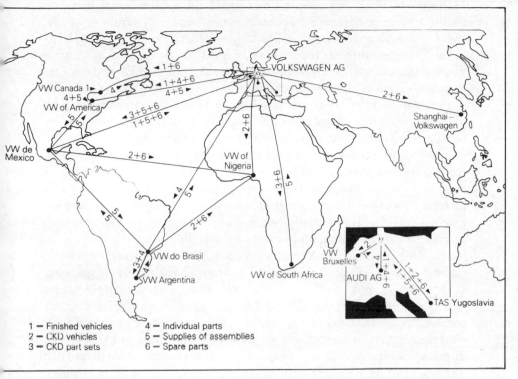

Figure 16   *Companies within the Volkswagen Group. This chart presents the worldwide interlinked supply system developed by Volkswagen. (Reproduced by permission of Volkswagen AG, Wolfsburg.)*

out the storm and is now fully recovered. The 'doctor's medicine' has worked!

Carl Hahn, the man

It would appear that an intimate knowledge of the industry is a substantial help when seeking to accomplish a turnaround. There are many cases where the 'doctor' has been new to the industry – Sir Michael Edwardes, who brought about the turnaround at British Leyland, is a case in point – but Carl Hahn was certainly asked to take command because of his past experience. In his case, that experience was almost exclusively within the car industry and included specialist knowledge of the American car market – and it was that market that had been one of the major problems for Volkswagen.

Born on 1 July 1926, he had cars in his blood. His father, also Carl

Hahn, was head of sales with Auto Union, a famous German manufacturer of cars and motorcycles that was later renamed Audi. Having taken a doctorate at Bern in Switzerland, he wrote at his father's suggestion to the chairman of Volkswagen in 1954 proposing the standardization of car parts. As a result he became the chairman's protege and by 1959 was chief executive of the US sales organization. However, having been twice passed over for promotion to the top job he left the company in 1972, only to be called back ten years later to take on the job he had coveted.[6]

It is indicative of his methods that he took the trouble to involve the workers at Wolfsburg in the planning and design of Halle 54, a fully automated assembly line. The application of automation has indeed made a great contribution, since it brings competitive pricing. Halle 54 has actually become a showpiece, with electric cars ferrying visitors down wide aisles to watch an army of robots at work. One great advantage of the robot is its continuing flexibility, since it can be adjusted to handle any model with equal speed and skill. Some 25 per cent of the final assembly is now carried out by robots of various types, cutting the time required to build a car by some 20 per cent. Cars go through Halle 54 at the rate of 3200 a day.

Manufacture in the US is, however, a different story. Hahn's approach to the problem over there has been to reinforce sales with imports. But imports are very susceptible to a fluctuating exchange rate, which has ranged from 4·2 to 1·7 DM to the US dollar. Hahn therefore sees the US manufacturing facility as a means of keeping 'his foot in the door . . . an insurance premium for tomorrow'.[7] Hahn not only has the advantage of knowing the American market intimately, but also that of having seen Volkswagen from the outside – twice! The company has certainly come a long way under his stewardship, but he is by no means resting on his laurels. To quote him once again:[8]

> Easy success comes only in the movies. . . . We haven't begun to realize our potential. Our competitive edge is our German engineering tradition. . . . We tended to bury that in the past by trying to bend to what we guessed local tastes wanted. A VW has to stand out for technically advanced transportation. . . .

There is no doubt that the quality of the engineering has been a great selling point for VW from the very beginning: reliability was the outstanding feature of the *Beetle* long before the Japanese really appeared on the European market. In the course of a discussion on the impact of the speed limit in various countries – there is none in West Germany, while in Japan the restrictions are severe – Hahn was quoted as saying (freely translated from French) that while Europeans, and particularly the Germans, are always concerned with performance, the Japanese concern themselves with the price and these are two very different attitudes. And when it comes to price, of course, the Japanese certainly 'have the edge', taking 13 per cent of sales in West Germany itself.

Hahn's wide experience outside West Germany and his fluency in several languages – he speaks English, French and Italian with nearly native ease – have contributed substantially to his appreciation as to what his customers are really looking for. This fluency has no doubt also contributed to the wide personal coverage that has been given to him in the technical press not only in his home country, West Germany, but also in France, Switzerland, South Africa, the US and the UK. [9, 10, 11, 12, 13]

The world as a market

Typical of Hahn's approach to marketing worldwide is, we feel, his comment on production in China:[7]

> China is nothing, it's six vehicles a day, but we consider it the most important project we have undertaken. It's like trading for Manhattan from the Indians. It's good when you're there at the beginning.

The company now builds substantially more than two million cars a year, two-thirds in West Germany and the rest abroad. The sales pattern is the converse of this, since only one third of its output is sold in the home country. There is no doubt that the *Golf*, launched in 1974 as a successor to the *Beetle*, has made a major contribution to the company's survival and revival. The first version sold over six million worldwide, while a new version, launched in June 1983, has sustained the success to such an extent that Volkswagen is now beginning to advertise the *Golf* as the successor to the *Beetle*. The *Beetle* became an ambassador for the 'Made in Germany' tag and was more than just a product. Indeed, it became a tradition. Beginning as the 'people's car' in its home country, it took on that role worldwide. It became so well-loved in the US as a second car that it often turned into the first car: it became a film star as Herbie the crazy Beetle: a car with a soul, with wit and intelligence. Company policy with respect to the *Golf* aims to have that model echo the Beetle history.

Volkswagen will stick to the tradition in that respect by making styling changes only rarely, but nevertheless new features will be introduced from year to year that improve the car's performance and keep the buyers interested. At the 51st International Automobile Exhibition in Frankfurt Volkswagen displayed the 16-valve engine for the *Golf*. This gives excellent acceleration coupled with low fuel consumption and exhaust emission. Another innovation is the *Golf* syncro – the first time an all-wheel drive has been made available on a saloon designed for large series production.[14]

Volkswagen seems to be doing extremely well almost everywhere except in its home market. Even in Italy, the home of Fiat, the company managed to surpass Fiat sales. During 1985 sales in the US rose by 25 per cent and profits doubled. In Spain, a most difficult market because of the tariff barriers, *Audi* sales nearly doubled in that same year, largely because of the partnership the company has formed with Spain's largest car manufacturer Seat (pronounced *Say-at*). Volkswagen stepped into the gap left when Fiat pulled out of its thirty-year relationship with this state-controlled Spanish group in 1980. Seat has lost money steadily for many years, accumulated losses since 1978 exceeding £800 million, and this despite the exceptionally creative accounting normally used in Spain to 'prop up' the balance sheet. Fiat pulled out because it was being asked to pump more money into Seat but so far Volkswagen has limited its assistance to technical help on the production lines, in quality control and purchasing. To achieve this some 200 VW engineers have come to know the Spanish company and its systems well enough and have helped Seat to set up its own distribution network throughout Europe. Seat in return has opened up the Spanish market to VW by putting the German group's cars on sale in Spain through the Seat distribution chain. It is also building VW Polos, Santana and Passat models under licence. Seat's production is expected to rise steadily to some 400,000 cars a year, of which some two-thirds will carry the brand name Seat, with the rest branded as VWs, all for sale both in Spain and Europe. It is anticipated that there will be a joint German–Spanish management. While Hahn is enthusiastic about this new acquisition he tempers his enthusiasm with a note of caution:[15]

> We have bitten off a great deal. Now we must chew it . . . consolid-
> ation with expansion. . . . Once we have entered a venture as big as
> this it might be an idea to forego other opportunities, however golden
> they might seem. We don't want to overstretch ourselves.

This is very sound advice – and not only for Volkswagen! We should all be listening. It seems that Volkswagen had learnt from its past experiences and the mistakes that have been made. Typical of Volkswagen 'overstretching' itself was its acquisition of Triumph-Adler in 1978. Having tried hard to nurse that company back to health, Volkswagen seems to have at long last given up the struggle. The company has now been sold to Europe's leading office automation company, Olivetti.[16] This should be to its mutual benefit, since Volkswagen will be able to concentrate on its main interest, car manufacture, while Olivetti will be consolidating its position in the European market, since Triumph-Adler is said to have some 30 per cent of the German market, 15 per cent of the US market, and 14 per cent of the office machine market worldwide.

Volkswagen is also entering into collaboration agreements with car manufacturers in China and Japan. Under a twenty-five year agreement signed with China, Volkswagen is to set up a modern car manufacturing plant in China designed to manufacture 100,000 *Santana* cars a year by 1989. Under a licence agreement with Nissan,

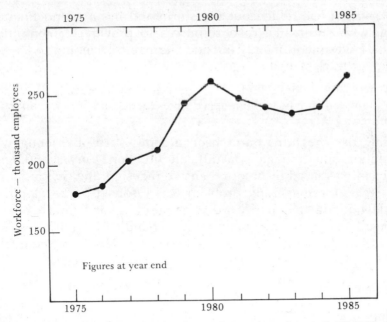

Figure 17   *The growth in the VW workforce. There was steady growth till 1980. After three years in decline, growth is now accelerating once again: from 3 per cent in 1984 to 9 per cent in 1985.*
Source: Company accounts.

the Volkswagen *Santana* will also be manufactured in Japan. On the other hand, Latin America remains a headache. The company has suffered as a consequence of the serious national financial and debt repayment problems of both Brazil and Mexico. While Volkswagen has a 40 per cent share of the Brazilian market, it may well take more than a decade for sales to recover to the million a year that were being sold in the early 1980s. While its Brazilian subsidiary has increased sales in 1985 and the workforce grew by some 27 per cent, the company still failed to make a profit. Volkswagen Argentina almost maintained its share of the passenger car market in that country, but Volkswagen de Mexico saw a slackening of sales in the second half of 1985.[14] However, all in all Volkswagen is in excellent health. Whereas many other car manufacturers have surplus capacity and surplus workers, Volkswagen is fully utilizing its capacity and is taking on extra workers to keep up with demand. Figure 17 illustrates the trend.

Summary

Volkswagen has ridden out the storm and has a sound financial base, with substantial cash resources to provide for continuing capital investment, mainly outside Germany. Listening to Dr Carl Hahn for the last time:[17]

> We feel, after a turnaround, we are now heading in the right direction with modern products, high-speed investments and an international linkage.

How has the turnaround been accomplished? By acting with resolution and courage in a difficult situation. The technological problem was faced by comprehensive redesign, the *Golf* replacing the *Beetle*, the marketing problem was resolved by developing a worldwide strategy – notice the exchange of cars and parts to be seen in Figure 16 – while overmanning was handled with firmness and resolution. Above all, the 'doctors' had vision. First Toni Schmücker and then Dr Carl Hahn knew precisely what they needed – and got it.

References

1   'It began back in 1934', Volkswagenwerk AG, November 1983.
2   DeMott, John S., 'Volkswagen is back on track', *Time*, 21 October 1985, p. 56.

3   Ball, R., 'Volkswagen hops a Rabbit back to prosperity',*Fortune*, no. 100, 13 August 1979, pp. 120–4 and 127–8.

4   Stallworthy, E. A., and Kharbanda, O. P., *Total Project Management*, Gower, 1983.

5   'Can Volkswagen regain its magic touch?', *Business Week*, 6 August 1984, pp. 50–3 and 56.

6   'Face to Face: Dr Carl Hahn of Volkswagen', *European Motor Business*, November 1985, pp. 1–11.

7   Brady, R., 'You will see more to come', *Forbes*, 28 January 1985.

8   Richman, L. S., 'Volkswagen regains some Beetle magic', *Fortune*, no. 113, 31 March 1986, pp. 30–3.

9   Wilkins, G., 'Carl Hahn of Volkswagen', *Car*, January 1985.

10 Seidler, E, 'Profitable Association', *Autocar*, 14 May 1986, pp. 57–9.

11 Guerithault, G., 'Une interview exclusive – Carl Hahn, le president de Volkswagen', *L'Auto-Journal*, 9 May 1986.

12 Rehsche, M., 'Technischer Fortschritt erschliesst neue Märkte', *Finanz und Wirtshaft*, 8 March 1986.

13 'Nationale "Eigenbröteleien" schädigen auch die Autokäufer', *Auto Motor und Zubehör*, 1 February 1986.

14 Annual Report, 1985, from the Supervisory Board and Board of Management of Volkswagen Aktiengesellschaft, May 1986.

15 Gooding, K., 'Volkswagen takes a rough Spanish road', *Financial Times*, 21 April 1986.

16 Friedman, A., 'VW to sell Triumph-Adler to Olivetti', *Financial Times*, 23 April 1986.

17 Gooding, K., 'How VW uses the world as its market', *Financial Times*, 7 March 1985.

Part Five

Working for success

17 The 'doctor' does it!

We have now gone through a number of case studies, from all parts of the world. We found company 'doctors' busy everywhere that we have looked: in the US, in several countries in Western Europe, in India and the Far East. We have even found the English and the Swedes succeeding in Japan, and an American in Britain. We have also seen that companies of any size may need a 'doctor', even the greatest of them. Did not what is possibly the largest company in the world, General Motors, make a loss and need a 'doctor' to pull the company round? Fortunately, that particular company found its 'doctor' in-house, but in most cases he had to be called in from outside. We are sure, too, that a similar sort of task is being performed with success in the many countries that we have not had the time nor the space to look at, for it is our view that the 'situation brings the man'. While it is true that all our 'doctors', so far, have been men, it is something that women can do and have done. There is the notable instance of Cathie Black, who joined the new magazine *USA Today* after succeeding in turning the magazine *New York* from loss to profit in just a few years. She seems to thrive on such a challenge, saying: 'I like dicey situations . . . I like startups and the new things and turnabouts'. Under her guidance the circulation of the monthly *USA Today*, which started at around 200,000 increased seven-fold in less than two years. The comment of those that deal with her is: 'Her orientation is on what she has that meets your needs rather than just selling you what she has'. With the popular and widely advertised chocolates from Rowntree in mind, *Black Magic*, the headline writers have made much play with her name, writing headlines such as: 'Has Black the magic?' and 'Can Cathie Black pull

USA Today out of the red?' What interests us, however, is that Cathie Black has a quality of mind that is essential in those who have to accomplish a turnaround: she is ready to face up to and meet the inevitable challenge and take hard decisions.

Having seen the 'doctor' at work in companies large and small, can we see any sort of pattern? We do not think so. What we *can* see, we believe, are certain particular qualities of mind and attitude which are common to the many and diverse characters we have seen in action. Many have sought to study and identify the essential requirements for those who would be chief executive and one such study went so far as to classify them into four groups:[1]

Craftsman   Jungle fighter   Company man   Gamesman

The distinguishing characteristics of these four groups can be summarized as set out in Table 15. It is undoubtedly true that the various chief executives we have watched lead their companies out of trouble and on to success could well be set under one or other of

Table 15 *Types of chief executive. This table details the characteristics attributed to the four basic types of corporate leader discerned by Macoby. (See Reference 1 at the end of this chapter.)*

Type	Basic characteristics	Other characteristics
Craftsman	Drive to build the best, competes only with self.	Only interested in work. His one goal is perfection. Derives great pleasure from building something better and better.
Jungle fighter	Kill or be killed. Dominate or be dominated.	Has a lust for power. Takes pleasure in crushing opponent and has fear of destruction. Only one place for him: the top.
Company man	Climb or fall. Looks for security rather than success.	Has a fear of failure and desires approval by authority. Is fearful and submissive.
Gamesman	Win or lose, still happy. Either triumphs or is humiliated.	Enjoys contest, looks for new options. Has pleasure in controlling the play. Considers work a game. Tense, dynamic.

three of the above four groups, but we will leave that most interesting exercise to you. None, we believe could be categorized as a 'company man' in the terms described. None were 'fearful and submissive'. Roger Smith, who wrought the transformation at General Motors which we describe in Chapter 9, might well have been thought to be a 'company man'. Indeed, some did see him like that – a 'greysuited executive'. Starting as an accountant, rising swiftly to the top, having never worked for any other company, he had all the outward characteristics of a 'company man', but when crisis came he displayed a very resolute spirit and did not shirk change. The typical 'company man' hates change because it is always an immediate threat to 'security', the one thing he always looks for and expects. So what have we learnt of the 'man at the top', the turnaround manager, the company 'doctor', the chief executive who stands out from all the rest as the one who can cope with trouble and win.

Managing a turnaround

The first thing that we have to realize is that there is a specific strategy involved in a turnaround: a turnaround has to be 'managed'. This is the key point made by Charles M. Williams in a paper with the eye-catching title: 'When the mighty stumble'.[2] He insists that executives must learn to manage adversity just as they have in the past managed success. We think it is true that one learns much more from adversity than one does from success. The trouble with success is that it can easily go to one's 'head'. Williams analyses four cases, of which the classic, Chrysler, which we deal with in Chapter 5, is one. There *must* be a plan and all, including those outside the company as such, such as the banks who have lent the money, must share in the sacrifices that will have to be made. This was where Lee Iacocca had to begin, but in our view the supreme example in this field was Umeo Oyama. Put in by the banks because he had a great reputation as a 'turnaround manager', the first thing he did when he took charge at the Ikegai Corporation was to get the banks to reduce their interest rate from 8 per cent to 4 per cent. In our view that was an achievement indeed! For the banks, of course, it was 'Hobson's choice', in that something is always better than nothing. Yet, surprisingly enough, there are many banks who fail to recognize this reality of life, stick to their 'principles', continue to demand the agreed rate of interest and eventually get nothing.

You will remember that it was Umeo Oyama who was much against the device of going bankrupt so that outstanding debt was written off. He said. 'The law shouldn't protect such companies'. Williams, too, has something to say on this aspect: for him it is not a favoured route to recovery. There is a popular adage: 'Owe the bank a thousand dollars and the bank has you in its grip – owe the bank many millions and *you* are in control'. In a sense that is true: how else could Iacocca or Umeo Oyama make advantageous arrangements with their creditors and, in particular, the banks. Iacocca went a step further, indeed he had to. He pursuaded the Government to guarantee the loan being made by the banks in the larger interests of the country. It was not just Chrysler at stake, but the US, or so it was alleged. Iacocca must have done his homework extremely well to make such a case and bring conviction to a hardheaded Senate Committee.

But of course it is better by far not to borrow, but to fund further investment from the earnings that are being made. Now that we have finished our case studies we think it has become apparent that there is no single turnaround strategy that can be adopted. Each case

Table 16   *Coping with crisis. Management has to cope with crisis when it comes and this table sets out some of the tools that have been used.*

Type of crisis	Management action
Strategic	
Threats to the potential of the company: its human resources, technology or sales.	Reorientate company strategy, disinvest, consolidate, diversify.
Financial performance	
Company has excessive loans, making a loss.	Improve efficiency, reduce costs, boost sales.
No liquidity	
There is threat of insolvency due to shortage of funds.	Seek bridging loans, change company's financial structure.
Insolvent	
Unable to satisfy bankers or other creditors: receivership certain.	Receiver can still save the company through successful composition with creditors, etc.

has to be studied and the various possible steps assessed and tailored to suit the particular circumstances. However, it is possible to set what we have seen in a sort of order and this has been done in Table 16. Here we set the possible steps that mangement can take against the type of crisis that has arisen. In many cases, of course, more than one of the 'types of crisis' will occur at the same time.

Forecasting disaster

Perhaps the most interesting aspect of the many case studies at which we have looked is that they all took the participants by surprise. This was true of them all: true even of General Motors. What brought that company up with a jerk was not the steady slide downwards, but the sudden sharp dip in its profits: so sharp that a massive profit one year became a loss the following year. Even the chairman, an accountant, was taken by surprise. Truly, when the crisis came, he grappled with it firmly and successfully, but had he acted earlier that particular crisis need never have arisen. Most company directors never think of crisis, never plan for trouble during good times: they are too busy. Then, when trouble comes, they are even busier and so still fail to stop and think, and plan.[3]

Of course, it should be possible to look ahead, assess if there is trouble ahead, and then take the appropriate steps to meet it and minimize its effects. Prediction is possible, as we ourselves have asserted, going on to demonstrate the various techniques that are available.[4] Yet these techniques do not seem to be used, even by those whom we would expect to understand them very well indeed. Two of our 'doctors' were accountants, working in the company they later 'turned round' and brought back to health. We have just mentioned Roger Smith of General Motors: David Roderick of US Steel (Chapter 5) was another 'quiet accountant' who took quite ruthless steps to transform the company when the need became apparent and still continues to do so. But why did they not use their skill and knowledge of accountancy techniques to discern the path their company was following, and take action at an earlier time? When they acted, they approached the problem very much as an accountant would be expected to do, using divestiture, diversification and acquisition as their main tools.

The quality of leadership

We have seen that the chief executives who have brought their companies back from the brink are very diverse characters, yet they must have and do have, some qualities in common. Above all, they must have the quality of leadership, a quality which, it seems, is inborn rather than learnt. One either has it or one hasn't. It is said that statistically speaking, by the time that you have brought eight people together at random, one of them will prove to be a leader and begin to assert dominance over the rest if they are put to a task. This is equivalent to saying that one in eight among us has 'leadership potential', but of course only a few of the potential leaders ever get the opportunity to become leaders. But perhaps the statistic is the reason why there always seems to be someone who rises up to meet the crisis when it comes.

We have also seen that this particular quality in the man (or woman) who leads a company, once there, seems to ensure success almost independently of the quality of the others, and particularly the management, in the company. Perhaps the reason for that is that one quality of leadership is that it brings out, develops and uses the best in others. A good leader can get the 'common man' to perform very uncommon deeds, thus leading to the emergence of an 'uncommon man'. According to Charles Darwin, men differ less in the sum total of their abilities than in the degree to which they use them. It is the leader who draws out these unused abilities and capabilities and thus makes all the difference.

While some of our 'doctors' made a 'clean sweep' of the existing senior management, most of them allowed the existing team to carry on. But, under their leadership, their performance was transformed. Perhaps Michael Edwardes, taking over at British Leyland, is an outstanding example in this. He himself said of the trouble in which British Leyland was in when he took over: ' . . .the real blame lay with management, for they failed in their duty to manage'. Yet those very same managers, under his leadership, worked successfully with him to transform the company and its operations. One of them, Sir John Egan, went on to lead Jaguar Cars towards resounding success, first within British Leyland and then with even more success once the company had been privatized and the 'dead hand of bureaucracy' had been finally removed.

Even bureaucrats can manage

Having just spoken of the 'dead hand of bureaucracy' – and that is what it usually is – perhaps we should assess once again those few cases we found, all in India as it happens, where a bureaucrat led a nationalized industry to success. While Peter Drucker is convinced that government, any government, is totally and utterly incompetent as an industrial manager, our case studies prove him wrong. We could even use British Leyland to demonstrate this. The case of British Leyland shows us quite clearly that it is not government as such, but the *type* of government that matters. Previous governments in the UK had funded British Leyland without question. The Thatcher Government asked questions, and called in Sir Michael Edwardes. Having done that, they let him get on with it. To quote the Prime Minister, Mrs Thatcher:

> He's the manager, I'm not the manager.

If only *that* situation can obtain, then there is hope, even for a nationalized industry.

This, it seems, was the position that was established both with Neyveli Lignite Corporation and more particularly with the Damodar Valley Corporation, whom we study in Chapter 6. The bureaucrats finally left the companies alone, although to establish that situation was a hard struggle. A 'leader' was needed, and one came along. Mr. G. L. Tandon wrought miracles at NLC, while Mr P. C. Luther fought off the bureaucrats (almost literally) at DVC. As Luther himself said, while the prevention of political interference was 'undoubtedly inconvenient, arduous and even hazardous, it is certainly not impossible'. His success, and the success of others running profitable companies under a governmental umbrella, is a powerful demonstration that it *can be done*. Government bureaucracy is therefore no excuse. The fault lies, as always, with the management itself. It lacks, above all, the right leader: a leader with courage, persistence and common sense, for those are the qualities we see coming to the fore in every effective leader that we have looked at. The leader doesn't need to have special skills. He doesn't need to be an accountant: we saw our accountants bringing in engineering expertise. He doesn't need to have any special knowledge of the industry in which he is working, although it can help. Sir Michael Edwardes came to British Leyland knowing practically nothing of the motor car industry, but he soon learnt. While Ian MacGregor had substantial experience of the steel industry when he came to British Steel, we would suggest that while that was a reason for him being chosen, it was *not* the reason why he succeeded. He went on from British Steel to British Coal, as it is now called, a very different industry, and is succeeding once again. Drew Lewis, a former Secretary of Transportation with the US Government, has been in the turnaround business since 1970. It is difficult to imagine, isn't it: a bureaucrat acting as a 'company doctor'. In 1982 he revitalized the floundering Warner Amex Cable company and more recently has been busy with Union Pacific Railroad. This company, it seems, may well present him with his toughest challenge yet, having much too much rail track and far too many employees. He is another 'doctor' with some hard choices ahead of him.

We have told the story of Ian MacGregor and his work at the National Coal Board (as it was then called) elsewhere, giving him and his efforts a whole chapter under the title: 'The anatomy of a coal strike'.[6] The issue at British Steel and again at British Coal has been the 'right of the management to manage' and in both cases it was the unions who were the chief antagonist, although the management structure did not lend itself to 'managers managing'. Another issue, not directly related to the mining industry, was the right of a man to go to his place of work without let or hindrance. That reminds us of a little story that came to our notice under the headline: 'The £1 million picket'.[7] Mr Silcock, a working miner, brought a profitable pit to a standstill with a one-man picket line. He picketed Markham Main Colliery, near Doncaster, because he had been sacked for breaching safety regulations. He picketed the pit for five days, and all 1200 of his colleagues refused to cross his picket line. As a consequence the Coal Board lost coal worth £800,000, while his colleagues lost £200,000 in wages. So the mentality which led to so much trouble in the coal industry is still there, but perhaps the most significant aspect of this little incident is that Ian MacGregor never said a word. All the responses were left to and made by the local pit management. It seems that the unions involved had agreed with the disciplinary steps being taken and were not at all happy with the strike action.

However, we have no doubt that British Coal will tread in the footsteps of British Steel: MacGregor is at the helm! British Steel demonstrates his competence. The 'doctor' has done it! That company has now announced its first post-interest profit for eleven years, but its new chairman, Mr Bob Scholey, said that the business needed to produce a surplus of at least £200 million a year to remain viable and self-financing. Now, with operations centred largely round five integrated steelmaking plants, the corporation could well be a prime candidate for privatization if there is a third Thatcher administration.[8] The need for one of those manufacturing centres,

Ravenscraig, is still in doubt, but British Steel are in any event pledged to keep it open until at least 1988.

Staying at the top

Some of the 'doctors' whose work we have surveyed seem to have set themselves up, as it were, as 'doctors' rather than chief executives, although they became the chief executive in order to carry out their task properly. Three 'doctors' we have looked at, Sir Michael Edwardes, Ian MacGregor (now Sir Ian) and Sir John Cuckney are all examples of chief executives who have made the rescue of an ailing company or corporation their profession. We met a similar example from Japan in the person of Umeo Oyama and there are many others who become, in effect, 'turnaround pros'. The turnaround becomes their business and they make a lot of money at it, as did Mr Oyama. For instance, there is Q. T. Wiles, who worked in close association with a San Francisco banking firm, Hambrecht & Quist, one of whose activities was the underwriting of high-tech companies. When such a company got into trouble, the bank sent in Wiles as a 'troubleshooter' and so successful was he that he was appointed chairman at the bank following the death of one of its co-founders, George Quist. Wiles adopted what we might call the 'Oyama' approach, taking up shares in the company he went to salvage. In this way he became chairman of five corporations, drew more than US$1 million a year in salary and owned some US$20 million in stock and options. Yet he has no management training, nor did he take a management degree. What is the secret of his success? According to Wiles himself he spends most of his time 'making sure people know what their jobs are'. As simple as that!

So far the 'pro'. But other chief executives have been successful in achieving a turnaround without being 'specialists'. Confronted with a situation that called for drastic action, they took that action and then remained in the chair to see the fruits of their efforts. There is no doubt that autocratic, decisive decision-making is crucial if a turnaround is to be successful. Change *must* be the order of the day and it has been suggested that the qualities demanded of a turnaround manager are not the qualities that are appropriate if the chief executive is to *run* the company. But some of the illustrations that we have taken and discussed do not support that idea. It seems that there are those who, while acting decisively when the occasion demands it, are equally prepared to let their staff exercise their own initiative once the crisis is past.

Summary

We have established, by example, that there are two roles which the chief executive can and should fill. Just as one can ride a horse with a 'slack rein' or a 'tight rein', so there are two ways of running a company. Some of the legendary figures in the management field, such as Tom Watson of IBM, Bill Hewlett and Dave Packard of Hewlett-Packard and Robert W. Johnson of Johnson & Johnson, while all believing strongly and sincerely in autonomy at all levels, were nevertheless all strict disciplinarians. While they gave their managers plenty of rope, they also realized that it was just possible that a manager might hang himself. So freedom was exercised within a reasonably rigid framework, a framework established by company policy and the company culture.

If this all sounds somewhat of a paradox, then all life is a paradox. It is recognized and accepted that in the classroom teaching can only take place if there is discipline. There must be regular attendance, punctuality, regular homework. Yet at the same time the good teacher seeks to allow pupils the freedom to express themselves and develop their own initiative. Similarly, in a well-run company, departmental autonomy is only effective if it operates within a disciplined framework. Stable, defined parameters within which one can work give people confidence and then they work better. Children are very much like that, you know. They *like* a disciplined and ordered structure to their lives. It gives them security and makes them feel safe. We leave it to you to apply the principle.

References

1 Macoby, M., *The Gamesman – the New Corporate Leaders*, Simon & Schuster, 1976.
2 Williams, C. M., 'When the mighty stumble', *Harvard Business Review*, no. 62, July–August 1984, pp. 126–39.
3 Loscocco, S. J., 'The "What-if" Director, Crisis aversion and Crisis management', *Directors & Boards*, no. 3, Summer 1978, pp. 20–6.
4 Kharbanda, O. P. and Stallworthy, E. A., *Corporate Failure: Prediction, Panacea and Prevention*, McGraw-Hill, 1985.

5 Edwardes, M., *Back from the Brink – An Apocalyptic Experience*, Collins, 1983.
6 Kharbanda, O. P. and Stallworthy, E. A., *Management Disasters: and How to Prevent Them*, Gower, 1986.
7 'The £1m picket', *Today*, 24 May 1986, p. 1.
8 Gribben, R., 'Steel faces "make or break" era', *Daily Telegraph*, 3 April 1986, p. 2.

18 Learning from experience

Can company management be taught? A question bearing even more closely upon our subject: can turnaround management be taught? There are certainly plenty of schools and colleges teaching business management in all its forms and the turnaround of companies in financial distress may well be touched upon. Are they successful? Perhaps. We ourselves have always maintained that experience is by far the best teacher, but that means learning on the job. While the pupil may then learn a lot, his company might well suffer much in the process. Nevertheless it can legitimately be considered to be part of the training process: learning the hard but expensive way.

We also know, and have said, that one can learn most from one's own mistakes. And he is a wise man indeed who can learn not only from his own mistakes but from those of others.[1] That is why we have sought to present the mistakes of others – that we *all* may learn and so prevent failure.[2] Here, in this book, we demonstrate success, rather than failure, the success of those who have the appropriate experience lighting up the road for others to follow. But the question remains: if experience is the best teacher, how can we best gain that experience?

The schools change course

It is interesting to notice that business management schools are beginning to change their teaching emphasis from the academic to the practical. The 'big three' business schools in Western Europe, INSEAD in France and IMI and IMEDE in Switzerland seem now to be relying less on the 'academic case study' method of teaching: the *forte* of the Harvard Business School. They are now seeking to introduce 'real life' into their teaching. For instance, the European Institute of Business Administration (INSEAD) worked in co-operation with Kronenbourg, a brewing concern, and part of the French foods group BSN, to develop a 'real life' situation. Krönenbourg was considering a new brewery in Europe, so its company executives discussed the proposal with the academic staff at INSEAD. Video films were made of these discussions, which then served as 'real business life' teaching material.[3]

Olivetti, whose experiences we discuss in Chapter 11, gave IMEDE of Switzerland an opportunity to enter a 'real life' situation when AT & T took a 25 per cent stake in the company. The Olivetti management had to determine what its relationship with AT & T and its personnel should now be. So sixteen managers from Olivetti spent two weeks in seminar seeking to think more 'internationally', while the students at IMEDE wrote a brief for Olivetti's marketing director. It is important in all this to recognize the origin of the current 'teaching tradition' in Europe. There had been no formal management education in the best-known universities, with the result that the European management schools took their ideas *and* their case studies – exclusively from the US, where schools such as the Harvard Business School had a long tradition. But one could hardly expect an American transplant to take root in European soil, nor did it. But now, it seems, the source of their inspiration is changing, and they are looking closer to home for their case studies.

It now seems that a certain divorcement between teaching and practice is starting to be recognized right where it all began, in the US, if the assessment of Abraham Zaleznik, professor of Leadership at the Harvard Business School is to be accepted. He is reported as saying:[4]

> In management education over the last two decades students have been taught to be utilitarians and calculators. . . . We have been abstracting people out of management as if they didn't exist. Business schools are now going through a self-searching process. The question is what kind of human beings are we producing by fostering this kind of experience?

Here we have a turnaround in Business Schools themselves! They most certainly need it. Professor Zaleznik is unique in being the only psychoanalyst with a tenured position in a business school, and his comment is a direct challenge to the prevalent teaching emphasis in business school curricula. What he is saying, in effect, is that the emphasis has been on the assessment and control of figures, when it should have been on the assessment and control of people. That is where the Japanese example, to which we have referred so often throughout this book, is so significant, since the prime emphasis in the Japanese system of management is so clearly on people. The employee is so very important: he is a member of the 'family' and you cannot become more important than that. The concept is perhaps best illustrated by the Japanese businessman we looked at in Chapter 4, Umeo Oyama. He certainly paid close and detailed attention to the figures, but he gave equal, if not more attention to the people: the employees and their attitudes. Remember the case where he greeted them all in the morning, then smelt their breath at night! Remember that plain, even stupid question: 'Does *your* wife powder her hip?' He was closely concerned with *his* people – and we believe that to be a common characteristic with all the 'doctors' whose manner of working and approach to the problems that confronted them we have been studying.

It is our thesis that when a company gets into trouble it is always the 'management' that is at fault, but *where* is the management at fault? Failure begins at the top. This is just like a tree, which always rots from the top: a simile drawn by one of the most respected of writers on management topics, Peter Drucker. No wonder the chief executive is so important, but of course he does not stand alone. Successful management, which demands a successful chief executive, will prevent failure, but what *is* successful management? Can we learn it at business school? Do they learn it at business school? Let us take a quick look at the literature on management, at those books which the budding manager may well be reading. It is our hope of course, that budding managers will read this book – and not only budding managers, but many who are now exercising their skills, since we believe that they may well be approaching management the wrong way.

The literature on management

The subject of management has attracted an enormous amount of literature from both academic and industrial circles. This is all to the good and a review of what has been written on the subject ought to make us wiser, provided we read with discernment. We found a book that asserted that it was going to take us 'back to basics' most informative.[5] The authors named three foundation blocks for good management:

'Back to basics' management
Interpersonal relations   } PEOPLE.
Effective communication

You will notice that the first item implies criticism of current management practice, while the other two are wholly concerned with people. And in all this, it is people who are the key to success: the proper management of people is crucial. The results are finally achieved, not by the chief executive, but by the people he directs. To manage the mass of employees he needs a management team, once the company gets over a certain size. Umeo Oyama, it seems, was able to greet every employee personally each morning, but that approach is beyond the reach of Roger Smith, chairman of General Motors. Roger Smith has to work through a multitude of management teams. Nevertheless, it is that multitude of individuals and above all their attitude to work, that is the key to success. We referred in the previous chapter to Macoby's classification of managers into four basic types. One of the examples he took was Andrew Carnegie, whom he described as one of the most intelligent and subtle 'jungle fighters' in the corporate world of his day. Carnegie was the founder of US Steel: we review the activities of the latest of his successors to that particular throne in Chapter 5 and there is no doubt that Carnegie was a great entrepreneur, even though the economic climate may well have favoured him. It is also very clear that figures mattered a great deal to Carnegie. He had a mind open to new ideas, new technology and new financial techniques, but only as a means of increasing profit. But he also recognized the importance of people, saying: 'Take away all my steel mills. Take away all my money. Leave me my people and in five years I will have everything back'.[6]

The importance of people

Still reviewing the literature, and seeing that it is the people in the business who are important, we ask ourselves: How does the manager manage people? We have already brought into question the academic approach to management, so let us now listen to an industrial manager whose academic qualifications brought him an academic post: he was, when he wrote the book we read, a senior staff member at the IBM Corporation's Information Systems Management Institute. He asserted that the present complex and competitive business world demands managers who not only have business skills, but also a highly developed acuity in *personal* matters.[7] He must be able to manage people as well as figures. The only point of issue, so far as we are concerned, is the implication that this is a new idea. In our view there has *always* been a need to manage people: it is no new thing necessitated by the growing complexity of the business world. According to Winters, an effective manager must be able, inter alia, to:

1 Make financial decisions.
2 Perceive the needs of the marketplace.
3 Implement the latest technological developments.
4 Communicate well with his people.
5 Motivate his people in order to accomplish the company's goals.

[margin handwritten notes: FIGURES; EXTERNAL SITUATION; PEOPLE]

Only the first item on the above list has anything directly to do with figures. The next two items demand sensitivity to the external situation, with a willingness to react, while the last two are wholly concerned with people. They have to be motivated, and motivation from the top can only be achieved if there is effective communication. We think it fair to say that every one of the 'doctors' whose approach to management we have studied have, in the course of redeeming a desperate situation, displayed outstanding ability in all of the above five fields and more. We have not been able to demonstrate in detail how they deployed their forces, as it were, but the manner in which they succeeded demonstrates their skill in all five of the above essential attributes. Since we are now looking at what we might well call 'people management', let us look a little more closely at those last two skills: communication and the ability to motivate people.

The importance of communication

Looking once again at the literature on the subject, there is no doubt that the importance of effective communication throughout the corporate structure is well recognized. Unfortunately it is also asserted that it is largely absent. Peter Drucker, whose reputation is such that we never dare ignore what he says, asserts in a book on the subject of management communication, that the great majority of us do not know what to say, when to say it, how to say it, nor to whom to say it.[8] A devasting assessment, but we believe it to be true. We ourselves, however, would go a step further: we would point out that the weakest link in the communications process is listening. If no one listens any attempt at communication just collapses.

The importance of listening

Since listening is an integral part of communication those who manage must realize its importance. It would seem that the chief executives who have figured in our case studies have, consciously or unconsciously, acquired the art of getting people to listen, because we can see from the results they achieved that they were indeed listened to, but the fact remains that the great majority of them fail to listen. We spend nearly half our waking hours listening: no, that is not true. We spend that time 'hearing things'. We do not necessarily *listen*: listening, though a vital skill, is rarely taught and the average listening efficiency is said to be a mere 20 per cent. Fortunately the importance of listening is now being realized by more and more business organizations and they are taking steps to deal with the problem. A bank in the UK, the Midland Bank, has advertised itself as the 'listening bank', although the advertising campaign went a bit awry in that the media dug up a lot of cases where the bank had patently *not* listened. Another illustration comes from Sperry, who has built a publicity campaign around the same theme, saying:

> We understand how important it is to listen. When you know how to listen, opportunity only has to knock once.

So we ask our readers: Do you listen? While you may well answer 'yes', we would still wonder.

Encouraging people to listen is such a vital element in effective management that we devoted a whole chapter to the subject (The project manager really must listen) when discussing the role of the project manager in project management.[9] We commend what we say there to your attention, since effective listening is relevant to all management, not merely project management. Indeed, we asserted there that 'all business is listening'. The basic components in communication are illustrated in Figure 18 and it is listening that links the message with the recipient. Without that the chain breaks

Figure 18 *Communication – the basic components. Communication consists of four equally important parts. Concentration is generally focused on the message and a breakdown often ensues when the communicator and the recipient are not given sufficient attention. (With acknowledgements for the idea to Mr A. Brown, see Reference 12 at end of the chapter.)*

down. So vital do we consider listening to be that one of us has conducted a series of courses and seminars on the subject. The first time that such a course was announced, the sceptics said: 'Listening? What's that? My hearing is perfect: what can *you* teach *us*?' Our answer: 'Yes, precisely. Our hearing is good too. We do not need a hearing aid, but we *do* need a listening aid.'

Listening is a skill we learn at our mother's knee. While it is the most used skill, yet it is never taught – merely 'acquired'. We are taught to speak, we are taught to read, we are taught to write, but we are *not* taught to listen. It has to be recognized that listening is a very active mental and physical process. This means that if someone tells you to relax, sit back and listen, you must not listen to him! You are not listening properly if you are relaxed, and there is sound scientific evidence to this effect. The heart beats a little faster and the body temperature rises slightly when you are really listening. This shows us that listening is hard work and needs effort on our part. But not only effort on our part. The communicator also has a role to play: he has to ensure that he is listened to. Figure 19 demonstrates that he too needs to do something about it.

There are two basic ways of communication: by word of mouth and in writing. We are now considering communication by word of mouth and we have made it clear that the recipient has to listen. It has also been established that in that context the attention to the

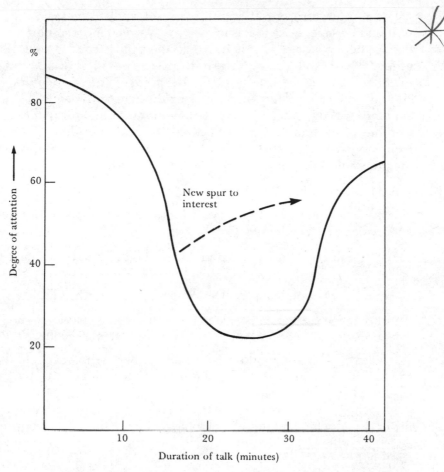

Figure 19 *Paying attention. This graph demonstrates an observed fact, namely that attention falls off very rapidly after some ten minutes into a talk (but not necessarily into a discussion) unless the speaker does something positive to regain the attention of his audience. And so few do!*

speaker is dependent both upon the length of the message and its quality. That is the significance of Figure 19. It demonstrates that, assuming an even quality of delivery of the message, attention falls off very rapidly after some 10 minutes, although it can revive again after some 30 minutes. However, if the communicator creates new interest, either by change of subject, change in tone of voice, or some other device, it is possible to create a new surge of attention, as illustrated in the graph. In this way a skilful orator sustains attention to his message.

Let us now turn our attention from the spoken message to the written message, since that is in many ways even more important. If the written message is not heeded, then all is indeed lost. The immediate lesson we can learn from Figure 19 is that written messages should be brief and to the point. Written memoranda should always be short and precise, though few may reach the standard of the fabled one-page memorandum at Proctor and Gamble. This tradition goes back to its past president, Richard Deupree, who was a stickler about the length of memoranda. A long memo would be returned to the sender with a note:

> Boil it down to something I can grasp.

If the situation was complex, or perhaps the writing was not clear and explicit, he would add:

> I don't understand complicated problems. I only understand simple ones.

Explaining his philosophy, Deupree was very forthright, saying:

> Part of my job is to train people to break down an involved question into a series of simple matters. Then we can all act intelligently.

It was the well-known novelist John Steinbeck who once said that the first step in writing a book (he referred to a novel, but we can assure you that it applies to books like this as well) was to get a one-page clear statement of purpose. Otherwise, he suggested, one will never get very far, and there is a lot of wisdom in this. The 'Deupree' style is still on at Proctor & Gamble, for a manager recently confided:[10]

> . . . I just submitted a set of recommendations . . . it ran to a page and a quarter and got kicked back. It was too long.

It was Peters and Waterman's study of America's best-run companies that demonstrated very clearly that people are not good at processing large amounts of new data.[10] It is said that the utmost that we can hold in our 'short memory', to which we have immediate access, is some six or seven discrete pieces of data. Rene McPherson, another company 'doctor', threw out 22 half-inch-thick policy manuals on taking over the Dana Corporation. He replaced them with a one-page statement of the company policy. Other managers: please copy.

Using what you've got

Still seeking to learn from the experience of others, while at the same time keeping in mind the literature on the subject, we thought it remarkable how rarely our 'doctors' had a management purge, or even an employee purge. It is true that at times thousands were made redundant, but that is not the same thing. Then they went because there was no work for them, not because they were not good at their work. This brings us to that last attribute of a good manager: his ability to motivate people. It seems that individuals can do a good job if they have the right environment and a good manager creates that environment. Bennett puts it thus:[11]

> The task is not to change people. People are perfectly alright the way they are. The task is not to motivate people. People are inherently self-starting. The task is to remove those things that demotivate them, to get them out of their way. Or, more precisely, to create those kinds of organizational structures that allow workers to get at problems and act in some independent ways so they can develop their skills at solving problems related to their own jobs.

Bennett sees the management team as the key potential resource for problem solving and the key to his approach is to encourage that which is in opposition – be it an individual, a department or a union – to change sides and function as part of the team. Thus the full potential of the organization is achieved and progress will be made. Reflect on our case studies and you will realize that you have seen this principle in action time and again. Many of our 'doctors' have done two key things in line with this policy. They have decentralized, breaking down the company into separate, autonomous units, each made responsible and given responsibility for their own activities. They have also got the workers 'on their side' and often the unions. Sometimes even the bureaucrats, in the case of a government-owned corporation. These are the real lessons to be learnt from the experience of others.

References

1 Kharbanda, O. P. and Stallworthy, E. A., *How to Learn from Project Disasters: True-life Stories with a Moral for Management*, Gower, 1983.
2 Kharbanda, O. P. and Stallworthy, E. A., *Corporate Failure: Prediction, Panacea and Prevention*, McGraw-Hill, 1985.

3   'Europe puts the business back into business schools', *Economist*, no. 291, 14 April 1984, pp. 79–80.

4   Collins, G., 'Putting human dimension into business school classes', *International Herald Tribune*, 1 November 1985.

5   Culligan, M. J., Deakin, S. and Young, A. H., *Back to Basics Management: The Lost Craft of Leadership*, Gower, 1983.

6   Brown, R, *The Practical Manager's Guide to Excellence in Management*, Amacom, 1979.

7   Winters, R. J., *It's Different When You Manage*, Lexington Books, 1983.

8   Parkinson, C. N. and Rowe N., *Communicate: Parkinson's Formula for Business Survival*, Prentice-Hall, 1977.

9   Stallworthy, E. A. and Kharbanda, O. P., *Total Project Management: From Concept to Completion*, Gower, 1983.

10   Peters, T. J. and Waterman, R. H., *In Search of Excellence: Lessons from America's Best-Run Companies*, Harper & Row, 1982.

11   Bennett, D., *Successful Team Building through TA*, Amacom, 1975.

12   Brown, A., 'Equipping ourselves for the Communications Age', *The Futurist*, no. 15, August 1981, pp. 53–7.

19   The challenge to management

Who are we to tell managements and managers around the world what is good for them? But we make no such claim: all we seek to do is to review the facts and draw out the lessons that are there to be learned from those facts. Good management is crucial to success and all our 'doctors', what ever else they did, have had to revise and reform the management structure with which they were confronted. Without good management failure will be at the door sooner or later. more often than not, sooner! We are convinced that good management can, and does, ward off failure. If the force of external circumstances is such that even good management cannot redeem the situation, it will at least minimize its traumatic effects.

But what is good management? Looking around the world, we have seen various styles of management, of which the Japanese style seems the most successful, seeing that it has brought that country from poverty to prosperity in some thirty years. However, it is obviously not possible to just 'copy' the Japanese style – except perhaps in Japan. You will remember that we found some *gaijins* who did just that (Chapter 14). It is certainly not possible to transplant a management style from one country to another, where the cultural values, history, traditions and business practice are so very different, although the Japanese themselves have a good try and usually succeed whenever they set up a factory in another country. We are sure, however, that the essentials can be assessed and the lessons applied: some of our case studies have shown this happening, not always consciously, so far as we know.

Did you notice that none of our 'doctors' did anything very remarkable, or very different, in terms of company management.

d, we would suggest that their management style, if we can call t, was very similar. What seems to be important is that the gement structure be straightforward, with no centralized iistration beyond that of providing policy guidance. What was *always* brought to the situation by the chief executive was common sense, hard work, integrity of purpose and sometimes ruthlessness. To act with speed and firmness is, more often than not, seen as ruthlessness, although we do not see it that way.

The importance of the individual

We have seen – and we make no apology for returning to this point once again – that if we continue to take Japan as our example, the individual there is always important. What is more, feeling that he means something to his company, he proceeds to identify himself very completely with his company. In introducing himself, your visitor does not describe himself as the finance manager, but as a 'Mitsui man' or a 'Matushita man'. This relationship between the individual and his company is so close that those who know Japan well will tell you that they can tell the difference between a Mitsui manager and Mitsubishi manager. Remember that these people almost invariably stay with the same company from the day they leave college or university to the day they retire. In the West, however, things are very different. Perhaps that difference is best illustrated by quoting the plaint of an auto worker (it was in the US). He said:[1]

> You really begin to wonder. What price do they put on me? Look at the price they put on the machine. When that machine breaks down, there's somebody out there to fix it right away. If I break down, I'm pushed over to the other side until another man takes my place. The only thing they have on their mind is to keep that line running.

A management approach that causes its employees to feel like that is well on the road to failure. The individual matters: the individual matters very much.

Out of sight, out of mind

Wherever we look we seem to find this basic difference emerging, manifested in the attitude employees have to their employment. Every year there are more and more companies operating on a multinational and even global basis, with offices and factories in other countries. Inevitably personnel are posted from the home country, usually to be managers and introduce the company techniques and knowhow in the distant location. It is always a difficult assignment, since a posting to another country, usually with another language and very different customs, can create a very stressful situation. Those who get on best are the ones who are able, although expatriates, to make their new location their *home*. Unfortunately, many expatriates seem to spend a lot of thime thinking about what is going to happen when they 'go back home' again: a thought that makes it very clear that they are *not* 'at home' where they are. They have some justification for thinking in this way, at least when their home is in the West – Europe or the US. One article on this subject made the point that when such people return to home base it is very difficult to get them back into the stream, especially when the home base is contracting in size, as it so often is these days.[2] It seems a very true saying for them: 'out of sight, out of mind'. That reminds us of a story we once heard in relation to that international multi-lingual forum, the United Nations Assembly in New York. The phrase 'out of sight, out of mind' is a colloquialism, and even the best of translators are not always *au fait* with colloquialisms. One translator at the United Nations certainly wasn't, for he translated the phrase 'invisible idiot'. Well, those who take on overseas assignments are certainly not idiots, although they may feel somewhat that way when they first arrive at the overseas location. But we were talking of their return. In a recent study by the Paris-based Intercultural Management Associates, all ten of the French multinationals who responded to the survey confirmed that it was difficult to fit in executives returning from foreign assignments. Based on its own experience, the Swedish car group Volvo has now designated someone at head office to communicate regularly with its executives abroad to let them know what is happening at home, especially in relation to job opportunities. This has not only reassured the expatriate – at long last he feels that somebody back home cares – but it has helped their placing when they finally return. Usually, of course, the standard of living and the emoluments on an overseas assignment are much higher than they are at home, and this is another source of problems.

The need for competent managers who can be sent abroad is a worldwide phenomenon. The US were pioneers in this area, but their failure rate is much higher than that of the Japanese.[3] Another survey showed that over 75 per cent of the eighty US corporations who responded found that between 10 and 40 per cent of their personnel assigned abroad had to be recalled or dismissed, because of poor performance, although their home record had been excellent. The Japanese corporations, however, reported very differently. Of the thirty-five who replied, 86 per cent reported a failure rate of less than 10 per cent, and in no case did the failure rate reach 20 per cent. The reason for this difference appears to lie in the fact that Japanese companies are willing to invest much more heavily in training and support, primarily because their staff are willing to stay abroad much longer than their American counterparts. Of course, if the American expatriates were better trained they too might stay longer, being better able to adjust to local mores.

Allowing for individuality

Not only is the individual important for his own sake, but he has a lot to contribute to the company, if only he is appropriately encouraged. Once again, the Japanese lead the way. Not only is there free and regular interchange of personnel across departments, which results in a 'new look' at things by the newcomers, but there is constant encouragement to present ideas for innovation or improvement. When such ideas are adopted – and they often are – the individual gets both the public credit and financial reward. Of these the public credit is possibly the most important. Elsewhere it can be very different. John DeMott tells the story of Stephen Wozniak, who went as a twenty-five year old designer (in 1975) at Hewlett Packard to his manager with an idea for a microcomputer. The company was not interested. So he left and started up his own company with a friend. Now his company, *Apple*, has become world-famous in the computer industry, with its 1984 sales topping US$1·5 billion.

It is this sort of incident, it seems, that has triggered off what is now being called 'intrapreneurship' in the larger companies, particularly in the US. Intrapreneurship is in effect the setting up of a small independent company *within* the main corporation. A new word, it seems, has been coined to describe this particular activity, and to differentiate it from entrepreneurship, but it has yet to find a place in the dictionary even though a full length book has been written about it.[4] The intrapreneur will be the creator or the inventor of the idea and his company gives him the task of bringing it to fruition. The development of its first 'plastic' car, the sports car known as the *Fiero*, by General Motors, was an outstanding example of intrapreneurship, an example which we have discussed in detail elsewhere.[5]

Giving scope for innovation

Having now introduced the concept of the intrapreneur and looking about us, we see that while it may be a new word, it is hardly a new idea. Peters and Waterman, whose book *In Search of Excellence* was published some three years before Pinchot's work, discuss precisely the same phenomenon, although they give it a very different name.[6] They used the term 'champion' to describe the intrapreneur in the large but innovative company, saying of him:

> [He is] so intent on innovation that its [the company's] essential atmosphere seems not like that of a large corporation but rather a loose network of laboratories and cubbyholes populated by feverish inventors and dauntless entrepreneurs who let their imagination fly in all directions.

The phrase 'dauntless entrepreneur' is hardly appropriate when applied to a young employee in a major corporation, whatever his attributes and whatever he does, so we endorse the invention of a new word to describe him – intrapreneur! To take another example, Lew Lehr, himself a notable intrapreneur, is quoted by Peters as saying of 3M, another successful company they researched:

> For many years the corporate structure has been designed specifically to encourage young entrepreneurs to take an idea and run with it. If they succeed, they can and do find themselves running their own business under the 3M umbrella. The entrepreneural approach is not a sideline at 3M. It is the heart of our design for growth.

So the idea as such is hardly new, but what is its relevance here? We have seen that an essential part of any turnaround is the development and encouragement of the innovative spirit. One reason for failure is often the fact that the innovative spirit has been stifled. This leads us almost inevitably to a management concept which is very relevant in this context: the principle of delegation. Crudely stated, the principle of delegation requires that the one in charge lets those to whom a task is given get on with it without interference.

The principle of delegation

The good chief executive will have recognized the importance of delegation and will apply it. James F. Beré, chairman of the Borg-Warner Corporation in the States, once put it this way:[1]

> The job [of chief executive] is not to make decisions . . . it is to put good people in place and judge if they are making good decisions. You give them the power. When they come in and say, 'How do I do something', I say: 'That's your problem.'

We do not need to elaborate here on the importance of this principle, having already seen how crucial it is in Chapter 3. All we need to do now is to remind you that it has been a powerful factor in the success of the 'doctors' whose work we have reviewed and to emphasize that the principle does not stop with the chief executive. It must go on all down the line, from manager to supervisor to foreman to the tradesman who tells his 'mate' what to do. All in their turn *must* delegate if they are to work efficiently. This, as we said, implies trust and confidence in one another and the ability to communicate. If you cannot communicate, you cannot delegate. That may sound a truism, but having seen earlier how important effective communication is, we now see that it *has* to permeate the organization from top to bottom. This is possibly the greatest challenge that there is to management: to ensure effective communication and proper delegation throughout the company. Everyone should know what is happening around them, what they are expected to do and how their particular area of effort fits into the whole.

Coping with change

The last challenge to management that we wish to assess is change. Change is inevitable. Reflecting upon our case histories, we see that while the world in which they worked was changing, many companies ignored what was happening until it was almost too late. They reacted to change far too slowly. Sometimes it was their sheer size that made it difficult to respond, as with General Motors: at other times it was a dogged hanging on to an outmoded concept. At one time the *Saturday Evening Post* and the company who owned it, the Curtis Publishing Company, were an American institution, but they have long disappeared. In the changing environment of the 1940s and 1950s the management could not respond, but held fast to the editorial policy they had pursued so successfully for so many years. The beliefs which had led to their success in the past blinded them to the new threats that arose, and they died. This is not unique. Many many companies have met the same fate for the same reason: blindness to the impact of change. The nature of the change will be different from case to case, but it is the inability to recognize change and its significance to the company that brings disaster. To take the very simplest of examples, the sharp rise in interest rates that occurred in the late 1970s added a severe and unexpected burden to many companies. The company that failed to recognize the situation and reduce its borrowing would eventually be in trouble.

Donaldson and Lorsch, following detailed clinical research into the practices, concepts and techniques of twelve very different companies, used the term 'strategic myopia' to describe this inability to cope with change.[7] Curious, isn't it, the way we cannot seem to get away from the use of human sickness to illustrate corporate distress. However, it is suggested that top managers fail to perceive environmental changes correctly or, having perceived them correctly, they have been unable to adjust to them because of the constraints within their company that are not compatible with the necessary change. It seems that these constraints are largely what we might call 'beliefs': customs, traditions and ways of thinking that have developed over the years – over successful years, and that is the trouble. The fact that they have brought success in the past gives them great strength. It is therefore suggested that a periodic audit of 'beliefs' is just as necessary as the financial audit. Whether management is willing to accept it or not, the external environment is all-important and *cannot* be ignored. So we have in effect a conflict between 'giants' and management has to resolve this conflict in the right way if the company is to survive. So powerful are the opposing influences, that one false step can quickly bring disaster. All we can do is to highlight the problem and the challenge it presents. The many examples we have studied show us that it can be met successfully and a company's health and survival ensured – and that in a wide range of different circumstances. So do not despair.

References

1   Beré, J. F., 'Turnover at the top – why executives are losing their jobs so quickly', *Business Week*, 19 December 1983, pp. 56–62.
2   Buchanan, S., 'Returning from overseas can mean a backward

step, *International Herald Tribune*, 30 October 1985.
3   Murray, F. T. and Murray, A. H., 'Global managers for global businesses', *Sloan Management Review*, Winter 1986, pp. 75–80.
4   Pinchot, Gifford III, *Intrapreneuring: Why you don't have to leave a Corporation to become an Intrapreneur*, Harper & Row, 1985.
5   Kharbanda, O. P., and Stallworthy, E. A., *Successful Projects: All with a Moral for Management*, Gower, 1986.
6   Peters, T. J. and Waterman, R. H., *In Search of Excellence: Lessons from America's Best-Run Companies*, Harper & Row, 1982.

20 Lessons for the future

The closing theme in Chapter 19 was 'coping with change'. Management *must* be able to cope with change and it is of course the future that brings change. While we would assert, and history demonstrates, that forecasting the future is *not* possible, there are still plenty of people who are prepared to tell us what the future holds. The essence of corporate planning is that one seeks to look to the future and most certainly corporate planning is fundamental to a company's success. Its purpose is to assess the long-term future of a company, and 'long-term' in this context is usually somewhere between five and twenty years. Five years certainly: the longer the period the more uncertain and speculative will the plan be. Among our case studies the forward look of Roger Smith was the most challenging, but only time will tell whether that plan will be realized. His project *Jupiter* is much further away than *Saturn*, but it might eventually materialize. What *is* important is that there should be a realistic goal in view. All our 'doctors' set up targets and then encouraged everyone to strive after those targets. There must be a purpose to give motivation.

Corporate planning is for the future and it is sometimes called long-range planning. There are some hundreds of books available on the subject, of which those by Hussey and Argenti are typical. [1, 2, 3] Any plan should be simple, short and straightforward. Although a corporate plan should consist of a few simple but significant statements, the formulation of those 'declarations of intent' will inevitably take much time and demand detailed discussion right at the top of the management tree. While the plan, when formulated, will be simple enough, arriving at that plan can be a very complex matter, since its primary purpose is to state the company's mission in life. Here the chief executive *must* take the lead, but he must work closely with his senior executives and the final plan must have the agreement of all. This is not decided in a moment: the development of a sound corporate plan can and should take anything up to a year and once developed it should be monitored at regular intervals.

Speculation is rife

We would contend that any system of forecasting which is predicated on a current trend must always be suspect. The oil crisis of 1973 is an outstanding illustration of the truth of this. There had been steady growth for nearly thirty years, but the upward curve collapsed overnight. The corporate plans of thousands of companies collapsed with it. Yet there are still those who analyse current trends, make projections and predictions – and there are those who listen to them with attention. The book by Naisbitt on the subject is a bestseller, so multitudes want to know what he has to say, yet the only data source he has is what is happening now.[4] His particular approach to the subject is based on the premise that new trends begin in the smaller cities. So he scanned some 6000 local newspapers and analysed over two million local articles about local events. The conclusion he drew from his study was that life by the year 2000 would be very different to what it was today. He discerned the following trends:

From	*To*
Industrial society.	Information society.
Institutional help.	Self-help.
Hierarchies.	Net-working.
Either/or situations.	Multiple options.

According to Naisbitt, a glimpse into the business life of the future shows us that:

- As our school system fails us, the corporation will become the teacher.
- In the US [the basis of his research] robots will replace operatives.
- The electronics, information and computer companies will grow to such an extent that they will replace the 'General Motors' and the 'US Steels' of today.
- To be really successful [also in the US] you will have to be trilingual: fluent in English, Spanish and computer language.

- You will tell the boss what to do. He will not tell you.

It is said that the seeds for the future outlined above have already been sown. That indeed is the basis of the forecast. But what do you think? Naisbitt mentions General Motors, but what have we already seen that company doing? It is not being *replaced* by an electronic company: it has bought up an electronics company (EDS) to assist in its progress towards its own declared objectives of reforming General Motors, using EDS as the catalyst.

The five-year plan

It is all very well to look ahead and speculate about what may happen by the year 2000, but of far more importance is what will happen in the next five years. Many countries, including the Soviet Union, and many companies have their five-year plan and it is that that is of real interest. To plan, they need to know what the world about them will be doing. It seems, for instance, that the developing countries, once thought of as of no account on an international scale, are now becoming a commercial force that will have to be reckoned with. There are now a number of multinationals who have their roots in the developing countries and they are growing and prospering – to the disadvantage, of course, of those who were there before them. Typical of such growth, though little heard of, is the Birla Group, based in India and the construction empire of Mendes Junior, based in Brazil. The number of such companies is growing steadily, their growth motivated by their urgent need to sell their wares world-wide. Export is facilitated by establishing a manufacturing base abroad and this is what happens. It is a reversal of the earlier trend, where companies based in the developed countries built factories in the developing countries.

As we review the literature, it seems that the greatest danger, as time passes, is that a company grows 'stale', for want of a better word. So its corporate plan should recognize the possibility and seek to cope with it. Toray Industries of Japan affords us a very good example in this. Founded some sixty years ago as a manufacturer of viscose rayon, it has kept up with the times and turned to the manufacture of other synthetic fibres as they came along. It is now a leading worldwide producer of both synthetic fibres and integrated high polymer chemical products. To celebrate its sixtieth year, the company has proclaimed a new philosophy. It says it will be creating new values through innovative concepts and technologies. But why? It is the reason that is interesting. Dr Yoshikazu Ito, the chief executive (a doctor in chemical engineering, not medicine) explains:

> Economists tell us that companies usually run out of steam after 30 years or so and must either diversify or go under. This year marks our sixtieth anniversary so we have to rejuvenate for the second time.

Thinking back to our case studies, it would seem that General Motors is once again an example. Its transformation came some thirty years after the inevitable revolution brought by the Second World War. It is also interesting to reflect upon Dr Ito's personal expression of what we have seen is fundamental to Japanese company management:

> Firing employees is good for nobody. The company's wealth is not confined to money alone, people are its greatest asset. The employee is the company's lowest common denominator and company assets should be forfeited before employees are laid off.

Socialist view ?

There is a trend toward this elsewhere in the world, but it is coming too little and too late, in our view. Time and again a successful, profitable company will close down a factory, to the devastation of the location where that factory is sited, just because its return is below average. While the protective policy and 'backward areas' development practised for instance in India, which results in a multitude of 'sick companies', may be going to the other extreme, it has a meritorious objective: the protection of the weak and helpless in society.

Coping with growth

All companies inevitably start small, and grow – and grow, if they are successful. Every company looks forward to such a future. The trouble is that when a company reaches a certain size, it seems that they almost always start to diversify.[5] This trend is probably worldwide, since while the original study was made in the US, Channon has observed a similar trend in the UK.[6] But while diversification leads to further growth, is exciting and challenging, there are hidden dangers. The future is at risk. How is that? The trouble is that the development of a new and unfamiliar product takes up the time and attention of senior management to such an extent that it begins to ignore its basic business. Since it is that business that is actually bringing in the profits, such neglect can be disastrous. An illustration from real life is once again the best way of driving home the lesson and the classic case, often quoted because of its tragic climax, is the US multinational United Brands Incorporated (UBI). Its diversification in the late 1960s and the early 1970s resulted in the neglect of its two basic lines, Fyffes bananas and Morrell meat. UBI got so interested in the new ventures that were being developed, that these became a substitute, in the eyes of the directors, for the original business. The inevitable consequence: substantial losses. The story achieved notoriety because the company chairman, Eli Black, took his own life by jumping off the top of the Pam Am building in New York City. Despite this sad story, diversification remains a good thing, provided always that it is approached with caution and does not start to dominate the company's activities. You will recollect that the problems at Metal Box in India (Chapter 7) were much accentuated by the chairman's devotion to his pet project, the ballbearing factory. This was diversification very much of the wrong sort, since diversification should always be into related areas that contribute to the 'main stream' activity in some way. The phrase we have encountered in this context is most expressive and easily remembered: 'Stick to your knitting'.

It will be seen from the above illustrations of the way in which some managements have coped with growth that success can be hazardous. Hirsch demonstrates this out in a paper that takes the example of the electric utility industry in the US and points out that the industry's unparalleled success over many years blinded its managers to the dangers inherent in technological progress.[7] Others have taken the example of the disastrous failure of the shuttle *Challenger* to demonstrate the same thing: that success had blinded the NASA management to the inherent dangers. It seems that NASA's legendary approach to everything, summed up in the phrase 'can do', had developed into an arrogant attitude that could be summed up in the phrase 'can't fail'.[8]

In conclusion

We have sought to set corporate planning in context by striving to demonstrate that the future really is and always will be uncertain. Even the professionals, it seems, are prepared at times to admit this, since we found a series of articles in one particular issue of *Long Range Planning* (August 1982) under the general heading: 'Corporate planning for the uncertain future'. The reasons for uncertainty were many and some of them we have already touched upon, but the leading article made the point that while planning, particularly under the guidance of an entrepreneural chief executive, has long been based on a 'hunch', life is now so complex that the professional forecaster is called in. 'Then', the writer of this particular article says, 'he in his turn realizes that he cannot provide a single line answer without qualifications. The qualifications get lost on the way to the decision maker and so the process becomes mechanistic'.[9] So the future is uncertain and all planning is suspect.

However, speculation is always fascinating and we thought we would bring this assessment of company prospects to an end by looking towards the stars – or better, perhaps, the planets. General Motors is our inspiration, with projects *Saturn* and *Jupiter*. Both the US and the USSR are very active in the development of 'space station' facilities for a variety of reasons, one of which is the near zero-gravity environment that is available there. The space shuttle programme in the US, operated by the National Aeronautical Space Administration has already attracted the interest of manufacturers of chemicals, semiconductors, pharmaceuticals, metals and other products. This has led to an impressive list of planned and proposed experiments in space which it is anticipated could well lead to substantial manufacturing operations there.[10] For instance, the Center for Space Policy (Cambridge, Massachusetts) has estimated that pharmaceutical production in space could account for annual sales of some US$27 billion by the year 2000. Another assessment (by Rockwell International of Pittsburg) forecast that by 1990 this could be a US$20 billion business. Taken together with the potential for electronic materials, semiconductors and space-processed glass, it would seem that the limiting factor is more than likely to be the availablity of space facilities rather than the finance, even although the absence of proven products at this time is liable to deter venture capital. Some of the newer and advanced materials developed and under development include new alloys, fine ceramics, high performance polymers and an increasing variety of composite materials for various extreme duties. The current demand for these newer materials in Japan alone is estimated at some US$3 billion per year, and this is expected to rise ten-fold by the year 2000. These developments bring projects in their train: projects inevitably calling for project managers able to meet the new challenges before them.

So far as the US is concerned, the government there seems to be doing its best to support such developments. Congress has appropriated US$175 million for basic research on the proposed permanently manned space station, while NASA is developing a very positive space commercialization programme. A leader in the field appears to be 3M, who has signed a joint two-year agreement with NASA, which provides for free shuttle transportation. In return, 3M will have to make much of the experimental data secured on board the shuttle public. Once again, in the characteristic 3M style to which we have already referred, full scope for individual initiative will be given by the creation of 'management teams' within the organization. Indeed, such teams are already in existence, for 3M has formed a space research team that includes chemists, physicists and engineers, together with administrative support personnel. The team will study and design experiments and also build the necessary hardware.

It is very clear that the prospects for new business, diversification and development are unlimited and endless. There will always be something new, even though we are not able at this time to forecast with any certainty what it will be or where it will take us. Not only that, but there will always be good managers and not so good managers, together with companies that are a success and some that are a disaster. But let us never forget that one man, alone, can achieve very little, even although in this book we have tended to concentrate our attention on the man at the top. The end result is not achieved by the chief executive, nor by him and his various management teams, although much has been said about their influence and impact on the end result. The end is in fact achieved by a multitude of workpeople, often scattered far and wide, in many countries, but one and all, in their turn, playing their small but significant part. They are, as it were, part of an international orchestra, scattered far and wide, but all responding to the 'baton' of their 'conductor', the chief executive – in our case, the 'doctor'. The result: a successful company that can well be likened to a harmonious symphony, a joy not only to those involved, but also those looking on.

We have seen that Japan can provide us with many illustrations and lessons in relation to good management and that essential element in good management: good leadership. So let us bring this book to its conclusion on a somewhat philosophical note by quoting Masao Kamei, the chairman of Sumitomo Electric Industries Ltd of Japan, at a 'Management Seminar' held in February 1986 at the Keidanren Kaikan in Tokyo. He looked first at the qualities necessary in the leader, and said:[11]

Of all the qualities necessary for good leadership, I think that personal magnetism – charisma – is most important. Napoleon, Oda Nobunaga and Toyotomi Hideyoshi were all a far cry from exemplary 'managers' and they would probably have received failing marks in that sense. But what they all possessed was an overwhelming personal magnetism which more than offset their shortcomings. A person with great magnetism is one who induces others to come to him for advice and assistance.

This seems to say that good managers, and especially good turnaround managers are born rather than made, but we would not despair. We still feel that the lessons that we have distilled from the examples we have taken from industry across the world can be learnt and applied.

References

1   Argenti, J., *Practical Corporate Planning*, Allen & Unwin, 1980.
2   Hussey, D. E., *Corporate Planning – Theory and Practice*, 2nd edition, Pergamon, 1984.
3   Hussey, D. E. (ed.), *The Truth about Corporate Planning: International Research into the Practice of Planning*, Pergamon, 1983.
4   Naisbitt, J., *Megatrends: Ten New Directions Transforming our Lives*, Warner, 1982.
5   Scott, B., 'Stages of Corporate Development', *Intercollegiate Case Clearing House*, Harvard Business School, Boston 9–371–294, BP 998, 1971.
6   Channon, D., *The Strategy and Structure of British Enterprise*, Macmillan, 1973.
7   Hirsch, R. F., 'How success short-circuits the future', *Harvard Business Review*, March – April 1986, pp. 72–6.
8   Burck, C. G., 'When "can do" business "can't fail"', *Fortune*, no. 113, 17 July 1986, p. 8.
9   'Corporate planning for the uncertain future', *Long Range Planning*, vol. 15, no. 4, August 1982, pp. 22–133.
10 'The $30 billion potential for making chemicals in space', *Chemical Week*, October 17, 1984, pp. 44–7.
11 Kamei, Masao, 'Trustworthiness and Foresight: requisites of good management', *JMA Newsletter*, 1 July 1986. (Translation of an article that appeared in JMA Management News, 10 May 1986.)

Indexes

Subject index

Author index